GOOD
MYTHICAL
MORNING

RHETT & LINK'S
BOOK OF MYTHICALITY

RHETT & LINK'S BOOK OF

# MYTHICALITY

BY RHETT McLAUGHLIN & LINK NEAL

WITH JAKE GREENE

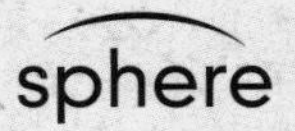

A CIP catalogue record for this book is available from the British Library.

First published in the United States in 2017 by Crown Archetype, an imprint of the Crown Publishing Group, a division of Penguin Random House LLC, New York

This edition published in the UK in 2017 by Sphere

1 3 5 7 9 10 8 6 4 2

ISBN: 978-0-7515-7057-1

Printed in Germany

Papers used by Sphere are from well-managed forests and other responsible sources

*Illustration and design credits appear on pages 268–269.*
*Cover design by Christopher Brand*
*Cover photograph by Peter Yang*

Sphere
An imprint of
Little, Brown Book Group
Carmelite House
50 Victoria Embankment
London EC4Y 0DZ

An Hachette UK Company
www.hachette.co.uk

www.littlebrown.co.uk

IN MEMORY OF BEN GREENWOOD

HIS FRIENDSHIP CHANGED OUR LIVES
BUT ENDED WAY TOO SOON

# CONTENTS

A MYTHICAL WELCOME
. . . 8 . . .

① LAUGH YOUR WAY INTO FRIENDSHIP
. . . 11 . . .

② GET LOST
. . . 29 . . .

③ MAKE A BOLD HAIR CHOICE
. . . 43 . . .

④ BUILD A TIME CAPSULE
. . . 59 . . .

⑤ EMBRACE IMMATURITY
. . . 75 . . .

⑥ PICK A FIGHT
. . . 85 . . .

⑦ EAT SOMETHING THAT SCARES YOU
. . . 101 . . .

⑧ UNLEASH A SIGNATURE DANCE MOVE
. . . 113 . . .

⑨ GET YOUR HANDS DIRTY
. . . 125 . . .

⑩ SAY "I LOVE YOU" LIKE IT'S NEVER BEEN SAID
. . . 137 . . .

11 INVENT SOMETHING RIDICULOUS . . . 149 . . .

12 GIVE THROWBACK THANKS . . . 161 . . .

13 VISIT THE FUTURE . . . 173 . . .

14 BECOME A SUPERFAN . . . 183 . . .

15 CONDUCT A WEIRD EXPERIMENT . . . 195 . . .

16 THROW A PARTY THAT DOESN'T SUCK . . . 207 . . .

17 RISK YOUR HEART FOR AN ANIMAL . . . 221 . . .

18 ISOLATE YOURSELF WITH YOURSELF . . . 237 . . .

19 SPEAK AT YOUR OWN FUNERAL . . . 247 . . .

20 STOP AND CELEBRATE . . . 257 . . .

A MYTHICAL FAREWELL . . . 264 . . .

SOURCES . . . 266 . . .

CREDITS . . . 268 . . .

ACKNOWLEDGMENTS . . . 271 . . .

YOU DID IT! You have officially made at least one good decision today. By opening this book you are opening yourself up to the very real possibility of increased Mythicality in your life. Why, exactly, you decided to open this book is not important. Maybe you heard that this book contains a skyscraper-shaped board game that builds character (true), a visual guide to slow dancing poses (true), apocalyptic-themed party ideas (true), and actual sheet music and lyrics for the song we want you to sing—and hopefully play on the organ—at our funeral (also true). Or maybe you opened this book because you wanted to see pictures from the time Link broke his pelvis (hilarious unless you were Link), or read about the time Rhett was confronted by a tattooed man while wearing a child's shirt (it didn't turn out well). Or perhaps you heard that one chapter of this book was written by our wives (a very risky decision) and another entire chapter was written from the future (the United States Department of Time Travel and Extraterrestrial Affairs will not permit us to confirm nor deny the validity of said chapter from the future). Regardless of your reasons, all that matters now is that, by opening this book, you have just merged onto the highway to Mythicality.

It would probably be helpful to tell you what Mythicality is (if you don't happen to know already). Here's a technical-sounding definition:

> **Myth•i•cal•i•ty** (mi-thi-ˈka-lə-tē) *noun*
> 1. the quality or state of being that embodies a synergistic coalescence of curiosity, creativity, and tomfoolery (sometimes referred to as curio-tomfoolivity), ideally experienced in the context of friendship and intended to bring goodwill to the universe. **Origin:** 2009; RhettandLinkish.

You may think you can't go around adding "-ity" to any word you want and then giving it your own meaning. But in the age of the Internet, you can—especially when there isn't already a definition that communicates exactly what you're trying to say. *Mythicality* is the word we've come up with that captures what's been at the heart of our friendship from the very beginning. We'll unpack it in layman's terms in a moment, but first, some background might be helpful.

We met in 1984 on the first day of first grade at Buies Creek Elementary School in Buies Creek, North Carolina, when our teacher, Ms. Locklear, held us both in from recess for writing profanity on our desks ("hell" and "dam" if you're wondering—spelling wasn't Link's strongest subject). She then sentenced us to coloring pictures of mythical beasts. We've been best friends ever since.

Over twenty years later, when YouTube was invented, we began uploading videos of questionable quality like "Cutting Strangers' Nosehairs at the Mall" and "The Unibrow Song." These videos are still online, although we strongly advise against watching them if you have an active cringe reflex. Surprisingly—and thankfully—enough people responded positively to these videos to encourage us to make more.

In 2009, we began to get a sense that there should be a name for this group of individuals who had collectively determined that we were more funny than obnoxious. So, we took the easy way out and asked them to name themselves. After members of the RhettandLinKommunity (an online fan site) threw around a number of suggestions including "Unicornholers" and "Rinkles," we all eventually settled on "Mythical Beasts."

Since then, we've gotten a little carried away with incorporating the term "Mythical" into our lives. In 2012, when we decided to launch a daily morning talk show, we naturally named it *Good Mythical Morning.* We founded Mythical Entertainment; created the Mythical Mail Boulder, the Mythical Mail

Museum, and the Wheel of Mythicality; and sold a Mythical Shoe, a Good Mythical Mug, and a Mythical Pomade. It's gotten a bit out of hand, we know.

Of course, this terminology has been a little confusing for those other than the Mythical Beasts. When we tell strangers that we have a show called *Good Mythical Morning*, we can sense their suspicion that the show only exists in our imaginations and that we are actually unemployed. But for us, Mythicality encompasses all of the qualities that we want our work, our friendship, and our lives to display. It's characterized by a desire to learn and do new things, an appreciation of originality, and a tendency to not take yourself too seriously. A person who is willing to risk pursuing these values—for the purpose of making the world a better place—is a true Mythical Beast.

We firmly believe that you can approach any aspect of your life with Mythicality, from the way you comb your hair to the way you say "I love you," and that's what we hope to demonstrate in this book. For us, it turns out that many of the experiences throughout our lifelong friendship, including hitchhiking, eating leeches and spiders, floating in a sensory deprivation tank, and even throwing balls at each other's balls have all helped to shape our understanding of what Mythicality is all about.

In addition to our stories, this book contains a collection of guides, charts, and activities to help you navigate a host of life situations with Mythicality, like a laughter compatibility test to take with a friend, a decision tree to consult if you get flipped off by a stranger, and step-by-step instructions on how to eat nasty foods (just to name a few). There are also Mythical merit badges at the opening of each chapter so you can track your progress (this is largely because we have a personal merit badge void that we've been trying to fill ever since we both dropped out of Cub Scouts after only one meeting). Of course, you can just read this book and not actually do anything we suggest. We have no way of knowing, unless you have one of the five copies of this book that has a small, imperceptible microphone and camera on the cover.

Because there are two of us, we will often write in the collective voice, just like we are doing right now. If it's helpful for you to imagine us using some sort of "talking harmony," feel free to do so. Also, since we are actually two distinct people, we will be speaking individually throughout the book. In those cases, it will look like this:

**RHETT** Hi, this is Rhett. When I'm saying something, you'll see this. I'm not 100 percent sure what it looks like, because I wrote this before we decided how to make it look when I'm talking. But I'm sure it's really cool.

**LINK** I'm Link, and this is what it will look like when I'm talking. It looks a little cooler than it does when Rhett is talking, don't you think? That's how you can remember that it's me talking: when it looks a little cooler. Also, I will be talking in a slightly cooler voice, so you can imagine that while reading my parts.

**IF YOU'RE NEW** to our Mythical world, welcome! (And don't be scared.) If you already consider yourself a member of the Mythical herd, thank you. One of the most Mythical parts of our lives is being able to share our work with Beasts worldwide. Without you, we would have never been given the opportunity to write this book. By choosing to read it, you're demonstrating that you want to be your Mythical best. If you stole the book, you can probably still return it—assuming you have not already drooled excessively on it or otherwise defaced it. If you can't work up the courage to return it, at least finish reading it. Then, give it to someone you care about. Oh, and stop stealing.

FRIENDSHIP LOLS
FRIENDSHIP GOALS
FRIENDSHIP LOLS
FRIENDSHIP GOALS

# LAUGH YOUR WAY INTO FRIENDSHIP

"WE WOULD SIT THERE, BENDING OVER IN BOISTEROUS SNICKERING, OUR FACES TURNING RED AS WE THOUGHT ABOUT RAINFOREST HAIR OR BRINGING DEAD DEER HOME TO OUR HUNGRY FAMILIES."

**WHEN WE UPLOAD** an Internet video, the primary response we're hoping for is laughter. That's a tad ironic, considering that we have no way to see or hear anyone laughing. Instead, we must scan user comments for comedic validation, and that means wading through remarks like "You guys are running out of ideas" or "Who else is eating chicken parm while watching this?" If we're lucky enough to stumble upon a "hehehehehehe," a "muahahaha," or even a coveted tears-of-joy emoji, it's not nearly as satisfying as hearing someone authentically burst into laughter.

Thankfully, we have each other. Before we were ever trying to get people on the Internet to indicate amusement with their keyboards, we were making each other laugh. To this day, we know we have succeeded in truly landing a joke when it causes us to begin giggling together like a couple of toddlers who just broke out of day care (we readily acknowledge that toddlers breaking out of day care is only funny for the toddlers).

There are probably best friends out there who spend most of their time together just somberly talking about impending global pandemics and financial collapse. We love a good apocalyptic conversation as much as the next person, but we've found that sharing a laugh is a true sweet spot where two hallmarks of Mythicality, humor and friendship, meet. It was this nexus of Mythicality that first opened the door to our lifelong companionship.

**LINK** From the time I was four years old until I met Rhett when I was six, I was determined to have a best friend. I was desperate for a best friend.

My first attempt to find one was in preschool with Brad McDonald. We had fun digging holes together, so I figured he was my best friend. Then, one afternoon while venturing into the bathroom just after Brad finished his business, I saw it: he'd forgotten to flush and had left behind a memento. It was orange. I'm talking cheese-puff orange. It was wrong to hold Brad's orange poop against him. He probably just drank a crap-ton (pun intended) of Fanta, or maybe he was secretly addicted to Creamsicles. But whatever the reason, it scarred me deeply, and I could no longer consider Brad my BFF. I guess I was a pretty ruthless four-year-old.

Young Link used a stuffed animal as a temporary best friend during his quest for a human best friend. Notice the chokehold.

My second attempt at best friendship came in kindergarten. Most days, the highlight of recess involved some kind of foot race, and I was determined to become friends with the fastest kid. I was among the slowest runners, but I figured that all great friendships should involve some realistic average speed, so that no duo is too fast or too slow. (I thought way too much about this.) Sadly, the fastest kid, Maurice Cameron, was already best friends with Lynwood Campbell. So I set my sights on the second-fastest kid, Matthew Enzor. I tried complimenting him after one of his silver-medal performances, only to realize that he was already committed to a best friendship with a slow-moving blond kid named JR. My search for a speedy best friend was going nowhere fast.

My third and final pre-Rhett best-friend-getting attempt came later that kindergarten year. I figured, since targeting the fastest kid had failed, why not try the biggest one? And Zac West was the size of a third-grader. Surely he would like a little friend to balance things out. I began talking to Zac, and he talked back. After a few days, he even asked me to come over to his house. This was working! He was gonna be my best friend! While at Zac's house, he asked if I wanted to "play wrestling." I loved wrestling, and anticipated Zac pulling out a full WWF pro wrestling toy set just like the one I had at home. "Yeah!" I told him excitedly. Before I knew it, Zac had me by the legs, upside down in a pile-driver position on his bed, and proceeded to jackhammer me headfirst off the bed and into the floor. His grandma was watching. I never went back to Zac's house.

On the first day of first grade, I met Rhett, and I knew that he was best-friend material. First off, he was tall, so there was the whole average-height-between-us factor. He was also pretty fast, even though it looked like he was moving slow because his legs were so long. I never saw his poop to gauge its orangeness, but he never attempted to pile-drive me, so I eased up on the background check. Plus, just a few days into our friendship, he asked if he could spend the night at my house, which meant that he knew that I was best-friend material too.

**RHETT** What Link didn't realize at the time is that I had some sort of inexplicable compulsion to invite myself over to spend the night at other kids' homes. It's strange, because as an adult, I like to spend the night in my own house, in my own bed. But as a child, I would jump at the first opportunity to invite myself over—sometimes in the first conversation I ever had with someone. I would just wait for a pause and say, "So you think I can spend the night at your house?" This was a surprisingly effective tactic in elementary school. Kids almost always just said, "OK, I'll ask my parents." And their parents almost always said yes.

I was fascinated with figuring out how other people's families worked—or more precisely, what they ate. I would open up their refrigerators to see what was in there (David Rogers's family were fans of cold cuts; Peter Dinklage's [not that Peter Dinklage] parents enjoyed large quantities of Capri Sun). I was also interested in what other parents would let us get away with (I watched *The Texas Chainsaw Massacre* at Adam Nicholson's house, and ate unlimited Cocoa Puffs at Tate Maddox's house).

So, when Link started talking to me, I wasn't looking for a best friend. I was just looking to infiltrate yet another home. When I invited myself, he didn't passively say that he'd ask his parents like other kids. He pounced: "Yes! Tonight. Tonight is good!" I was a little taken aback at his eagerness.

When I showed up at his house, I proceeded with my usual family evaluation. He had a stepdad named Jimmy who started a big fire in the backyard and then threw cups of gasoline on it. This seemed unsafe, so I was very into it. They also had a pantry full of Little Debbie treats of nearly every variety. I wasn't accustomed to this, so I had two fudge rounds and two oatmeal creme pies in under ten minutes.

Later that night, as I lay there trying to go to sleep, I noticed that there was something different about spending the night at Link's house. It wasn't just that I smelled like a bonfire, or that I had never experienced a sugar

Young Rhett thinking about the contents of various friends' refrigerators.

high quite like a Little Debbie sugar high. It was that I was laughing. We were laughing. A lot. I don't recall the specifics of what made us laugh that night, and I can only imagine how silly and stupid it was. I'm sure it was the typical six-year-old boy fare of saying the word "butt" and laughing for three minutes straight, but it was an intense, infectious laughter. We made *each other* laugh.

**LINK** I had no idea that Rhett was thinking any of this. I was just happy that he hadn't tried a wrestling move on me. But I remember that roaring laughter as well. I had never laughed like that with a friend. I figured that this was what best friends did.

Our ability to make each other laugh uncontrollably served as the foundation of our friendship, and every time we did, we poured a little more cement onto that foundation. Our adolescence was defined by our relentless commitment to amuse each other, and the setting for this was often the balcony at Buies Creek First Baptist Church.

Instead of listening to Pastor Rogers preach, we would take the little white cards used for reserving a spot at the Wednesday-night family dinner, turn them over, and write absolutely ridiculous "Deep Thoughts" on them. We were inspired by *SNL*'s recurring "Deep Thoughts with Jack Handey," but as you can see, we didn't exactly achieve the comedic genius that Jack did.

These may not strike you as precursors to a career in comedy, but at that point it didn't matter that no one else found this stuff funny. When we passed the cards back and forth during the church service, it took everything in us to contain our laughter. We would sit there, bending over in boisterous snickering, our faces turning red as we thought about rainforest hair or bringing dead deer home to our hungry families. Mrs. Lanier, one of our schoolteachers, was in the choir that sat behind Pastor Rogers, giving her a great view of the whole congregation. Each time Rhett and I would begin to lose it, she would shoot a look up to the balcony directly at us like the Eye of Sauron.

**RHETT** Mrs. Lanier's scolding didn't stop us. We continued to view every setting as an opportunity to crack each other up. This was captured perfectly in the notes we wrote to each other in our high school yearbooks (see pages 16–17).

I thought it was funny to sign a name other than my own as I waxed eloquent about fart blossoms, and Link figured I would appreciate him rewriting Merle Haggard lyrics—Haggard's our favorite singer (more on him later)—in order to brag about his manhood and contemplate the possibility of using it as currency. We were both right.

IT WOULD PROVE strategic that we didn't spend all of our time just trying to make each other laugh. We learned pretty early on that we could also make our friends laugh at us. We sought to turn every class project and event into a vehicle to deliver our comedy to an audience.

When we were told that Buies Creek Elementary would be holding its first Fall Festival in 1991—and that it would feature a bake sale, games, and live musical performances in the school auditorium—we asked our teachers if we could sing a Halloween-themed song. Without knowing our full plan, they agreed.

Naughty by Nature had just released their new hit rap single, "O.P.P.," and it had taken our

Our parents used these cards to reserve a spot at the always tasty Wednesday night church dinner, while we used them to try to make each other laugh in the church balcony. The top one is Rhett's and the bottom is Link's. They are both supremely stupid.

**Reservation** **5:45 P.M.**

**WEDNESDAY NIGHT FAMILY DINNER**

_____ ADULT ($3.00 ) PLATES

_____ CHILD'S PLATE (½ Regular Plate) ($1.50)

_____ OPTIONAL PLATE ($1.50) (Burger, chips, pudding)

☐ Permanent Reservation for this school year.

☐ Weekly Reservation for _____________ (date).

NAME: ______________________________ Phone: ______________

(IF YOU CANNOT BE PRESENT, RESERVATIONS MUST BE CANCELLED BY TUESDAY NOON! YOU MUST PAY FOR THE MEAL(S) IF YOU FAIL TO SHOW AND HAVE NOT CANCELLED!)

Sometimes I think of the hair on my head as a tropical rain forest. And when I go to the barber to get my hair cut, right before the barber starts to cut my hair, I stand up and say "Hey, you're about to kill millions of little animals and destroy our earth!" Then I sit down and say, "Just kidding."

When I ride down the highway, I see dead deer on the roadside. I'll pick these deer up and put them in my trunk, when I get home, I show my children all the deer and they say "Daddy, why are there tire marks on all of them!" and I reply, "I am a great hunter and I found these dead deer on the side of the road where they were hit, and I caught them!" That day I felt like a hero

Rhett's heartfelt note to Link.

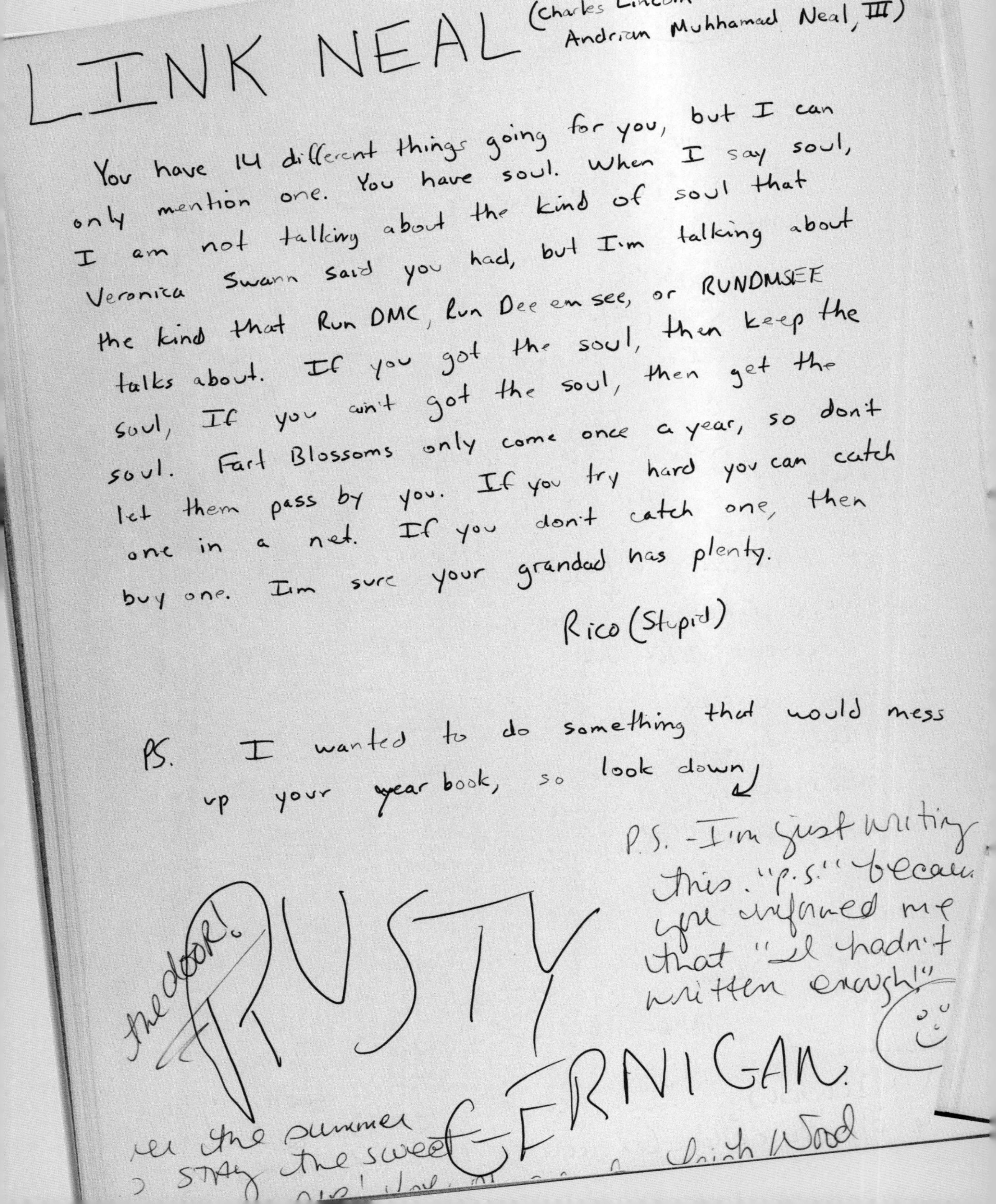

LINK NEAL (Charles Lincoln Smith Johnson Andrian Muhhamad Neal, III)

You have 14 different things going for you, but I can
only mention one. You have soul. When I say soul,
I am not talking about the kind of soul that
Veronica Swann said you had, but I'm talking about
the kind that Run DMC, Run Dee em see, or RUNDMSEE
talks about. If you got the soul, then keep the
soul, If you ain't got the soul, then get the
soul. Fart Blossoms only come once a year, so don't
let them pass by you. If you try hard you can catch
one in a net. If you don't catch one, then
buy one. I'm sure your grandad has plenty.

Rico (Stupid)

P.S. I wanted to do something that would mess
up your year book, so look down

P.S. - I'm just writing this "p.s." because you informed me that "I hadn't written enough!"

RUSTY the door!

GERNIGAN.

... the summer
... STAY the sweet
...

... Wood

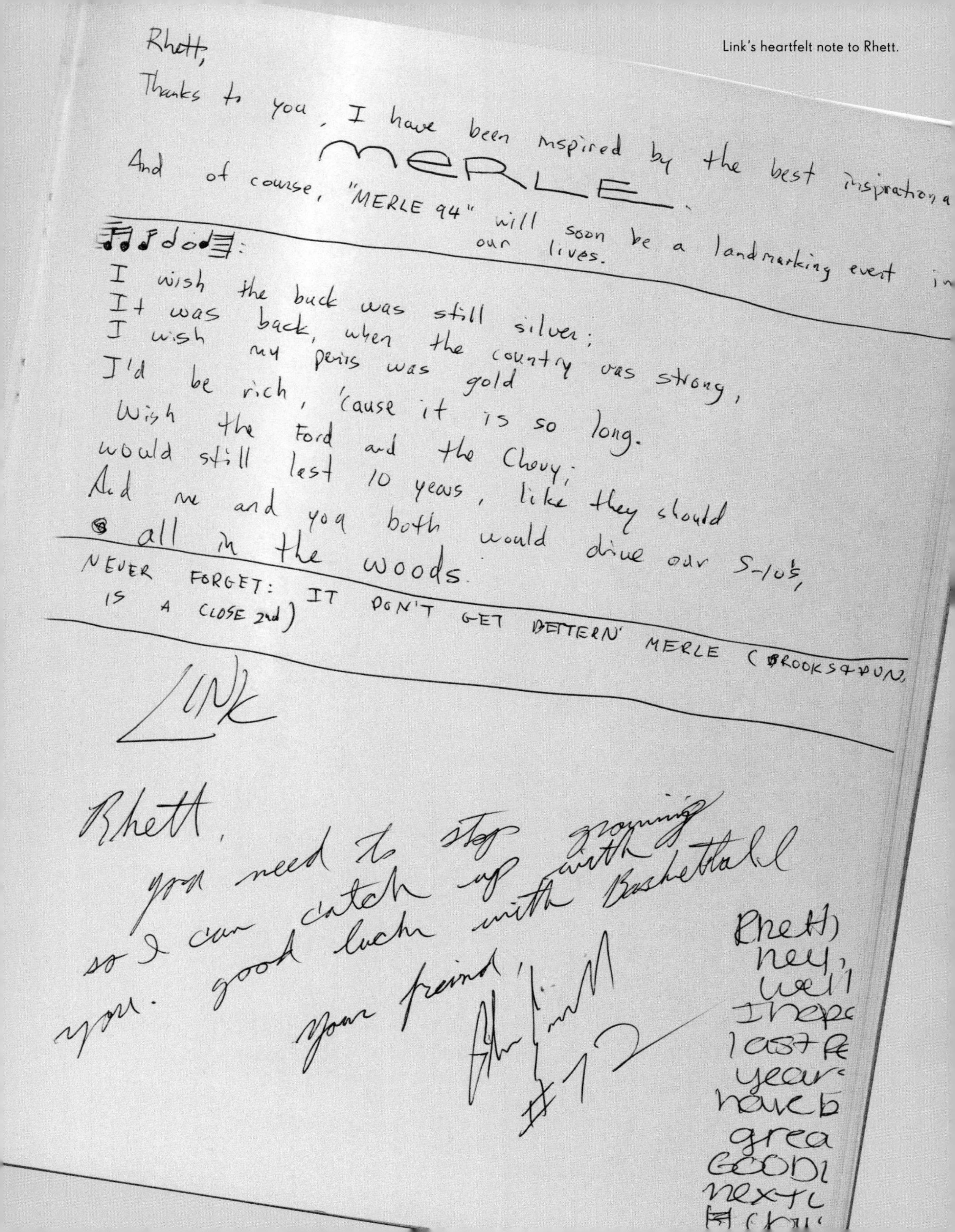

Link's heartfelt note to Rhett.

Rhett,

Thanks to you, I have been inspired by the best inspiration a[...]

MERLE.

And of course, "MERLE 94" will soon be a landmarking event in our lives.

♫♫ :

I wish the buck was still silver;
It was back, when the country was strong,
I wish my penis was gold
I'd be rich, 'cause it is so long.
Wish the Ford and the Chevy;
would still last 10 years, like they should
And me and you both would drive our S-10's,
all in the woods.

NEVER FORGET: IT DON'T GET BETTERN' MERLE (BROOKS & DUN[N] IS A CLOSE 2nd)

LINK

Rhett,
you need to stop growing
so I can catch up with
you. good luck with Basketball
your freind,
[signature]
#12

Rhett,
hey,
well
I hope
last fe[...]
years
have b[...]
grea[...]
GOOD L[...]
next [...]
[...]

school by storm. None of us had any idea what the lyrics meant, but that didn't really matter, because we decided to overhaul the song and turn it into what we considered to be a hilarious rap about All Hallows Eve. We simply replaced "O.P.P." with "Hall-O-Ween." It was the same number of syllables, fitting the chorus perfectly. Thankfully, we were able to find the actual original lyrics we wrote down in 1991 (see pages 20–21).

Our teachers didn't necessarily appreciate us suggesting that the student body was free to "dress like a junky" for Halloween, and no one actually threw their hands in the air when we asked. That didn't matter. We had developed our own sense of humor that served as a language between the two of us. If we were operating solo, we may have been discouraged by the lack of response. But because we had each other—and we were convinced that what we were doing was hilarious—we were willing to shamelessly put ourselves out there.

Years later, when we joined YouTube in the summer of 2006, the potential for a captive audience increased exponentially beyond those gathered in the Buies Creek Elementary auditorium. And even though the initial response to our first videos was lukewarm at best, we kept moving forward, using our ability to entertain each other as motivation.

People often ask us how we've managed to remain friends for so long, and they sometimes ask in a slightly accusatory manner, as if they assume that our friendship must have been manufactured by the top brass at YouTube in order to generate clicks. It's difficult for people to believe that two kids can meet in first grade and then choose to work together for a lifetime. Granted, it's a little unusual. But it's not a conspiracy like the moon landing, Tupac's death, or a spherical Earth. We're actually best friends, and one of the reasons is that our job is to make each other laugh nearly every day of our lives.

Maybe we would still be best friends if we were in a different line of work. We could have been librarians, spending our days amusing each other by reorganizing books counter to the Dewey Decimal System, or massage therapists doing celebrity impressions while administering couples' massages. While both of those careers sound incredibly fulfilling and profitable, there's no doubt that it has been easier to maintain our BFF status because of our profession.

We're not trying to pressure you into convincing your best friend that the only way you're going to sustain your friendship is by starting a YouTube channel together. (You shouldn't start a YouTube channel. We don't need the competition.) But maybe you're on a best-friend hunt like Link, and you've already tried and failed with the fastest people you know. Our first piece of advice is to place less importance on your potential friend's foot speed. You're only increasing the chances that you're the one who's going to get eaten by a grizzly bear when the two of you finally go on that Yellowstone camping trip.

Instead, find a friend you can laugh with. There are few things that set the bond in a Mythical friendship better than that. Getting stranded on a deserted island together or being held captive by a cannibalistic tribe is probably more effective, but it's hard to organize such things, and we doubt it's worth the risk.

Rhett considered Link his best friend, despite Link's claw hands.

Sitting on the hood of a car with the doors open is hilarious if you do it right.

Box
Beet

Beet Box Beet Beet
Box

I'd like to have your attention for
just a little minute,
so I can bust a rhyme and
tell you what's in it.
It's about a holiday that's
coming up,
so listen closely to this rhyme
and don't iterrupt
We're in the house, the auditourium,
and straight from BC where we're
coming from.
Rhett + Link on the microphone,
rocking so hard you think you in the
Twilight zone
It's kind of funky,
a little bit spunky,
You can dress like Frankinstein,
or you can dress like a junky
The holiday is halloween,
where you can walk outside,
and see what you never seen.
It's a time to read books
by Stephen King,
and also a time to hear your
doorbell ring,
It's where you give candy, in the little

Box Box Beet Box Box Beet + Box

These are the original handwritten lyrics for the masterpiece "You Down with Halloween?" (a parody of the then popular hip-hop song "O.P.P." by Naughty by Nature), which we performed at the [illegible] Buies Creek Elementary Fall Festival.

handy,
All the way from Almond Joy
to the good + plenty,
Be aware for the wolfman,
If you want to keep your right leg
+ left hand
cause he'll come + get you
in the middle of the night,
what you think about that, Yeah right
It's just something you never seen,
and here comes the chorus,
HALLOWEEN.

Halloween is a spooky time,
but to tell you the truth, that's
why I wrote this rhyme.
for you to listen to,
and if you don't mind, I'd like
you to do,
something, a little bit crazy
c'mon party people and don't be lazy
throw your hands in the air with
the beat,
Because, you know the beat is kind of sweet
Well let's get back to the main issue,
about how haloween really really gets you

# GMM'S BIGGEST LAUGHS

**EPISODE 573:**
***Upside Down Glasses Challenge***
Link miserably failed at pouring liquid into a bottle while wearing special prism glasses.

**EPISODE 719:**
***Will It Cookie? – Taste Test***
Rhett adopted a Scottish accent and exclaimed, "Brother Link breaks out the beans & franks . . . cookies!" to help Link eat a haggis cookie.

**EPISODE 680:**
***Testing the Butter Cutter***
Rhettina suggested that she would brush Linkita's hair back to signal when she wanted to speak.

**EPISODE 166:**
***How to Make Someone Sound Like an Idiot***
Link gave a severely slurred speech about cinnamon-buns ice cream while using a homemade "speech jammer."

**We don't spend the night at each other's houses anymore so we can have giggle-filled sleepovers. We leave that to our kids. Our most epic bouts of laughter happen on *Good Mythical Morning*.**

**EPISODE 451:**
***Spotting a Fake Laugh***
After watching footage of Link fake-laughing, Rhett laughed and said that laugh was fake, which made him laugh again. Real. They both laughed.

**EPISODE 457:**
***Squeezable Food Test***
Link squeezed a solidified log of soggy Frosted Mini-Wheats into Rhett's mouth.

**EPISODE 674:**
***Weirdest Things Found in Toilets***
Rhett role-played as a naked man found by police waist-deep in a porta-john: "Man, if I told y'all, you wouldn't believe me!"

**EPISODE 473:**
***Introducing Pool Pants***
Link filled Rhett's "pool shirt" with water and showered under a huge leak from Rhett's belly-button region.

## THE LCT (LAUGHTER COMPATIBILITY TEST)

The following is a quiz to determine how compatible your sense of humor is with your friend's (or enemy's or spouse's or sibling's or anyone else's, really). Write down your answers separately, and then compare at the end.

1) Which phrase is funniest?
   a) Granny panties
   b) Jelly belly
   c) Crotch rocket
   d) Poot

2) Which kitten-related scenario is funniest?
   a) A kitten in a business outfit
   b) A kitten with devil horns and a goatee
   c) A kitten wearing lederhosen
   d) A puppy on a kitten's grave

3) Which haircut is funniest?
   a) Ponytail mullet on a businessman
   b) Bowl cut on a businesswoman
   c) Weird Al curls on a baby
   d) Mohawk on Jesus

4) Which schadenfreude moment is funniest?

   Your pushy, arrogant boss . . .

   a) doesn't know he has a booger hanging out of his nose
   b) is not caught by the team during a team-building trust fall
   c) gets fired
   d) pees his pants during a PowerPoint presentation

5) Which nickname is funniest?
   a) Biscuit
   b) Bubbles
   c) Rebecc
   d) FlossBoss

6) Which dumb thing makes you laugh the most?
   a) Good pun
   b) Knock-knock joke
   c) Ironic T-shirt
   d) Poot

7) Which funny face is funniest?
   a) Puffy cheeks
   b) Fish lips
   c) Taco tongue
   d) Fake redneck teeth

8) Which one of these characters is most likely to be funny?
   a) Clown
   b) Stand-up comedian
   c) A college professor who wears jeans
   d) Grandmother with a glass of whiskey

9) Which of these pranks is funny without crossing the line?
   a) Scaring someone when they walk in the door late at night
   b) Cling wrap on the toilet seat
   c) Writing "poot" on a sleeping friend's head
   d) Banana peel on the floor of a nursing home

10) A dirty joke is funniest coming from . . .
   a) A small child
   b) A public official
   c) You
   d) A grandmother with a glass of whiskey

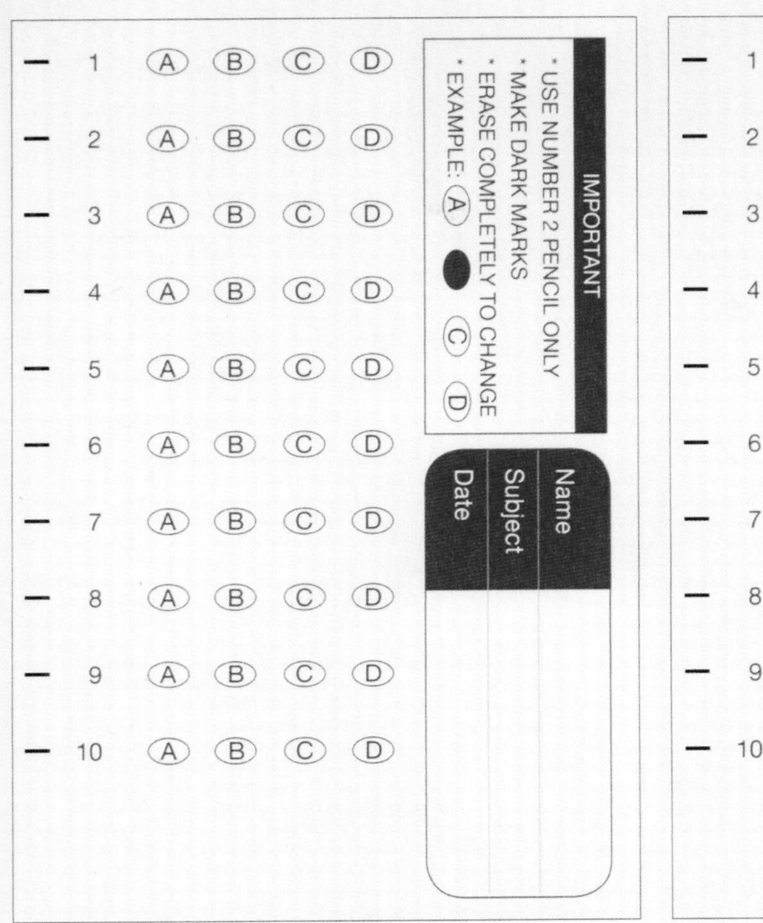


1 A B C D
2 A B C D
3 A B C D
4 A B C D
5 A B C D
6 A B C D
7 A B C D
8 A B C D
9 A B C D
10 A B C D
IMPORTANT
* USE NUMBER 2 PENCIL ONLY
* MAKE DARK MARKS
* ERASE COMPLETELY TO CHANGE
* EXAMPLE: A C D
Name
Subject
Date

## COMPARE YOUR RESULTS

| | |
|---|---|
| 10 answers the same | You cheated. |
| 6–9 answers the same | You are two halves of a comedic whole. Matching tattoos would not be out of the question. |
| 5 answers the same | Fill up the cooler and throw on some tunes because you've found a road trip buddy! |
| 3–4 answers the same | We're not saying you shouldn't be best friends, but we are saying that we hope you have a strong shared interest outside of comedy. |
| 1–2 answers the same | You probably share a third friend that both of you connect with better than each other. |
| 0 answers the same | The fact that you grew up near each other and went to the same school is masking the truth—you are mortal enemies. |

IN MIDDLE SCHOOL, WE SET OUT TO WRITE A SCREENPLAY FOR A FILM CALLED *GUTLESS WONDERS.* WE FILLED THE STORY WITH THINGS THAT MADE US LAUGH AT THE TIME. WE'VE DECIDED TO TAKE THE TWO-PAGE OPENING SCENE AND ANALYZE IT THROUGH A MODERN LENS TO SEE IF THE CURRENT RHETT AND LINK WILL LAUGH AT THE STUFF THAT THE YOUNG RHETT AND LINK THOUGHT WAS FUNNY.

FADE IN:

SCENE 1: INTRO

Peaceful scenery. Rhett speaking in English accent.

ENGLISH ACCENTS MAKE PEOPLE TAKE YOU SERIOUSLY, EVEN IF YOURE TRYING TO BE FUNNY. THIS WAS A GOOD INSTINCT.

RHETT VO

In the great era of time we call the late 70s, two-landmarking events occurred. Rhett McLaughlin and Link Neal were born.

Cut to Rhett as a baby.

RHETT VO (cont'd)

Rhett emerged from his mother's womb, his body weighing 6lbs 5 oz, and his gargantuan noggin weighing 7lbs 8 oz, for a total weight of 13lbs 13oz.

OF COURSE, OUR HUMOR HAS ALWAYS BEEN PRETTY SELF-CENTERED. THIS HASN'T CHANGED SIGNIFICANTLY.

LARGE HEADS ARE ALWAYS FUNNY. THIS JOKE WORKED. HOWEVER, ENLARGED CGI BABY HEADS MAY BLOW PRODUCTION BUDGET.

Cut to Link as a baby.

RHETT VO (cont'd)

Link came into this world, his body weighing 6lbs 3oz, and his unbelievably huge noggin weighing 8lbs 4 oz, for a total combined weight of 14lb 7oz.

THIS WAS AN OPPORTUNITY TO INTRODUCE A NEW JOKE, BUT WE WENT WITH THE BIG HEAD ANGLE AGAIN. A MISS. PLUS, BUDGET DEFINITELY DOESN'T ALLOW FOR TWO CGI HEADS.

Cut to both.

RHETT VO (cont'd)

Little did they know at this young age that one day they would come be to be known as the two of the greatest blooming idiots to ever walk the face of this green, blue, brown - with hues of yellow - earth.

SELF-DEPRECATION TAKES THE EDGE OFF THE SELFISH COMEDY. SMART MOVE.

UNNECESSARY SPECIFICITY WAS AND STILL IS FUNNY.

Good Ole Boys starts while showing both as babies.

WE DIDN'T UNDERSTAND MUSIC LICENSING AT THE TIME. THIS SHOULD READ "ROYALTY-FREE GOOD OLE BOYS SOUNDALIKE."

Cut to CREDIT: Starring

Cut to Rhett and Link as young kids playing "catch" with one another, hitting each other with the ball. They start fighting.
CREDIT: Link Neal

VIOLENCE CAN BE FUNNY, BUT THE DETAILS ARE IMPORTANT. WE SHOULD HAVE BEEN MORE SPECIFIC, LIKE "LINK BITES RHETT'S EAR."

CONTINUED:

Cut to young Link fishing, has a "big one", young Rhett comes out of the water. They fight.

SEEMS LIKE WE ARE BUILDING TO SOMETHING HERE. AGAIN, NOT BAD, BUT MORE DETAILS ARE NEEDED. LIKE, "RHETT BITES LINK'S EAR."

CREDIT: Rhett McLaughlin

AFTER THE MAN-FISH JOKE, YOU WANT A THIRD BEAT THAT IS EVEN BETTER. A SIMPLE GOLF DIVOT JOKE IS A STEP BACKWARDS, AND A MISS.

Young Rhett playing golf. Swings; shows divot fly, shows it hitting young Link in the face. They fight.

COMEDY COMES IN THREES, SO THE THIRD FIGHT IS THE RIGHT CALL. BUT, AGAIN WITH THE DETAILS. THIS HAS TO BE THE FUNNIEST BEAT. EXAMPLE: "RHETT AND LINK BITE A THIRD GUY'S EAR."

CREDIT: Screenplay by Rhett M. and Link N.

Good Ole Boys fades out.

Cut to farmer played by Rhett standing in front of his field.

FARMER

THIS IS WHERE THINGS BEGIN TO GO OFF THE RAILS. NOT ONLY ARE WE ALREADY PLAYING ANOTHER CHARACTER, BUT IT'S A CLICHÉ.

Yeah, I remember those boys.
(spits)
Back in the summer of '83 they whizzed all over my tobacco crop. Huh, a'course it still ended up the best tastin' stogies we'd had since '77.

WE STILL RESORT TO POTTY HUMOR REGULARLY—MORE THAN WE WOULD LIKE. THIS ONE'S NOT BAD, ESPECIALLY CONSIDERING WE USED THE WORD "WHIZZED" WHICH IS INHERENTLY FUNNY.

CREDIT: Produced by Link N. and Rhett M.

Cut to Phil Juby watering the lawn.

WE WANTED MICHAEL JUBY'S DAD, PHIL, TO BE IN OUR MOVIE BECAUSE HE WAS THE COOLEST DAD WE KNEW. PROBLEM IS, WE DIDN'T GIVE A JOKE. THIS MONOLOGUE HAS NOTHING TO OFFER. MISS.

PHIL

Ohhhh. I knew those kids. They'd always press their faces against my kitchen window when we were eating supper. They looked real hungry so I threw some scraps out to them. Maaannnnn, they attacked those things like wild hyenas!

CREDIT: Featuring: Ronald McNeill, Chris Gardner, Trent Hamilton, Jason Keenan, Michael Juby, Phil Juby, Brendon Tart, Sue Capps, Diane McLaughlin, and Jim McLaughlin.

Cut to Link as an old woman.

CROSS-DRESSING CAN BE HUMOROUS, BUT A CONFUSED, OLDER WOMAN IS SIMPLY ANOTHER CLICHÉ. THIS WAS AN OPPORTUNITY TO INTRODUCE ORIGINAL CHARACTERS, AND WE DIDN'T.

OLD WOMAN

Wh- Wh- Who? I can't- I won't- I don't know-
(points at camera)
Wh-Wh-What's that contraption sonny?
(gets frightened)
(yells and runs)
It's a b- b- bazooka! Help! Help!
Bazooka!
Bazookaaaaaaaaaaaaaaaaaaaaaaaaaaaaaaa!

SOMEONE THINKING A CAMERA IS A WEAPON COULD HAVE BEEN FUNNY, BUT THE AUDIENCE CAN'T SEE THE CAMERA. WE DIDN'T THINK ABOUT THAT. FAIL.

CREDIT: Directed by Rhett M. and Link N.

PICK A DIRECTION
AND GO!

# GET LOST

"ONCE RHETT GOT HIS LICENSE, WE RE-CREATED THE 'GETTING LOST' ROUTINE ON A LARGER SCALE IN HIS PARENTS' DODGE DYNASTY. HE'D ROLL UP TO MY HOUSE, I'D GET IN, AND WE'D PICK A DIRECTION AND DRIVE."

**WE DIDN'T HAVE GPS** growing up, just directions. We're not talking about a robotic lady in our pockets telling us exactly when to turn left. We relied on a handwritten list of turns, road names, and distances, like this:

Go 3.2 miles on Old Buies Creek Rd.
Take a Left on Hwy 27 at the First Baptist Church
Go 1.7 miles until you see the Second Baptist Church.
Take a Right on Sheriff Jerry Joe Johnson, Jr. Rd.
Go 0.8 miles. The Third Baptist Church is on the Left.
If you pass the Methodist Church without a steeple, you've gone too far.

We would take this sheet of paper with us in the car or on our bikes. If we misplaced it—or a rogue wind blew it into a ditch—we probably ended up lost. We may have even had to stop and ask another actual person for directions. THIS IS HOW WE LIVED. It was so barbaric.

Things are different now. It's difficult to get lost. Sure, you might read a news story about some dude spending a year lost at sea, having to decide whether or not to eat his dead friend or his own legs, but that kind of thing doesn't happen to you. No, you can pull out a phone and find your exact location on a map of the entire world pretty much anytime. If you're asked how long it will take to walk to Fuquay-Varina, North Carolina, from virtually any location in North America, you can give an answer in under twenty seconds (assuming you know how to spell Fuquay-Varina, which is never a sure thing).

We were lucky to have grown up during a unique navigational era—somewhere between the present day and a forgotten time when people used the stars, the sun, or the old "licking your fingertip and holding it up in the wind" technique to get around. (That last one might actually just be for kicking field goals but whatever.) As kids, it was pretty easy to get lost, and we did it a lot. Turns out that getting lost with a friend is a pretty Mythical thing to do.

**LINK** We lived on opposite sides of our hometown, Buies Creek. On any given Saturday morning, we'd meet at the graveyard. We met there for two reasons: First, saying "Let's meet at the graveyard" made us feel like gangsters. More practically, it was our best guess as to the halfway point between our houses. (Looking at Google Maps today, it turns out that I was a little farther away, but Rhett had to cross a major highway on his bike and go up a hill—so it kinda evened out.)

Link knew that, if you're going to get lost, always bring a shoulder-mount video camera along.

After we met up at the graveyard, the operative question was very simple: "Which direction should we go today?" We didn't use actual navigational terms like north or south, but rather a simple point of the finger accompanied by "that way." After deciding on a direction, we'd start pedaling. We had no helmets, no food, and no water. Just ourselves and our bikes.

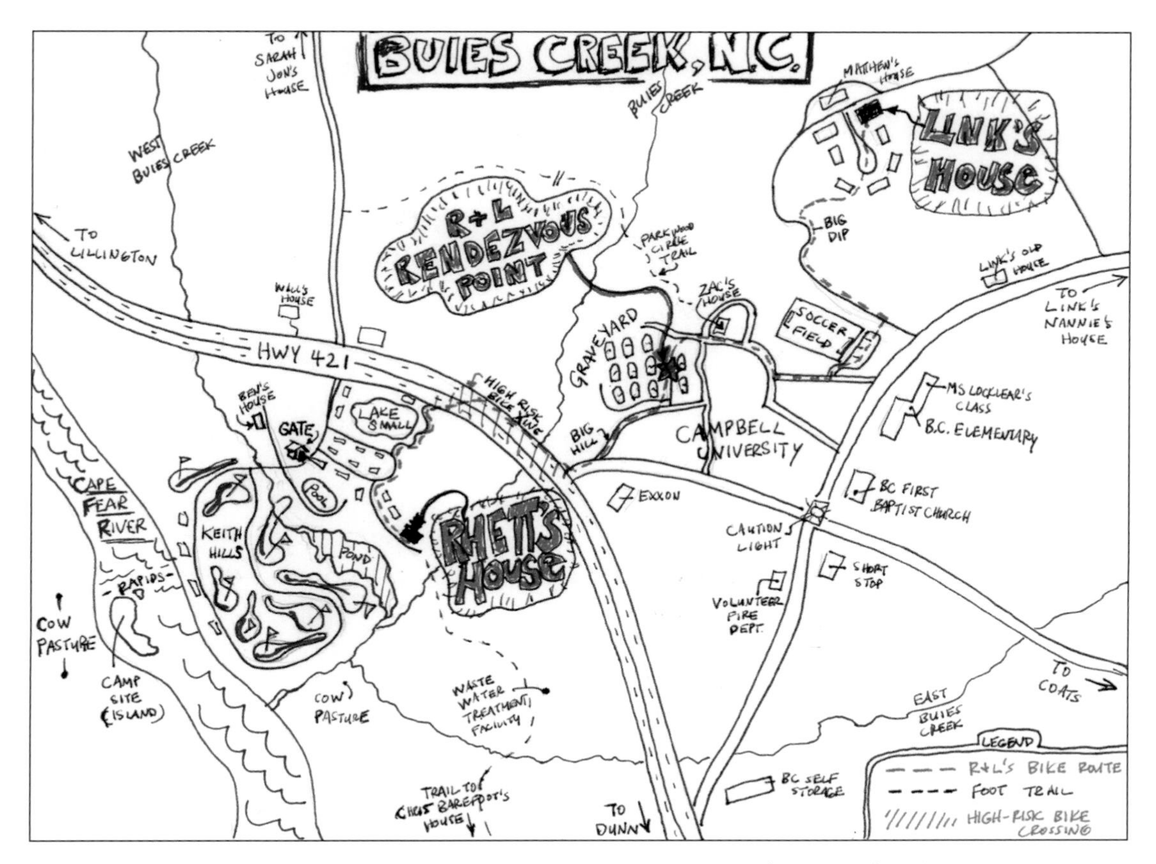


Living on opposite sides of Buies Creek required us to select a sufficiently central (and spooky) rendezvous point.

**RHETT** We seldom stuck to paved roads, opting instead to explore the woods. My bike was a Walmart special, while Link's bike was a little nicer and said YOSEMITE on it. Having no point of reference for Yosemite National Park, he pronounced it YO-seh-might. One Saturday we followed a forest clearing that fanned out from the local wastewater treatment plant. After a few miles, it ran into a dirt road we had never seen before. We rode along the road until we were ambushed by two wildly aggressive pit bulls, who chased us for a few seconds before they were called off by a young boy. It was our classmate Chris Barefoot's little brother. Strangely, he was wearing shoes at the time.

Rhett wore camouflage so that it looked like a bike was driving itself through the woods.

After seeing a house, we put it together that this was where the Barefoots lived. We were suddenly struck with a strange feeling of accomplishment. Lewis and Clark followed the Missouri River and saw the Pacific Ocean—Rhett

Here we are, lost somewhere in Africa. No, wait, scratch that. It's the zoo.

and Link followed a sewage clearing and saw the Barefoots' house. We continued on the dirt road until it hit the highway, at which point we gained an appreciation for just how far we'd come. It was too late in the day to go back through the woods, and we would've had to ride our bikes on a four-lane highway for miles if we took the road. So, we decided to do something we'd only seen in the movies. We stood next to the road and stuck out our thumbs. After ten minutes or so, a truck driven by two good ol' boys stopped and asked us where we were going. We said, "Back to Buies Creek," and they responded, "Hop in." We threw our bikes and ourselves into the truck bed and rode down Highway 421 like two kings on a palanquin. We were freaking hitchhikers. House-discovering hitchhikers, to be exact. (A disclaimer: we don't recommend hitchhiking if you don't live in Buies Creek, NC, in the 1980s.)

**LINK** Once Rhett got his license, we re-created the "getting lost" routine on a larger scale in his parents' Dodge Dynasty. He'd roll up to my house, I'd get in, and we'd pick a direction and drive. We'd put in a mixtape full of songs by Merle Haggard and listen to the first side as we traveled down the road, eventually crossing the Harnett County line. There was no discernible difference in the landscape once we entered a neighboring county—just more endless blacktop cutting through farms and communities so small they weren't even considered towns. Still, it seemed like a foreign land and made us feel like pioneers. There was something electric about the unknown, about giving ourselves over to the fate of North Carolina country roads for a couple of hours. It was precisely the fact that we didn't know the end that made it worth the drive.

With its streamlined front and boxy rear, the Dodge Dynasty embodied the most groundbreaking automotive design of the 20th century.

Once the first side of the mixtape was done, we'd stop driving. If we were lucky we'd find a convenience store that we'd never been to before and drop in to get a cold Mello Yello before flipping over the tape and driving home. A few weeks later we would pick a new direction. We were addicted to the process of choosing a direction and just going. Eventually, we explored just about every road in Harnett County. If there is ever a "Draw a Map of Harnett County from Memory" contest, we would stand a good chance at winning.

**WE DIDN'T KNOW** it at the time, but our tendency to drive without a destination prepared us well for adulthood. When we set out into the recesses of rural North Carolina years ago, we were fostering a sense of discovery that scratched our Mythical itch of curiosity. We were reinforcing the idea that sometimes the most important part of the journey is just deciding to go. (We have gone through the trouble of creating an inspirational quote poster for you because that last sentence was so good. Just flip the page.)

To be clear, we haven't done much literal "pick a direction and drive" lately. The smog levels in Los Angeles are already bad enough without us taking joyrides across town. And if we decided to ride bikes instead, getting lost and hitchhiking might turn out a little differently here than it did in Harnett County. We might get a ride home, but we'd probably have to give up our bikes for it (or at least the front wheels).

Instead of driving, we've applied the principle of getting lost to our careers. Since starting our business together, we've sat down a number of times with the intention of planning our next steps. This has always been a relatively difficult exercise, because we're much better at picking directions than destinations. In 2007, when we decided to try to make a living on YouTube, there was no guidebook to follow. We didn't know anyone who had tried it. We didn't even know what to call it. "Internet comedy" sounded like some sort of pyramid scheme that you recruit your friends into. *You can be an Internet comedian without leaving your house, adding hundreds of dollars a week to your pockets! Join today!* We ended up calling it "Internetainment." Regardless of the name, if we had really thought about trying to make a living through online video, we might have convinced ourselves that it was incredibly stupid for two men with wives and children to try such a thing.

All we knew was that we wanted to continue creating together for a small but growing audience, so we kept heading in that direction. As we kept moving, the pieces began to fall into place around us, and most of it was outside of our control or ability to predict. It was a bit like showing up at Chris Barefoot's house. We came out of the woods and just realized we were there.

Since the beginning, nearly every significant development in our career has followed this rule: moving forward without knowing a specific destination can lead to some pretty remarkable adventures. *GMM* is no different. More than 1,000 episodes later, it's still becoming whatever it is. In the meantime, we'll keep the Merle mixtape playing and see what county line we cross next. Hopefully it's not Cumberland. Fayetteville has some rough spots.

Sometimes
the most important
part of the journey
is just deciding to go.

# THE BEST AND WORST PLACES TO GET LOST

**(WITHOUT A CAR OR A BIKE)**

**We recognize that not all of the Mythical Beasts in the world have access to Yosemite bicycles or Dodge Dynasties, so we wanted to outline the best and worst places to get lost using other common modes of transportation that might be more accessible to you.**

## 1 ROLLER BLADES

**BEST PLACE TO GET LOST ON ROLLERBLADES:**
***AN EMPTY SPORTS ARENA.*** The wide, smooth concrete walkways are perfect for blading. You will feel like you are doing time trials at Daytona. Plus, the lack of people means you can blade without a tinge of self-consciousness—commonly known as "Rollerblading Embarrassment."

**WORST PLACE TO GET LOST ON ROLLERBLADES:**
***ROLLER-SKATING RINK.*** No matter where you go in the facility, you will be seen as an imposter. Don't risk it.

## 2 SCOOTER

**BEST PLACE TO GET LOST ON A SCOOTER:**
***THE US PACIFIC NORTHWEST.*** Scooters are cool here, and you can always fall into an existing scooter herd if you begin to feel vulnerable.

**WORST PLACE TO GET LOST ON A SCOOTER:**
***SOUTHEASTERN UNITED STATES.*** The vehicles are big and the roads are narrow. There is no room, and people might hit you with their trucks just for kicks.

## 3 JET PACK

**BEST PLACE TO GET LOST WITH A JET PACK:**
***ANYWHERE ON EARTH.***

**WORST PLACE TO GET LOST WITH A JET PACK:**
***THE RINGS OF SATURN.*** Unless you are really good at dodging ice and controlling particle density.

## 4 SEGWAY

**BEST PLACE TO GET LOST RIDING A SEGWAY:**
***TOKYO.*** Just throw on a cartoon mascot costume and gingerly lean forward.

**WORST PLACE TO GET LOST RIDING A SEGWAY:**
***YOUR EX'S FAMILY REUNION.*** You would basically be trying to navigate a human minefield of humiliation at roughly 5 mph. Most likely while wearing a helmet.

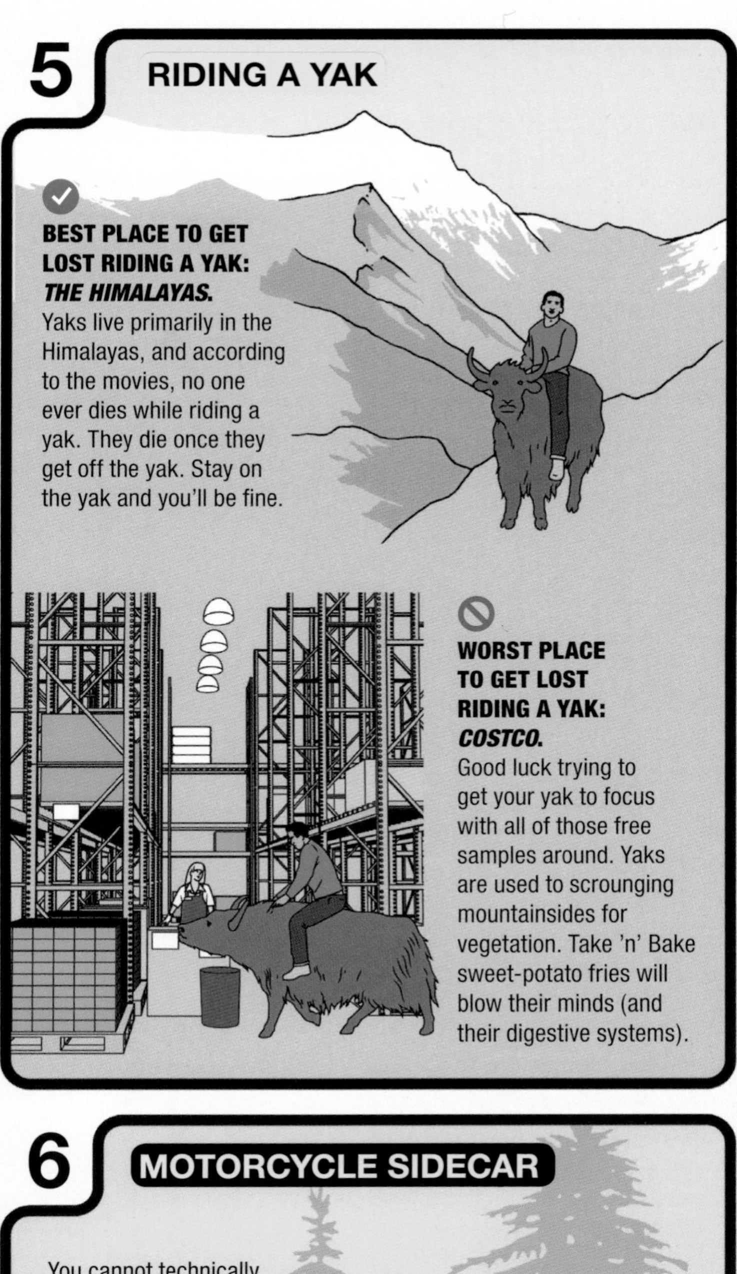

## 5 RIDING A YAK

**BEST PLACE TO GET LOST RIDING A YAK:**
***THE HIMALAYAS.***
Yaks live primarily in the Himalayas, and according to the movies, no one ever dies while riding a yak. They die once they get off the yak. Stay on the yak and you'll be fine.

**WORST PLACE TO GET LOST RIDING A YAK:**
***COSTCO.***
Good luck trying to get your yak to focus with all of those free samples around. Yaks are used to scrounging mountainsides for vegetation. Take 'n' Bake sweet-potato fries will blow their minds (and their digestive systems).

## 6 MOTORCYCLE SIDECAR

You cannot technically be lost in a sidecar.

THE

# "WHELEPHIGEONOLE"

## THE MYTHICAL BEAST THAT NEVER GETS LOST

The recent discovery of clustered regularly interspaced short palindromic repeats (CRISPR for short) DNA editing has opened up the very real possibility of custom genetically engineered organisms in the not-so-distant future. When that day comes, we plan on trying to talk the scientists into creating a whelephigeonole. Why? Because it will look extremely cool, and it will be the only animal in the world that is literally incapable of losing its whereabouts.

THE ECHOLOCATION OF A WHALE
Toothed whales (and dolphins) bounce sounds off objects and the seafloor in order to determine their position. Plus, getting inside the whelephigeonole and plunging into the ocean depths like you're James Cameron in a submarine seems fun.
THE STEREO SMELLING OF A MOLE
Moles don't see or hear very well and yet they are able to locate food very efficiently above or below ground by utilizing their amazing nostrils, which can process and compare smells similarly to how our ears process and compare sounds. Of course, the ability to dig large underground tunnels will make the whelephigeonole a favorite pet of drug cartel kingpins, but nobody's perfect, right?
THE GPS OF AN ELEPHANT
Elephants have incredible spatial reasoning, which allows them to mentally chart the most efficient course to locations up to twenty miles away. They also have a trunk, and putting trunks on genetically engineered animals seems like a good idea.
THE ELECTROMAGNETIC NAVIGATION SKILLS OF A HOMING PIGEON
Homing pigeons are believed to use the magnetite in their beaks to detect magnetic signposts and form a navigational map. Also, the ability to fly means that you'll be able to ride the whelephigeonole around like Falcor from The Neverending Story.

# HOW TO GET UNLOST

**THE RISK OF GETTING LOST FOR FUN IS THAT YOU END UP GETTING LOST FOR REAL. WE'VE COMPILED A LIST OF THE PLACES IN WHICH PEOPLE GET LOST MOST OFTEN, ALONG WITH SUREFIRE WAYS TO GET YOURSELF FOUND.**

## 1. THE MALL

It's happened to the best of us. You look at the mall map with the "You Are Here" point marked, and you might as well be looking at ancient Mesopotamian inscriptions. No need to panic. Priority number one is food. Follow the smell of every cuisine on Earth mixed together. This will lead you to the food court. Grab all the free samples. Then put your shirt on inside out and grab all the free samples again. Now nourished, follow the distinctly different smell of every perfume on Earth mixed together. This will lead you to one of the department stores on either end of the mall. Do not follow the smell of one perfume, because this will lead you directly to a lady who will aggressively sell you said perfume. Avoid her and her cohorts and move quickly to the parking lot for fresh air. Hopefully you parked nearby. If not, hitch a ride on a mall-cop cart to your vehicle.

## 2. THE ZOO

(ON THE PATH)

We've all been there. You're at the zoo and all you want to do is see the chimpanzees or the elephants, but the winding pathways get you all turned around until it seems that no matter where you go you always end up in front of the boring "desert reptiles" exhibit. Don't worry. All you have to do is wait for a family with four or more children to come by. Families of this size have learned to plan zoo trips meticulously in order to maximize animal sightings and minimize uncoordinated bathroom breaks. Follow them for the rest of the day, and you will see all the cool stuff. Stay at least fifty feet away so as not to frighten them.

## 3. THE ZOO

### (INSIDE THE TIGER HABITAT)

First things first: recognize that you aren't actually lost. Sure, you feel disoriented, but that's just a result of the concussion you suffered when you fell into the tiger enclosure. No matter, the tigers (yes, there are two of them) are headed your way and they look hungry. Don't waste time looking at the wall. You can't climb it. The fake swimming hole is a possibility because you've never actually seen the tigers swim in it, but you shouldn't risk that either. Instead, immediately make yourself puke. Nothing is more pungent than vomit consisting of hot dogs, nacho cheese sauce, and churros. It also happens to be a tiger delicacy. When they begin to devour it, climb on their backs and then reach up for the railing. If the large family you have been following is worth their salt, they will have formed a human chain long enough to pull you to safety.

## 4. IN SPACE

We are going to assume that you are lost well beyond the Milky Way, because everyone knows that if you get lost in our galaxy, all you have to do is to triangulate your location using the Orion, Perseus, and Sagittarius arms of the galaxy, and then ride the solar winds home like you're in the carpool lane. Anyhow, for the sake of argument, let's assume that you are lost in Zebulor or maybe the Varinian System and your transworld-navigation system is running low on Shartilliam. Check your dead cyborg companion's cache. Did he pack an A-490 or a BiddybiddyBot for backup? If so, use it to call out to the closest space-junk freighter and drift off into cryosleep for a few light-years. If you don't have a dead cyborg companion (or if you're a firstborn albino Demi), you'll have to make an emergency landing on the nearest planet and hope that it's inhabited . . . so you can find someone to eat. Or, you can just try your best to wake up because you're clearly dreaming.

## 5. A NEW CITY YOU'VE NEVER BEEN TO

Try Google Maps or duck into a coffee shop and ask for directions.

DEFEAT
THE
HAIR
OF

# MAKE A BOLD HAIR CHOICE

"WE WERE SO KEEN ON ACHIEVING THE PLATINUM-BLOND LOOK THAT WE CAME UP WITH A PROCESS THAT INCLUDED BLEACHING OUR HAIR TWICE, DYEING IT BLUE, THEN BLEACHING IT AGAIN. THIS ENSURED THAT THERE WERE LITTLE TO NO TRACES OF YELLOW LEFT. JUST WHITE, BRITTLE, HIDEOUS HAIR."

THERE IS A huge TV screen just to the right of the camera on the *GMM* set that displays the video feed of what is being captured. If you've watched the show, you've seen us checking ourselves out in it. We're supposed to use it as a monitor—so we can keep things in frame—but we employ it almost exclusively as a mirror to ensure that our coifs stay tamed. Our editors could easily create a montage of all the times we've made hair adjustments just before we deliver our show teaser in each episode. It would be at least ten hours long. If you were to accuse us of caring more about our hair than is normal or necessary, we would have a difficult time defending ourselves.

We care about our hair.

If/when the apocalypse finally comes, we will gladly toss aside our concerns over our hairstyles, or at least adopt a different approach. Extremely intimidating hairdos—like a series of large conical spikes—will potentially be useful for striking fear into rival camps in order to pillage them, but we can discuss that in another book. Currently, we still live in a relatively safe society where fashion and style are legitimate forms of expression. So, it seems like it's not too superficial to write about hairstyles. Pretty superficial. But not embarrassingly so.

Plus, you can't deny that it's a bit strange that we humans have retained hair in just a few strategic places, the main one being right there on the tops of our heads. As long as our species continues to grow this curious skull cover, it's an opportunity to make a statement, a chance to set ourselves apart from one another. And since originality and creativity are hallmarks of Mythicality, expressing yourself with your hair is a pretty Mythical thing to do. However, this requires making a definitive choice. This may seem simple, but plenty of people fail to make a decision about their hair and instead let it make the decision for them—allowing their hair to just sort of "happen" on their heads. As you will soon learn, we were once victims of this kind of hair indecision. Thankfully, we've emerged on the other side. We invite you to join us on a journey through our hair adventures that we hope will be helpful to you, especially if you are presently suffering, as we did, from Hair of Defeat.

Like most everyone, the first several years of our lives were characterized by our mothers making all hair-related decisions. Based on the available photo evidence, those decisions were limited to simply combing all of our hair straight down in every direction from the crown of our heads. We choose to believe that this was fashionable at the time.

While we began to have some limited say in our hairstyles during our elementary school years, we were still somewhat bound by the places our parents took us to get haircuts.

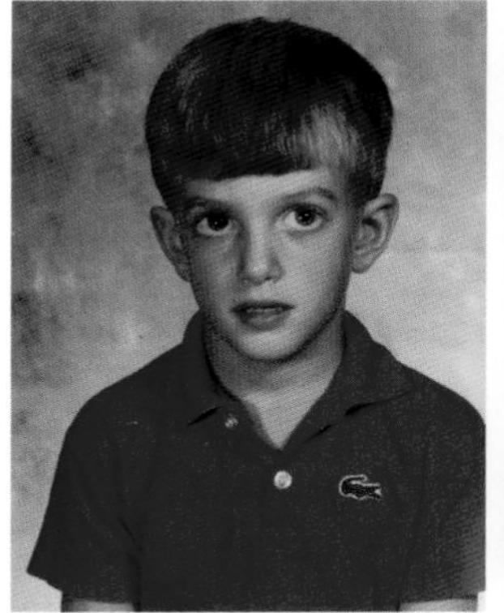

Not only did we have matching haircuts as youngsters, but we also sported Lacoste crocodile polos. Link appears more confident in this look than Rhett.

**RHETT** There was one barbershop in my town, owned and operated by Rudolph Blanchard. My father and brother got their hair cut there—along with 99 percent of the men in Buies Creek—so I did as well. I would sit down in Rudolph's chair and he would ask me, "What'll it be this time?" It didn't take me long to learn that, no matter what I said, Rudolph was going to give me one haircut: the "Rudolph." It was a short, simple part. I sported the Rudolph, along with nearly every other male in a three-mile radius, for many years. It never failed me.

Rhett went from boyhood to young manhood without ever departing from the "Rudolph" haircut.

**LINK** I was in the 1 percent of Buies Creek males who didn't go to Rudolph. Instead, my mom took me to Cindy the Beautician, who also cut my mom's hair. Like Rudolph, Cindy apparently knew of only one approach to cutting a boy's hair, but the outcome was distinctly different: the bowl cut. Of course, the bowl cut wasn't a particularly original hairstyle in the '80s for boys of my age, but considering that every other dude had the "Rudolph," I really stood out. The normally plain bowl cut almost seemed bold. Even though Cindy would reset the bowlishness of my haircut each time I returned to her, the pressure of being surrounded by so many Rudolphs led me to occasionally comb my hair into more a Rudolph-esque part.

LEFT: Link was equally proud of his bowl cut and his jack-o-lantern. MIDDLE: Peer pressure pushed Link's bowl cut into a slight part to mimic the "Rudolph." RIGHT: At times, Link was compelled to fully part his hair (and wear a completely Coca-Cola–themed outfit) to fit in.

**HIGH SCHOOL REPRESENTED** a shift to true autonomy in hairstyle management. Unfortunately, having been restrained by the low level of experimentation that Rudolph and Cindy were willing to flirt with, we were slow to push the limits of our hair potential.

Rhett with the "Modified Rudolph" in high school, a time when his head had yet to fully grow to match his neck.

Nothing says Merry Christmas quite like Link's mushroom hair and Rhett's lazy eye.

**RHETT** I was so overwhelmed with trying to adjust to the spindly, Plastic Man–like body that puberty had given me that I opted to take a simpler approach to my hair. I maintained what you might call a "Modified Rudolph," awkwardly straddling the line between an original "Rudolph" and a total buzz. There was just enough length to indicate that my hair was about to part if it were a little longer—a "pre-part" if you will. I was like a flower whose petals were caught in a perpetual state of almost blooming.

**LINK** I, on the other hand, began to truly express myself. And by express myself, I mean get the same haircut that every guy on the soccer team had. We didn't have a name for it, but the approach was pretty straightforward. It involved growing the hair on the top of your head out to what we considered long (approximately four inches), then shaving the sides and back down to buzz level. This resulted in my silhouette closely resembling a mushroom. I loved my mushroom hair. When I supplemented it by growing a weak goatee, I was convinced I had achieved the look that I would carry to my grave. It was the perfect hairstyle.

**BUT THEN WE** started a band. The Wax Paper Dogz. Yes, that's right, "dogz" with a *z*. It was 1994; switching *s*'s with *z*'s was fashionable at the time. Over a very short stint, our band tore through a number of musical genres, including '70s easy listening, country, and classic rock, eventually settling into some kind of a 311 rip-off rap-funk-rock thing. While our music didn't get us anywhere near a record contract, it did send us into a whole new world of coiffure.

Taking more than just our musical queues from 311, we decided to make the much-less-original-than-we-thought-at-the-time move of bleaching our hair. This started us down a road that left our scalps burned and blistered more than a few times. We were so keen on achieving

We thought we should bleach our hair because we were in a band. It's worth noting that we sounded just as bad as we looked.

We rotated through several hairstyles in college, all while maintaining our tradition of semi-regular shirtlessness.

the platinum-blond look that we came up with a process that included bleaching our hair twice, dyeing it blue, then bleaching it again. This ensured that there were little to no traces of yellow left. Just white, brittle, hideous hair (sections of which would just break off and blow in the wind like a dandelion). We began to treat our poor hair like a canvas, even donning red, white, and blue for a mind-blowing performance on the stage at the town of Lillington's 1996 Fourth of July celebration. We were so cool.

College at NC State University was a time of further hair experimentation. We both majored in engineering (Rhett civil and Link industrial), and our rather boring studies may explain why we oscillated between a number of styles, sometimes sporting the bleached look from our band days while occasionally assuming tight buzz cuts. Interestingly, we each had poofy hair for a time, which would be an early precursor to Rhett's current hairstyle. Our only hair rule in college was that we couldn't commit to any style for too long. We had to keep changing (and keep our concerned relatives concerned).

When we graduated and began to work as engineers, our previously expressive and dynamic hair configurations began to settle into a very sad state. It's as if our hair was some kind of indicator as to what was going on inside of our souls as we toiled away at mind-numbing calculation after calculation. Naturally, there was a bit of an expectation as to what kind of hair was acceptable among junior engineers. Nowhere was it stated that our hair needed to assume a lifeless and unprovocative appearance, but given that we were required to wear collared shirts tucked into dress pants, it was clear enough. These were our unfortunate days of hair indecision.

Remarkably, we both adopted the same haircut. We never discussed it or planned it. One day we were living wild and free as college students, never knowing what hairstyle was coming next, and then, all of a sudden, we were sitting in cubicles with totally uninspired mats of hair on our heads. We'd given up on making a statement with our hair. But make no mistake, hair is always making a statement. During those days, ours only said, "This is hair." We had Hair of Defeat.

LEFT: Rhett may have been forcing a smile, but he and his hair were defeated. Even his nephew, Micah, knew something had gone horribly wrong. RIGHT: The look on Link's face communicated that he was suffering from deep hair indecision.

When we made the decision to leave engineering for good to start working together in comedy, our hair slowly began to come back from the dead. The more we became locked into this new career together, the more our hair responded. Just like it had symbolized our discontent during those engineering days, our hair began to signal that we were finally realizing our dream of creating together. We were ushering in a new hair era. A new haira. That should be a word.

**RHETT** It was at this point that my hair began to literally reach for the skies. Like I mentioned before, I had briefly tried a poofy updo in college one summer, but I lost heart upon returning to school in the fall. This time was different. When I applied massive amounts of pomade to convince my hair to defy gravity, I was saying, "Look at me! I'm an already freakishly tall man who is using his hair to make himself obscenely tall by adding a full two inches to his stature." Eventually, I would even abandon my horrid chinstrap by growing a full beard, finally settling into the look that most Mythical Beasts are familiar with.

After beginning to work together making Internet videos, Rhett's hair went up, and Link's hair went down (and out). There's even a song about it.

**LINK** My hair also began to reach new heights, but not by going up. No, my hair sprouted wings and took flight. My wings could have never flown in my engineering job, where I had to be taken seriously, but afterward my hair was released like a carrier pigeon with a message. That message was "I'm an Internet comedian, and I'm not even sure if that's a real job, but it means I can have hair like this!"

Alas, after nearly a decade of letting my hair fly around the Internet, I decided that it was time to ground the bird. I think I had said everything I wanted to say with that particular hairstyle, and honestly, I believe it might have overstayed its welcome. And so, in late 2015, I clipped my wings. Even though I've been in this business long enough to know how much the Internet is resistant to change, I had no way of anticipating the level of reaction to my decision. But I had no regrets. It was time for my hair to say something new about me. I'm still not entirely sure what my new hair says. Maybe it says, "I was tired of my old haircut and I think this new one looks pretty cool." I trust its message will be revealed over time.

**Betty Ochoa** @BettyLamont27 Dec 21
#riplinkswings NOOO IM CRYING NOOO NOT NOW NOOOOOOO WHYYYYYYYYYYY NOOOOOOOOOO WHYYYYYYYYYYYY THE WINGS WERE AWESOME AND WHYYYYYYYYU NOOOO.!!

**krista** @itsmekristae Dec 21
Link cut his hair and I could literally cry. #RIPLinkswings

in reply to @linklamont

**gmm pugs tobuscus** @gmmandp... Dec 21
@linklamont did link really cut his hair #riplinkswings he isn't the same awesome dork anymore

The Internet cried when Link clipped his wings.

**RHETT** In early 2017, I embarked on my latest haira. My hair has always been a bit wavy, but I've spent most of my life attempting to calm the seas with combs and blow dryers. After years of resistance, I made the decision to let my hair follow its heart, if only for a time. The hair wants what the hair wants. And apparently my hair wants to look like the North Atlantic during a squall. Who am I to stand in its way?

Link's latest iteration of hair. Simple, aerodynamic. No wings.

Rhett is letting his hair follow its heart.

WHO KNOWS WHAT shapes our hair will take in the future. We reserve the right to change our hairstyles as we age, even if that means bringing back the "Rudolph." But that's not the point. The bottom line is that we escaped the depths of the valley of hair indecision, and we are currently exercising our freedom to definitively sculpt our manes into whatever style we choose.

You may not be free at this particular time to experiment with your hair. Maybe you have a job with certain guidelines, or if you're still living at home, your parents may have a say in your hairstylings. Working within those particular parameters is totally fine, but just make sure that you're not currently experiencing Hair of Defeat. Make a bold decision about your hair, and go for it.

It won't be easy. Hair indecision is actually very common, and having it can be a way to fit in. But if you want your hair to be Mythical by saying something about you, or serve as an indication of the way you feel, then make the change. When you finally enter your own new haira, you'll be glad you overcame your hair indecision. And if for some reason you end up regretting it, just shave it all off. It'll probably grow back.

# The Chinstrap
## A TALE OF REGRET

I inherited a weak chin from my mom's side of the family, and ever since I discovered hair growing on the lower half of my face in high school, I have been attempting to use it to create the illusion that I actually have a normal chin.

This is me without a beard—but with a perm—from the prom scene in *Buddy System*. I trust that it is patently obvious why I have sought to augment my face with hair.

I regularly grew a goatee in college. It wasn't a full goatee, because there were serious connectivity issues between my mustache and beard. It was more of an overgrown soul patch. It added some dimension to my face, but left quite a bit exposed. Shortly after college, my beard began to fill in, allowing me to see the potential to use my facial hair to accomplish something I had been hoping to do for years: establish a jawline. Thus, my chinstrap phase began. Although I love horses and agree that much of modern technology is a vice, I definitely was not trying to apply for a position on an Amish farm. I would have grown a full beard were it not for the persisting mustache-beard gap. The beauty lowlight of my life occurred during the years where my Hair of Defeat coincided with my chinstrap, which happens to be the precise time we were getting our start on YouTube.

I would like to take this opportunity to officially apologize for the chinstrap. While I feel that extenuating—as well as genetic—circumstances left me with little choice, there had to be a better way. I was afraid that my full beard would be too patchy, and in my defense, the "weak hipster beard" look wasn't a thing in 2006. Thankfully, around the time I was turning thirty, my beard was beginning to experience its full potential, and I was finally able to absorb the hideous chinstrap into a fully formed beard. I promise it won't happen again. Thanks for understanding.

I have to believe that our YouTube career would have experienced a quicker start had I not worn the chinstrap.

# Taming the Unibrow

I too had a genetic facial hair hurdle to clear. My nana's branch of the family tree, the Buchanans, all suffered from *persistent gapless brow syndrome,* aka the unibrow. Some were more pronounced than others. Great-Granny Shirl probably endured the occasional pluck back in her dating days; but Uncle James sported a thick shelf of forehead forestation that stretched uninterrupted from temple to temple.

During the beginning of my freshman year of high school, I was looking in the mirror and realized it was happening to me. A hair bridge was forming between my otherwise island-like eyebrows. I tried to tell them they'd be happier apart. But they couldn't be reasoned with . . . because they were hair. *This can't be happening,* I worried. *It's my freshman year.* Facial things like this (feel like they) determine the fate of the rest of your life. I had to do something.

The next day I showed up to class with a space between my eyebrows exactly the width of a Gillette Sensor razor. I'd altered the trajectory of my high school career with one single swoop. It was so easy. And so wide. I clear-cut the forest, but I really only needed to make a nature trail.

In homeroom, Rhett asked, "What did you do?!" I said, "I took care of it." He said "It's gonna grow back thicker, man. Don't you know you gotta pluck?" He must've been reading *Cosmo* or something. That afternoon Rhett's dad was driving us home. I remember Rhett saying, "Dad, Link shaved his eyebrows with a razor. Tell him they're gonna grow back thicker; tell him he's gotta pluck." It was a little embarrassing to get grooming advice from my friend's dad, but I did switch to plucking from there on out. And for some reason I didn't want to tell my mom I was plucking my eyebrows, so I would sneak in her bathroom and borrow her tweezers while she was watching *Entertainment Tonight.*

Today, I'm a proud plucker. But I *do* shave a patch of hair on each of my shoulders that's exactly the width of a Gillette Sensor razor.

I promise this is not a Glamour Shot. I also promise that I will never again have this much bare space between my brows.

# Unfortunate Hairstyles throughout History

MAKEOVER -EDITION-

# MARIE ANTOINETTE

**THE PROBLEM:** Only an out-of-touch, elitist monarch with her head in the clouds would think that a hairstyle that looks like a cloud would endear her to the masses.

**OUR SOLUTION:** A simple pixie cut that says "Forget what I've said about you silly peasant revolutionaries. I'm still, I'm still Mary from the block (please don't put my head on the block)."

## NAPOLEON

**THE PROBLEM:** Are you the greatest military leader the world has ever seen, or his overworked and underappreciated accountant?

**OUR SOLUTION:** A gargantuan "Phil Spector in court" bouffant. Napoleon was a small man with big ambitions (hence the whole Napoleon complex thing). By making his head seem as large as possible, he would finally have a physical trait to match his massive personality—as well as a place to hide extra croissants.

## MEDIEVAL MONK

**THE PROBLEM:** The whole point of the monk's classic tonsure haircut was humility. They figured that you couldn't fall victim to vanity if you had a ring of hair around a bald spot. They were right.

**OUR SOLUTION:** If a monk's hair was supposed to keep him from focusing on himself, why not go all the way? Letting the hair grow into an impenetrable 360-degree hair curtain creates a distinct "Cousin It" effect that is sure to maximize embarrassment.

## JULIUS CAESAR

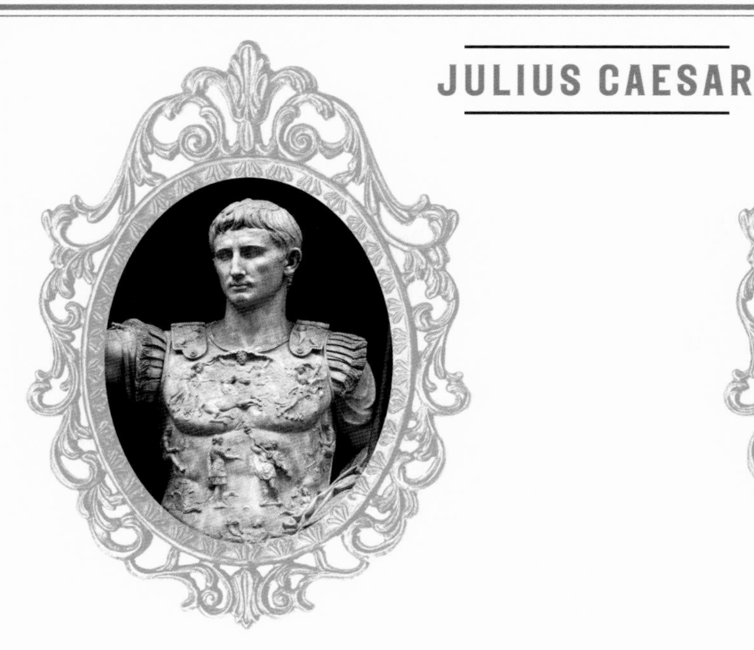

**THE PROBLEM:** Achilles had his heel, Julius Caesar had his receding hairline. Why not own your hairline and mow the lawn, rather than try to landscape your way to a full head of hair? Nothing says "I'm vulnerable" like a man who is obviously self-conscious about his hairline. No wonder Brutus took a run at Caesar when he wasn't looking.

**OUR SOLUTION:** Shave it tight like Mr. Clean or Michael Jordan. Clean, powerful, timeless. If you are worried about not looking youthful, add an earring.

## GEORGE WASHINGTON

**THE PROBLEM:** It's easy to overlook the absolutely ridiculous nature of the first president's hair. But there's a reason that no one else sported this look. It's horrendous.

**OUR SOLUTION:** This one's easy. All George had to do was turn his hair upside down and he would have had the flyest presidential hair of all time.

SAVE IT
FOR LATER

# BUILD A TIME CAPSULE

"IT MEANS A LOT THAT RHETT WROTE DOWN THE DETAILS OF THAT NIGHT. NOTHING SAYS 'I CARE ABOUT YOU' LIKE A WRITTEN REMINDER THAT YOU REPEATEDLY MADE THE OL' PENIS/PELVIS JOKE WITH A HOSPITAL NURSE."

**IN FIRST GRADE,** we learned about time capsules from Ms. Locklear. We were immediately fascinated by the idea that we could send important messages to the deep future simply by choosing a collection of items to be preserved and discovered later. However, just learning about time capsules wasn't enough. We wanted to make our own.

Picking the right container was key. It had to be the kind of enclosure that could safely hold our precious cargo for generations. But more important, it had to be something two first-graders could acquire. Ultimately, we landed on a cardboard paper-towel tube sealed at both ends with duct tape. We were six.

Then came the contents, the real heart of our message. We had to choose these objects carefully. We determined it would be best to include one item from each of us, as well as one collective offering.

**LINK** I offered up a GI Joe figure. "Doc" to be exact. I thought that if anyone could survive years underground in a duct-tape-sealed cardboard tube, it was a doctor. And to be honest, Doc was my most expendable GI Joe figure. I never saw much need for a medic on my pretend battlefields since there was never any actual blood.

**RHETT** I figured that the people of the future would want to know how the people of the past ate. Plus, I was—as usual—thinking about food. I reasoned that a pack of crackers, specifically the bright-orange cheese crackers with peanut butter sandwiched between them—commonly called "Nabs" throughout the South—were a great representative foodstuff of our era. I had never seen a pack of Nabs go bad, no matter how long my dad left one in the glove compartment of his Caprice Classic. Also, Nabs were the only food I had on hand that could comfortably fit into a paper-towel tube.

**FINALLY, WE DETERMINED** that our time capsule should accommodate the unlikely possibility that aliens, not humans, would ultimately unearth our buried treasure. Without stopping to consider that extraterrestrial invaders might not understand English, we wrote a note to them. Unfortunately, neither one of us has any memory of what we said in that letter three decades ago. Seeing as how we could barely write anything without the assistance of that special paper we used at school to make sure our letters lined up properly on the page, our message was undoubtedly short and sweet. Something along the lines of "Dear Aliens, Please take care of Doc and enjoy the Nabs. Love, Rhett & Link."

When our time capsule had been tightly secured with ample amounts of duct tape, we transported it to one of the many tobacco fields near Link's house. In retrospect, burying a time capsule in a field that is tilled and planted every year wasn't the brightest idea, but we never thought about that. All we knew was that the soil was soft, and we could count the rows of tobacco to remember the exact burial location. We deposited our cardboard time tube about six inches below the surface, made a mental note of how many tobacco rows deep we were, and proudly returned home.

The next day, our excitement grew as we pondered who might find our time capsule at some distant point in the future. Then it dawned on us that maybe we didn't have to wait for someone else to find it. Maybe *we* could just dig it up when we were old. But what if we died in a tandem skydiving accident as teenagers? Maybe we should just wait until next year. But what if we both experienced a sudden and unexpected regression in rudimentary mathematics, causing us to forget how to count rows of tobacco? You see where this is going. Shortly after our conversation, we went back out to the field, easily found the disturbed earth, and dug up our time capsule less than twenty-four hours after it was buried. Again, we were six.

Thinking back, it makes sense that we retrieved the time capsule the next day. Not only because poor Doc would have been torn limb from limb and mixed thoroughly with Nabs by the metal discs of a tobacco cultivator, but because our time capsule wasn't really about some point in the far future; it was about our particular "now." Those silly items in that inadequate container buried in an ill-advised location said something about six-year-old Rhett and Link. On one hand, they said that six-year-old Rhett and Link were idiots when it came to proper time-capsule construction and burial. But they also said that we wanted to take the time to mark a moment in our lives in a significant and original way.

Over the years, we've repeatedly tried to mark particular points in our lives so we could revisit those memories later, and we've expanded our efforts beyond traditional time capsules. Turns out there are a lot of different ways to encapsulate time that don't involve actually burying anything but still preserve the memories. And it can be even more fun when you rope other people into it, like we did in college.

During our freshman year at NC State, we were roommates in Room 24 of Syme dorm. While many of our friends were putting flimsy futons in their rooms, we opted for a more substantial piece of furniture with its own sense of history. At the local Salvation Army thrift store, we spotted an extra-long, twenty-plus-year-old couch adorned with a hypnotizing floral pattern. We brought it home and christened it "Mr. Fly." After setting Mr. Fly against our wall, we felt he needed some company. So just above him, we hung the fully unfurled inside cover of Lionel Richie's first solo album, featuring Lionel lying on what appears to be a gymnasium floor in white pants, striking the coolest lounging pose in the history of lounging poses. Then, in order to timestamp the moment, we each did our own Lionel lounging pose impersonation while lying on Mr. Fly, had the pictures developed (it was 1996), and posted them on the adjacent wall.

But we didn't stop there. We decided that each and every person who came into our dorm room would be required to imitate Lionel's pose and have their pictures taken as well. Eventually, our dorm room wall was lined with pictures of our friends and dormmates, all of them doing their best Lionel poses with varying degrees of success. (Hint: the key to the pose is in the hand and finger placement, as well as a head held perfectly perpendicular to the ground.) We called our photo wall "Project Lionel," and it didn't take long before random students began to show up from all over campus just to be a part of it.

You have reached the home base of...

# *Project Lionel*

**You may be wondering...**
**What is Project Lionel?**

For your information, Project Lionel is an in depth process instigated by Rhett McLaughlin and Link Neal, residents of this very room. It consists of you, the guest to our room, entering the premises and posing as Lionel Richie himself on our couch, "Mr. Fly". We will take your picture and add it to our Project Lionel "Wall of Fame" if you would like to participate.

Your participation is wanted!!
Knock if you have questions!!

And a very important note: It costs money to process all this film that we are using on your pictures. Please leave a donation inside. We make double prints of every pose, so if you would like to purchase your very own picture of your pretty self, you can have it for ~~$1.00~~. .50 big sale

See the Project Lionel "Operation Indicator" below to see if Project Lionel is currently in session. Rhett and Link are busy, so Project Lionel cannot operate constantly.

MARIA MATTHEWS. HIGH SCHOOL HISTORY TEACHER.

GREGG HARISFIELD. MECHANICAL ENGINEER IN WA.

COLE MCLAUGHLIN. STILL RHETT'S BROTHER.

SHELLY MOORE. SINGER/SONGWRITER.

RODERICK F. BROWN. CORPORATE LAWYER IN NC

TOMMY RUTLEDGE. SOLD HIS AWESOME PONTIAC FIREBIRD FOR SOME REASON.

JACQUI MCLAUGHLIN. STILL IN NO WAY RELATED TO RHETT.

TERESSA GUTWEIN. NOW RHETT'S SISTER-IN-LAW.

MATTHEW ENZOR. INVENTOR OF THE SCISSOR SPOON.

JOHN ENZOR. STILL PLAYIN' BASS.

SUE CUMMINGS. STILL LINK'S MOM.

LINK NEAL. SEMI-PRO PEANUT BUTTER EATER.

KELLY BROWN. STILL RHETT'S EX-GIRLFRIEND

RHETT MCLAUGHLIN. UNSUCCESSFUL PART-TIME FOSSIL HUNTER.

HEATHER WILSON. MARRIED A BUSH PILOT.

CHRIS LANIER. HAS SIGNIFICANTLY SHORTER HAIR NOW.

When we look at the pictures from Project Lionel today, we see more than just the horrific hairstyles, questionable configurations of facial hair, and misguided fashion choices. We see the people who were in our lives at that pivotal time when we were experiencing our first taste of adult independence. Taking the time to turn the purchase of a sofa into an art project was worth it.

The two of us on a snowboarding trip that we returned home from with fully intact pelvises (something we would soon not take for granted).

A wounded Link is escorted from the hospital by our roommate, Gregg.

**LINK** We have never regretted making the decision to pause and creatively document a moment in our lives, good or bad. I am especially grateful that Rhett took the time to record the details of me breaking my pelvis while snowboarding when we were juniors in college. That winter, we drove up to Hawksnest Ski Resort in the mountains of North Carolina with some friends. That's about all I remember, because I wiped out so hard that all the details between driving up the mountain and later sitting on a donut pillow back home have been lost.

**RHETT** Luckily, I remember all of the sensational details of Link's ordeal during that trip. I also remember thinking as it was happening that I must write the entire event down because it was so hilarious. I transcribed the events of our trip in a short story entitled "The Tragedy." We've included an excerpt from that historical document on pages 66–67.

As you can see, the key words that the doctor wanted to emphasize were *fell, concussion,* and *broken pelvis*. Makes sense. However, Link didn't take this note too seriously. When I arrived in the ER for the second time, Link held up the sign and said, "Hey, Rhett, I've got a broken penis!"

He told us about his apparently malfunctioning penis a number of times. He was really amusing himself, and every time he would laugh he would follow it with a moan because of his broken PELVIS, not penis. He read the sign to me a couple of times, then he got that I've-just-come-into-reality look on his face. I asked, "How many times have you read that, Link?" He said, "Once."

After a day of relaxation and pain relief, Link was released like a restless coyote into the wild. His mind came back and he began to laugh with us about all that had happened. We took him home in the Dynasty just as we had taken him there. To this day Link doesn't remember snowboarding that night at all. He probably never will. The important thing is that a few lucky individuals will never forget it, and I'm one of them.

**LINK** It means a lot that Rhett wrote down the details of that night. Nothing says "I care about you" like a written reminder that you repeatedly made the ol' penis/pelvis joke with a hospital nurse. Of course, if this were to happen today, Rhett would probably just record the entire episode on his phone, post some of the funnier moments online, and then we'd end up selling a T-shirt that says HOLD ON. I'M JUST COMING TO. EVIDENTLY I'VE HURT MY LEFT HIP. But I think there's something even more special about him going through the trouble of documenting my adventures in pelvis-cracking.

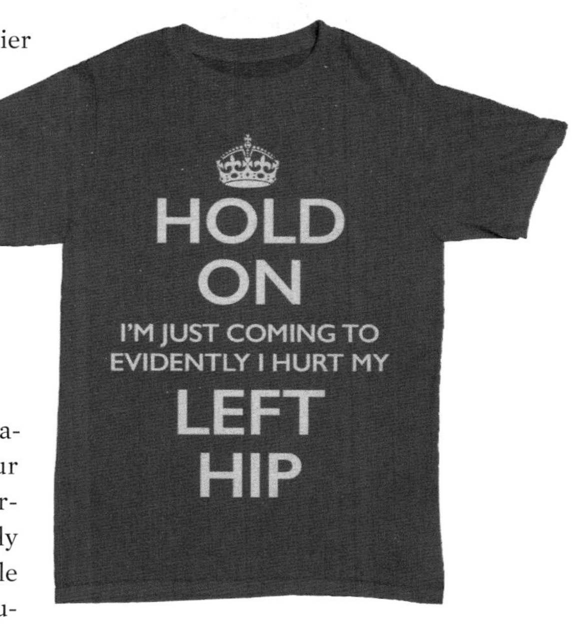


SOCIAL MEDIA HAS given us the ability to catalogue and share every significant moment of our lives. While we're both thankful that large portions of our years on Earth were not extensively documented, it is remarkable that most people born in this millennium will have the opportunity to share a virtual scrapbook of their entire existence with whomever they wish.

This ease with which we can archive ourselves online may make building a time capsule or writing a piece about your friend's pelvis injury seem less necessary. We have to admit, a Snapchat story featuring Link lying in a hospital bed confusing his pelvis with his penis sounds incredible. But simply using existing social media tools to capture your life isn't exactly Mythical, because it's not original. Everybody already does that. If you want to create a Mythical record of an event, you'll take the time to remember something in a unique way. And by doing so, you'll likely have an even stronger and more significant memory each time you revisit it.

Note: we feel obligated to state that we are not publicly advocating scrapbooking. While we are well aware that scrapbooking might be a perfectly logical application of this chapter, we cannot in good conscience openly endorse the practice. So we are taking a neutral stance. If you choose to scrapbook, we will not try to stop you. Just know that once you enter the world of scrapbooking, it can serve as an unexpected portal to becoming a cat lady.

We can, however, freely advocate building a time capsule. We also highly recommend Lionel Richie–themed photography projects. Since we already did the Lionel Richie album pose, may we suggest re-creating Lionel's epic "jumping on a pole for no apparent reason" photo found on the inside cover of his 1983 album *Can't Slow Down*. This will require commandeering a stripper pole, and we can't help you there. Also, covering a friend's harrowing ordeal (with or without a broken pelvis) like you're some kind of embedded war journalist is definitely a Mythical idea. Other options for historicizing an event include oil paintings, poems, ballads, commemorative tattoos, documentaries, and T-shirts, just to name a few. You'll notice a pattern. All of these options are relatively permanent. Less permanent historical markers, such as cakes, tree carvings, or shaving something into the side of your head will fade with time, and therefore are less Mythical.

Whichever route you choose to commemorate your next significant life event, just remember to make it Mythical and you won't ever forget it, even if you get a concussion.

# The Tragedy

As experienced by Link Neal
and told by Rhett McLaughlin

## The Jump

On our fifth and final run, Will and I cleared the table top jump and stopped short of the second one and waited for Link to come. Well, Link came all right, and he came with style. He, like a pro, bounced off the tabletop jump in full composure, and landed it. It was at this point, when Link neither stopped nor slowed down, that I thought, "Man, Link's going for it." Link had told Gregg earlier in the evening that he should go "balls to the wall." He's a man true to his word.

Charles (Link is known as Charles in formal circles) carved back and forth skillfully as he progressed to the steep jump. It was then that Will yelled out, "Link!! You're going to bust!" Bust, it turned out, would be too gentle of a word. Link nailed the face of the beastly incline, was hurled 8 to 10 feet in the air, obviously lost control while in the air, and disappeared over the horizon. I don't recall what I thought at that point, but I remember Will following Link over the jump (much slower), and me doing the same. That's when I saw Link, laid out about 40 feet from the jump, being consoled by Will. Will asked, "Link, are you hurt?" Link responded, "My hip is hurt." Will suggested, "Take your board off and walk it off." I believe that no matter how badly one male is injured, if the first person on the scene is another male, the instructions for therapy will always be "Walk it off."

## Signs of the Concussion

Link said to me, "I think I'm going to faint." He placed his head between his legs, then raised it, and I noticed a completely blank look on his face. He said, "Hold on . . . I'm just coming to." I was confused, for it appeared as if Link had "been to" for about 5 minutes. He followed this phrase with, "Hold on . . . I'm just coming to." I looked at Will, we both laughed. He was joking, right? Then he says, "Hold on . . . I'm just coming to. Evidently I've hurt my left hip." After a few seconds, in which Will and I questioned Link repeatedly to no avail, he said, "Hold on . . . I'm just coming to. Evidently I've hurt my left hip." This broken record conversation continued for about 20 minutes. I asked Link who he was, he said Link. I asked him who I was, he said Rhett. He then became angry at our remedial interrogation. He was fully aware of his surroundings, but fully aware over and over again. He was continually forgetting anything and everything he or anyone else said. He was "coming to" repeatedly, and I was getting the biggest kick out of it.

## The Hospital

Link saw that the nurses had put an IV in his left arm. He didn't like that too much, and he realized just how much he didn't like it about 5 times. He would look down and say, "Oh man, they put an IV in my arm." The conversation would progress a little, and then he'd say, "Oh man, they put an IV in my arm." I had a little fun at his expense. Before they wheeled him off for a CAT scan, I asked, "Hey, Link. Did they put an IV in your arm?" Link said, "I hope not!" He then looked down and said, "Oh man, they put an IV in my arm."

Later, Gregg, Mark, Will, and I all went back to see Link. He was lying in the same bed, except this time he had in his hand a big yellow sign.

CHARLES NEAL
FRIDAY, JAN 8
1999
FELL SNOWBOARDING. YOU ARE
IN WATAUGA MEDICAL CENTER.
YOU HAVE A CONCUSSION +
A BROKEN PELVIS.

# THE GMM TIME CAPSULE

IN 2012 (season 2 of *Good Mythical Morning*) we began one of our first fan-mail projects. Using an old ammo box, we created the "Mythical Time Capsule," filling it with notable mail items from various Mythical Beasts that we highlighted on the show every Thursday. Then, at the close of season 2 during our Mythical Christmas Special, we carried it deep into the woods to bury it, where we found our friend and fellow YouTuber, Julian Smith, burying Santa. He offered to throw the time capsule in with Santa. As you might imagine, the burial was a bit fictionalized (Santa is real, but Julian Smith is not a murderer). But we must now regretfully admit that the entire burial was fictionalized. We never buried it because we were told that the wooded area we visited was soon to be razed and turned into a park. So, we brought the Mythical Time Capsule back home and buried it in our studio storage closet. We honestly always planned to bury it in actual dirt at some point in the future; we just haven't reached that point. The good news is that this allowed us to pull out the contents and snap pictures of them for this book. The Mythical Beasts sent us some weird stuff. Maybe we should actually bury it now?

KEY: 1 Swedish meatballs recipe (in Swedish) from Felix K. 2 Cardboard box with Rhett's beard hair 3 Tape recording from Michael P., Leah P., and Jessie P. 4 Twinkie from Kaitlyn 5 Zebra finger puppet from Christina 6 Kangaroo scrotum from Michaela 7 "Non-perishable" bacon from Laurel 8 Book (*Rhett & Link and the End of the World*) from Ruthie and Deborah 9 Fake mustaches 10 Little TARDIS from Sophia 11 Duct-tape bow ties from Erin W. 12 Birthday card and recipe for cake from Lindsey S. 13 Possum skull from Hammond and Deanna 14 Pentium 4 processor from Malcolm 15 Fake blood from "Rub Some Bacon on It" music video 16 An instructional manual for a drink dispenser 17 Hot Wheels DeLorean from David F. 18 Logo necklace with Buies Creek soil from Tim 19 Old pair of earbuds from Seth 20 Carrot, cucumber, and cauliflower seeds from Crystal 21 Pack of shredded dollar bills from Jessie E. 22 Squirrel tail from Drew 23 Comic book, Uncanny Avengers #1, from Etai A. (The Tacopotamus) 24 List of 2012 facts & statistics and 2012 timeline 25 *Good Mythical Morning* optical illusion generator 26 "Lock Locker" from Emily (a small piece of poster board with two pouches for a lock of each of our hair)

1
2
3
4
5
6
7
8
9
10
11
12
13
14
15
16
17
18
19
20
21
22
23
24
25
26
DAGENS RECEPT
Köttbullar med gräddsås
Swedish meatballs
Keep on doing your show!
Bye
Felix Kozma
I live here
Rhett & Link
AND THE END
OF THE WORLD
MAKING YOUR DRINK DISPENSER WORK
Carrot
Danvers Half Long
PACIFIC NORTHWEST
Cucumber
MARVEL
UNCANNY AVENGERS #1
FEATURING PREVIEWS OF:
IRON MAN #1
ALL NEW X-MEN #1
INDESTRUCTIBLE HULK #1
Deodorant Soap
GOLD
Go
Mtia
Mrig
2012 Facts + Statistics
Average income: $50,964
Price of a gallon of milk: $2.79
Price of gold per ounce: $1720
Price of a movie ticket: $8.20
Price of a first class stamp: $0.45
World Population: 6,973,738,433
THE LOCK LOCKER 2012
Rhett McLaughlin
Link Neal

# OUR GOLDEN FRIEND-AVERSARY TIME CAPSULE

In 2005, a year before Queen Elizabeth's eightieth birthday, one of her loyal subjects, an Australian man named Jim Frecklington, decided to build Her Majesty a special gift to mark the occasion. Specifically, Frecklington constructed a coach comprised of priceless artifacts from British history, including pieces of King Henry VIII's warship, the Mary Rose; wood from the door of 10 Downing Street (the headquarters of Her Majesty's government); decking from the royal yacht; and fragments from Sir Isaac Newton's apple tree. The coach took nine years to build, which means Frecklington delivered the birthday present eight years late, but we think it was worth the wait.

Watching a YouTube video of the queen riding to Parliament in the Diamond Jubilee State Coach, we started brainstorming about what kind of vehicular time capsule we could build to commemorate our Golden Friend-aversary in 2034 (it may seem far away, but if we don't start planning now, we'll be late like Frecklington). We believe that we have conceptualized something that will adequately pay homage to the first fifty years of our friendship.

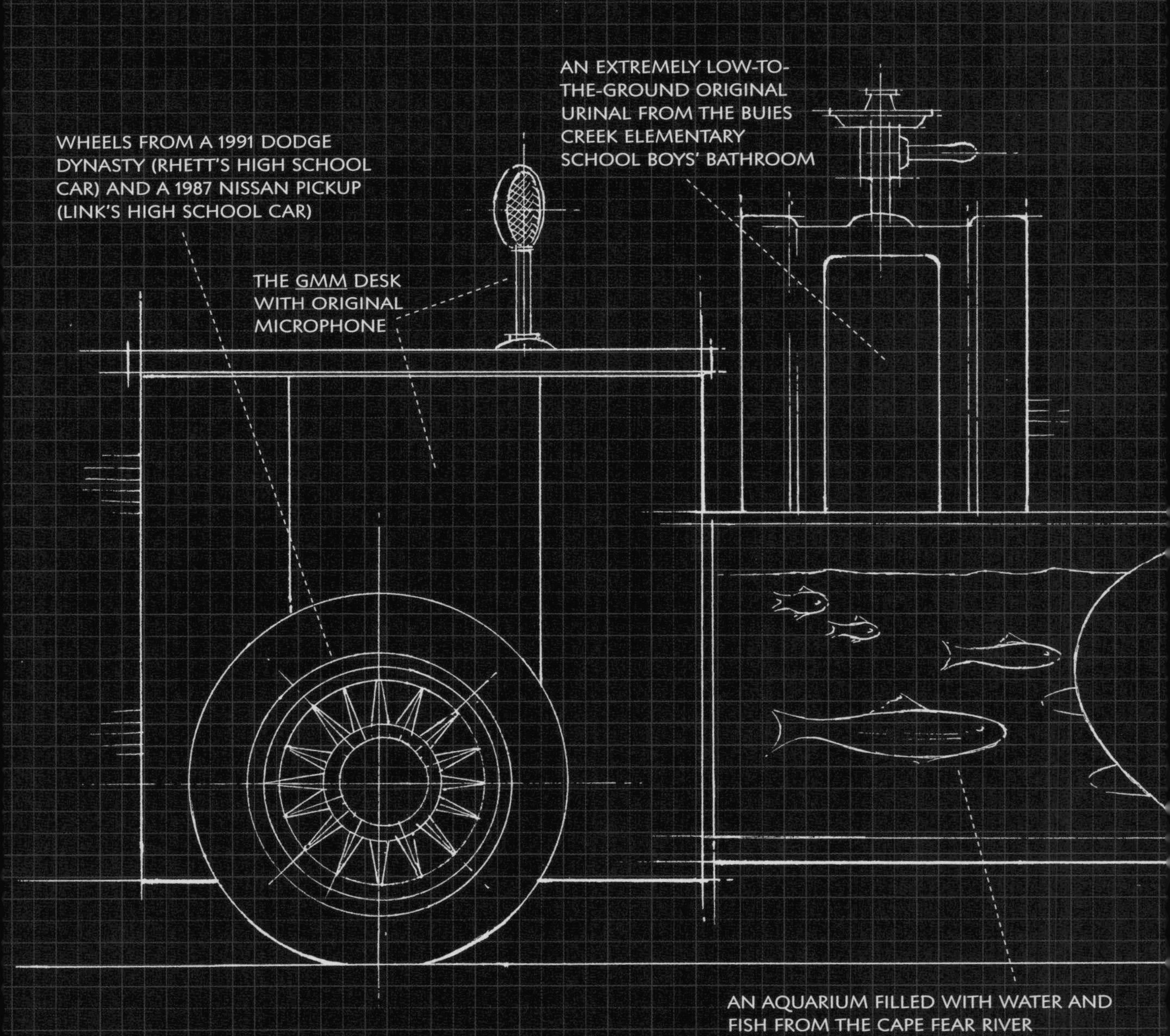

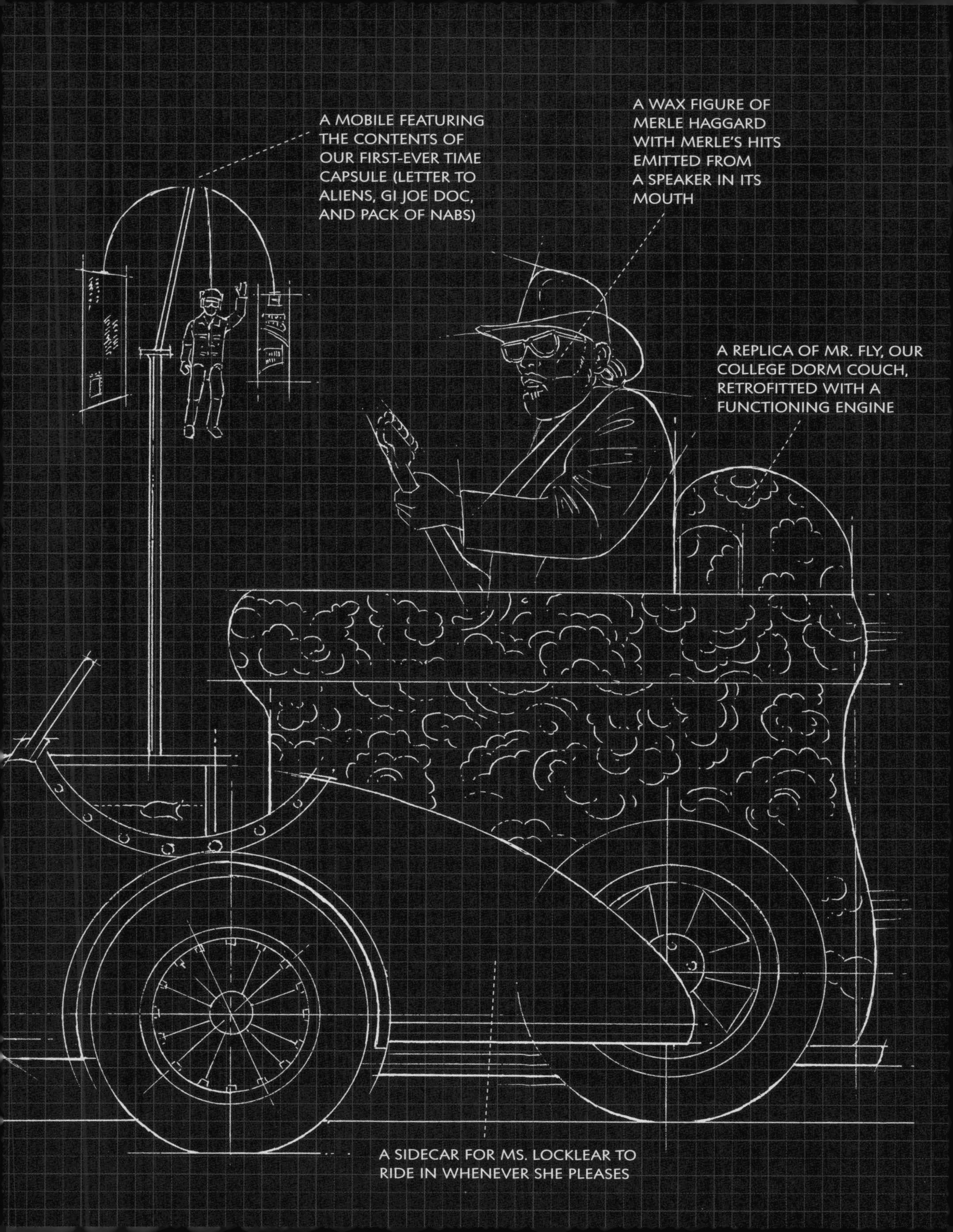
A MOBILE FEATURING THE CONTENTS OF OUR FIRST-EVER TIME CAPSULE (LETTER TO ALIENS, GI JOE DOC, AND PACK OF NABS)
A WAX FIGURE OF MERLE HAGGARD WITH MERLE'S HITS EMITTED FROM A SPEAKER IN ITS MOUTH
A REPLICA OF MR. FLY, OUR COLLEGE DORM COUCH, RETROFITTED WITH A FUNCTIONING ENGINE
A SIDECAR FOR MS. LOCKLEAR TO RIDE IN WHENEVER SHE PLEASES

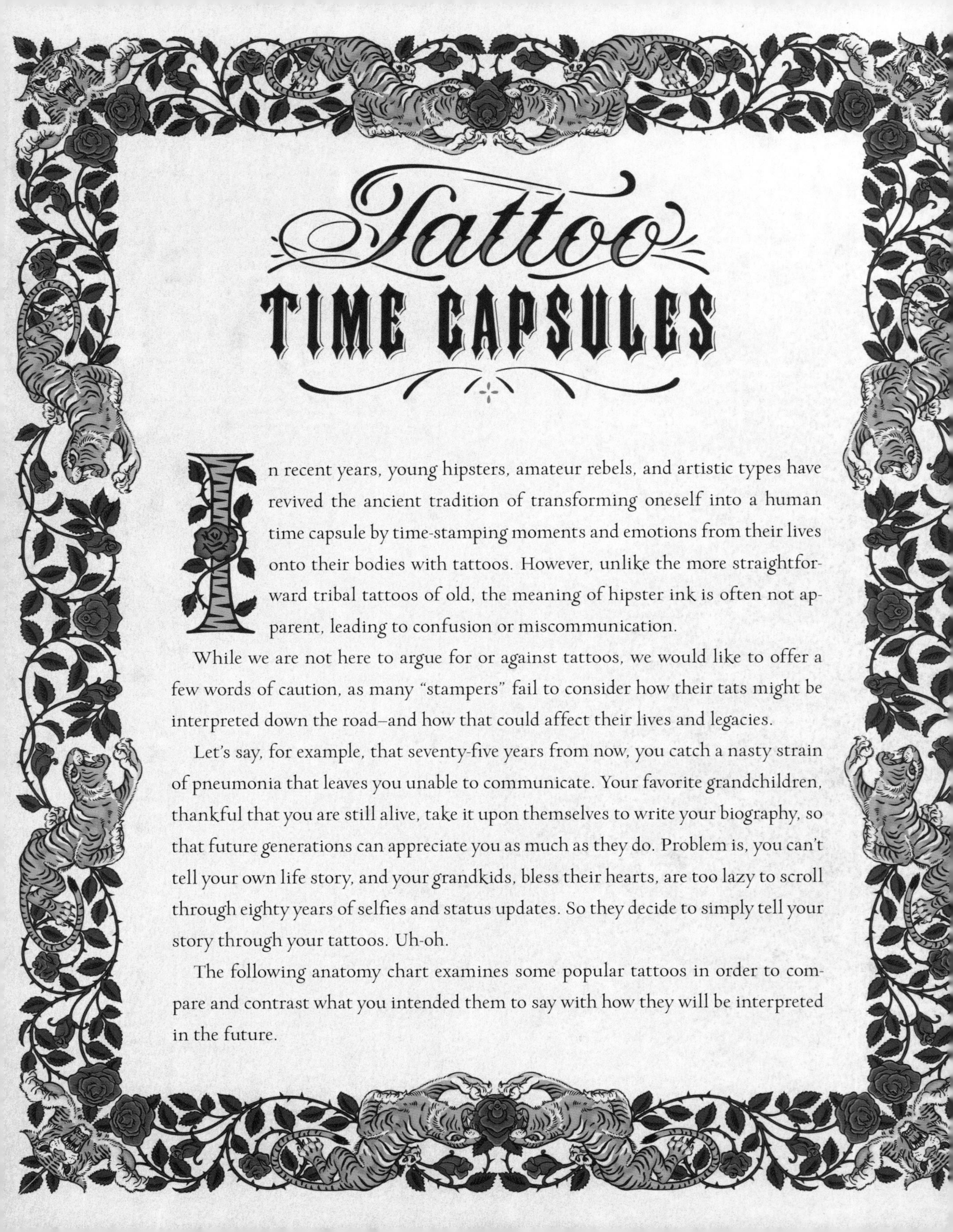

# Tattoo Time Capsules

In recent years, young hipsters, amateur rebels, and artistic types have revived the ancient tradition of transforming oneself into a human time capsule by time-stamping moments and emotions from their lives onto their bodies with tattoos. However, unlike the more straightforward tribal tattoos of old, the meaning of hipster ink is often not apparent, leading to confusion or miscommunication.

While we are not here to argue for or against tattoos, we would like to offer a few words of caution, as many "stampers" fail to consider how their tats might be interpreted down the road–and how that could affect their lives and legacies.

Let's say, for example, that seventy-five years from now, you catch a nasty strain of pneumonia that leaves you unable to communicate. Your favorite grandchildren, thankful that you are still alive, take it upon themselves to write your biography, so that future generations can appreciate you as much as they do. Problem is, you can't tell your own life story, and your grandkids, bless their hearts, are too lazy to scroll through eighty years of selfies and status updates. So they decide to simply tell your story through your tattoos. Uh-oh.

The following anatomy chart examines some popular tattoos in order to compare and contrast what you intended them to say with how they will be interpreted in the future.

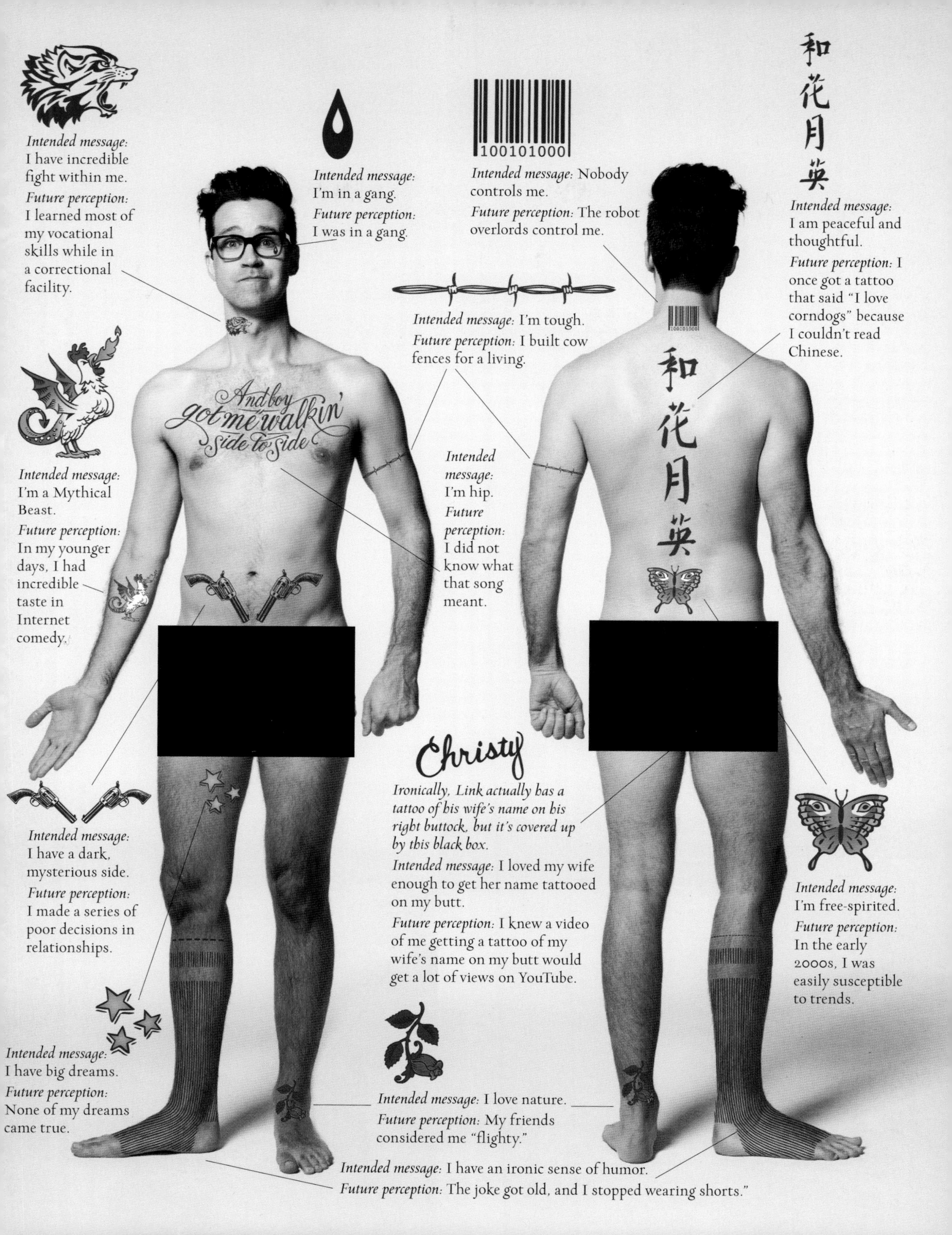
Intended message: I have incredible fight within me.
Future perception: I learned most of my vocational skills while in a correctional facility.
Intended message: I'm in a gang.
Future perception: I was in a gang.
100101000
Intended message: Nobody controls me.
Future perception: The robot overlords control me.
和花月英
Intended message: I am peaceful and thoughtful.
Future perception: I once got a tattoo that said "I love corndogs" because I couldn't read Chinese.
Intended message: I'm tough.
Future perception: I built cow fences for a living.
And boy got me walkin' side to side
Intended message: I'm a Mythical Beast.
Future perception: In my younger days, I had incredible taste in Internet comedy.
Intended message: I'm hip.
Future perception: I did not know what that song meant.
Christy
Ironically, Link actually has a tattoo of his wife's name on his right buttock, but it's covered up by this black box.
Intended message: I loved my wife enough to get her name tattooed on my butt.
Future perception: I knew a video of me getting a tattoo of my wife's name on my butt would get a lot of views on YouTube.
Intended message: I have a dark, mysterious side.
Future perception: I made a series of poor decisions in relationships.
Intended message: I'm free-spirited.
Future perception: In the early 2000s, I was easily susceptible to trends.
Intended message: I have big dreams.
Future perception: None of my dreams came true.
Intended message: I love nature.
Future perception: My friends considered me "flighty."
Intended message: I have an ironic sense of humor.
Future perception: The joke got old, and I stopped wearing shorts."

LOOSEN UP

# EMBRACE IMMATURITY

"LUPÉ'S GUYS CAME BACK WITH TWO FIFTY-GALLON DRUMS FULL OF MILK ON THE FORKLIFT, PULLED THE PLUGS, AND MILK BEGAN TO RAIN DOWN ON US. IT WAS AS IF WE HAD PIERCED THE VERY FLOOR OF HEAVEN ITSELF."

IN MIDDLE SCHOOL, we invented a game. We never named the game, mostly because it was never the kind of game we intended to tell anyone else about, much less recount at the beginning of a chapter of a book. Plus, it was difficult to come up with a name that captured its true magic.

**RHETT** The gameplay was simple. We would sit across from each other in my bedroom, no more than six feet apart, with our legs spread. We would then take a small Nerf basketball and roll it at each other's nuts. The only rule was "You can't protect your nuts." There was no point system. We just played until someone's nuts hurt too bad to continue.

**LINK** It's worth noting that if we had never played this game, we would probably have much larger families. And while we love our children dearly, we don't want any more kids. So, in some ways, we're thankful for NutBall, or Balls to the Nuts, or the Great Nut-Off (see, nothing really does it justice) for keeping our lives manageable.

**RHETT** I recall one particularly heated game of Nutpocalypse (that's not bad). I lived in a two-story home and my room was directly above the living room, my father's sanctuary, where he enjoyed weekly episodes of *Matlock* (a classic lawyer crime drama we highly recommend for those of you aching to see a white-haired, sleuthing side of Andy Griffith). Anyhow, in the room above *Matlock*, our game was getting intense. After each increasingly forceful impact, the recipient would keel over in wincing pain, and the offending ball tosser would laugh loudly

Rhett's dad didn't just love *Matlock*. He also loved taking us to the zoo and buying us both purple gorilla T-shirts.

in gonad-busting triumph. As we sat there trying to come down from yet another laugh attack resulting from an accurately placed roll right to the groin, we heard it: someone was ascending the stairs at a frantic pace. We got quiet and quickly closed our legs so as not to be caught in the awkward position of dual leg-spreadedness with your best friend. The door flung open to reveal my dad, wearing his comfort clothes: a V-neck undershirt, tighty-whities, and dress socks. He looked like a man who had been violently wrenched from a pivotal *Matlock* moment, just as ol' Ben was about to extract another confession from a bewildered defendant.

Dad gritted his teeth and yelled, "What the hell are y'all doing up here?!"

Let's just say we didn't answer with "Uh, we're throwing this Nerf ball at each other's nuts." Not that it would have mattered. Dad's mission was accomplished the moment we stared back at him in stunned/scared silence. Quick as he came, Dad was back downstairs, enjoying another predictable *Matlock* denouement (spoiler alert: Matlock solved the case!) and we started another round of Testi-Kill (I think that's it!).

**LINK** While we don't throw objects at each other's nether regions as much as we once did, it would be incorrect to assume that we have outgrown our penchant for sophomoric pursuits. A large portion of *Good Mythical Morning* consists of us doing things that might cause Rhett's dad to come upstairs and ask us what the hell we're doing. It's not a sophisticated show. I once played the mouth trumpet while Rhett put a towel over his head and peed into a bag strapped to his leg.

**RHETT** We probably should be interrupted by my dad from time to time, but as it turns out, he thinks the stupid stuff we do is pretty funny. This is most often communicated via texts from my mom that say things like "Your dad thought it was funny when you peed in the bag."

One of the more ridiculous yet fulfilling things we've done (repeatedly) is bathing in substances other than water. It started with dust baths. After learning that some animal species regularly take them, we decided to try our own on the show. Our dust bath involved filling a baby pool with dirt and rolling around in it. While we didn't experience any of the purported benefits of bathing in soil, we did notice something else as we made mud hats for each other and created dirt angels by lying down and flapping our arms and legs: pure joy.

Months later, we followed our dirt baths by taking ice baths. It probably didn't hurt that we sang along to the *Frozen* theme song as we froze—or that Link found a rogue can of Sprite in his bath—but getting so cold that we needed to hold hands for emotional support was so invigoratingly stupid that it left us with an incredible high.

We followed up the ice baths with a ranch-dressing bath (should've worn goggles) before planning what turned out to be the most significant bath of our lives thus far—our giant cereal bath.

**LINK** We had a ten-episode *GMM* miniseries called Backup Plan, in which we searched for alternative careers to fall back on just in case "Internetainment" doesn't work out. On one particular episode, we visited Organic Milling, a cereal manufacturer. This was an especially momentous trek for me, considering my lifelong love affair with the undisputed king of bowled breakfast foods. Of course, we could have just visited the cereal factory, seen how they made it, sampled its sugary goodness, and gone on with our lives. But we didn't.

Animals do not know what they're talking about. Bathing in dirt does not make you clean.

We're guessing that professional athletes do not make these faces when taking ice baths.

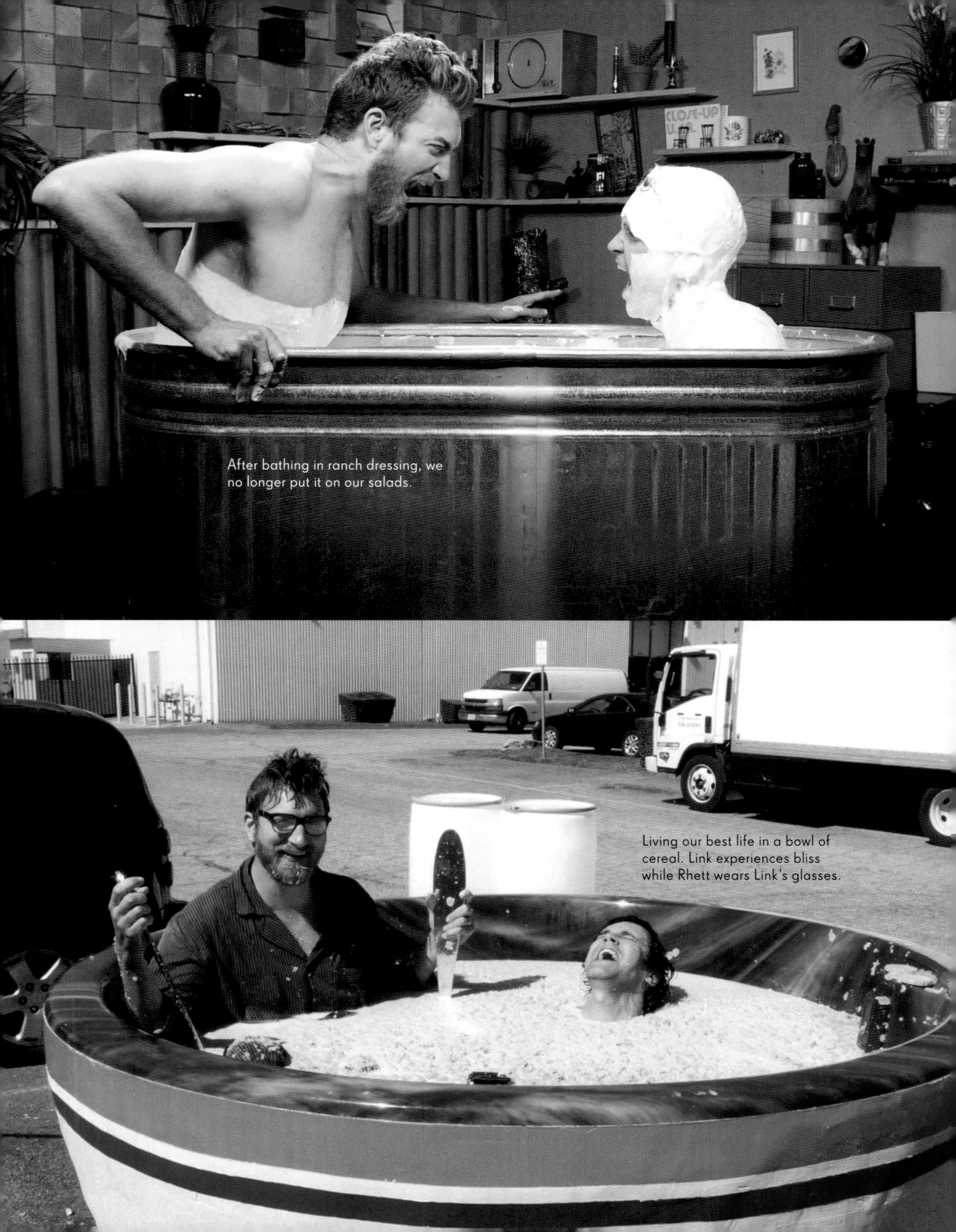

After bathing in ranch dressing, we no longer put it on our salads.

Living our best life in a bowl of cereal. Link experiences bliss while Rhett wears Link's glasses.

We loved our cereal bath so much that we took another dip for this book. As it turns out, standing in cereal is also amazing, especially when you know you're about to sit in it.

Instead, we asked our crew to find an old hot tub on Craigslist and turn it into a giant cereal bowl. This is the kind of thing you ask for, expecting that someone will say it can't be done, but our crew proceeded to make a cereal bowl perfectly capable of accommodating two pajama-clad adult men. Then we asked Lupé, the VP of Organic Milling, to provide us with enough cereal and milk to fill our huge bowl. Surprisingly, she said yes. I get the feeling that this is the kind of thing Lupé had been wanting to see her entire cereal career.

Lupé instructed her employees to haul out a five-hundred-pound bag of cereal on a forklift. They proceeded to untie the bottom of the bag, bringing forth a landslide of cereal—a cerealanche—right into our laps. As the massive weight of the cereal began to lock our legs into place, I had one thought: I may be killed by cereal, and it'll be worth it. Then, Lupé's guys came back with two fifty-gallon drums full of milk on the forklift, pulled the plugs, and milk began to rain down on us. It was as if we had pierced the very floor of heaven itself.

EVEN THOUGH WE stayed in the cereal bath until it became more of a mushy oatmeal bath, and we were only able to consume a small fraction of it—the leftovers were given to horses; no lie—it remains one of the most gratifying experiences we've ever had. It may seem unnecessary for two fully grown men to immerse themselves in cereal. That's because it is. But that doesn't mean that these kinds of pointless and childish acts should be reserved for children.

Children know something that we all too often set aside once we enter adulthood—that one of the best things in life is an experience designed to give you nothing more than glee. Of course, you can't spend all your time acting childish, or you'll end up living in your parents' basement until you're forty, sitting in the dark eating Cheetos your parents paid for, watching *Game of Thrones* using their HBO password. You don't want to be that person, but you also don't want to be an adult who never embraces immaturity, because you'll miss out on Mythicality.

# 20 Ways to Embrace Immaturity

## CHECKLIST

1 ☐ Wear your undies on the outside.

2 ☐ Drink from the dog dish.

3 ☐ Say "ya dig?" at the end of all of your sentences.

4 ☐ Walk like a cartoon character.

5 ☐ Repeat everything your friend says.

6 ☐ Go on a Bigfoot hunt in your backyard.

7 ☐ Let a kindergartner plan your day.

8 ☐ Turn every meal into a smoothie.

9 ☐ Sing yourself to sleep.

10 ☐ Walk a balloon animal on a leash.

11 ☐ Sustain a text conversation using only Disney quotes.

12 ☐ Buy a Whoopee Cushion and use it.

13 ☐ Have a serious conversation in a bounce house.

14 ☐ Go to school/work in a costume you made yourself.

15 ☐ Make people guess what you're thinking.

16 ☐ Play hide-and-seek.

17 ☐ Kidnap your boss's/teacher's coffee cup and write a ransom note.

18 ☐ Commit to an imaginary friend.

19 ☐ Cover your ears and make noises when someone says something you don't like.

20 ☐ Blame a fart on someone else.

***Matlock,* the TV show,** ran for nine seasons (196 episodes) from 1986 to 1995. All across the country, tighty-whities-wearin' dads like Rhett's tuned in every week to watch no-nonsense attorney Ben Matlock crack cases and expose the bad guys in the courtroom. The storylines were as predictable as Matlock's wardrobe (gray suit), and hardworkin' guys like Rhett's dad, trying to make their way in an ever-changing world, were able to rely on Matlock to dispense a weekly dose of good ol' common sense and justice.

Today, we're dads struggling to maintain the balance of work, marriage, and fathering kids from Generation Z (yes, that's what they're calling them—it makes them sound like the last generation ever). We too could use someone like Ben Matlock to turn to each week. That's why we want to reboot the Matlock franchise for our time. We'd call it *Matlock Reloaded.*

**LEAD ACTOR:** Reginald VelJohnson, known for his role as Carl Winslow in *Family Matters*. In the '60s, Andy Griffith was the perfect TV father who made his living in law enforcement. In the '90s, Carl Winslow was that same mix of lovable dad and principled cop. Like Andy, Reginald is perfectly primed for a new life as a crotchety case jockey twenty-five years later.

**PREMISE:** These days, nobody cares much for scripted courtroom drama, but there is still an appetite for reality TV courtroom shows—especially if there's a twist. For *Matlock Reloaded,* Judge Reginald deals exclusively with "family matters." Is little Timmy seeking a divorce from his parents because they're limiting his screen time? Are siblings Lilly and Billy fighting over their late father's priceless clove cigarette collection? Judge Reginald will swing his giant gavel of justice (it really is giant . . . and inflatable) to set things straight.

**SIDEKICK:** It's time to resurrect the career of Jaleel White in a big way. He's the bailiff who can't help but let out a snorting laugh at Judge Reginald's courtroom jokes. He also routinely drops important evidence as he's carrying it across the courtroom, giving him the perfect opportunity to say his catchphrase, "Did I do that?" America will love this!

★ ★ ★

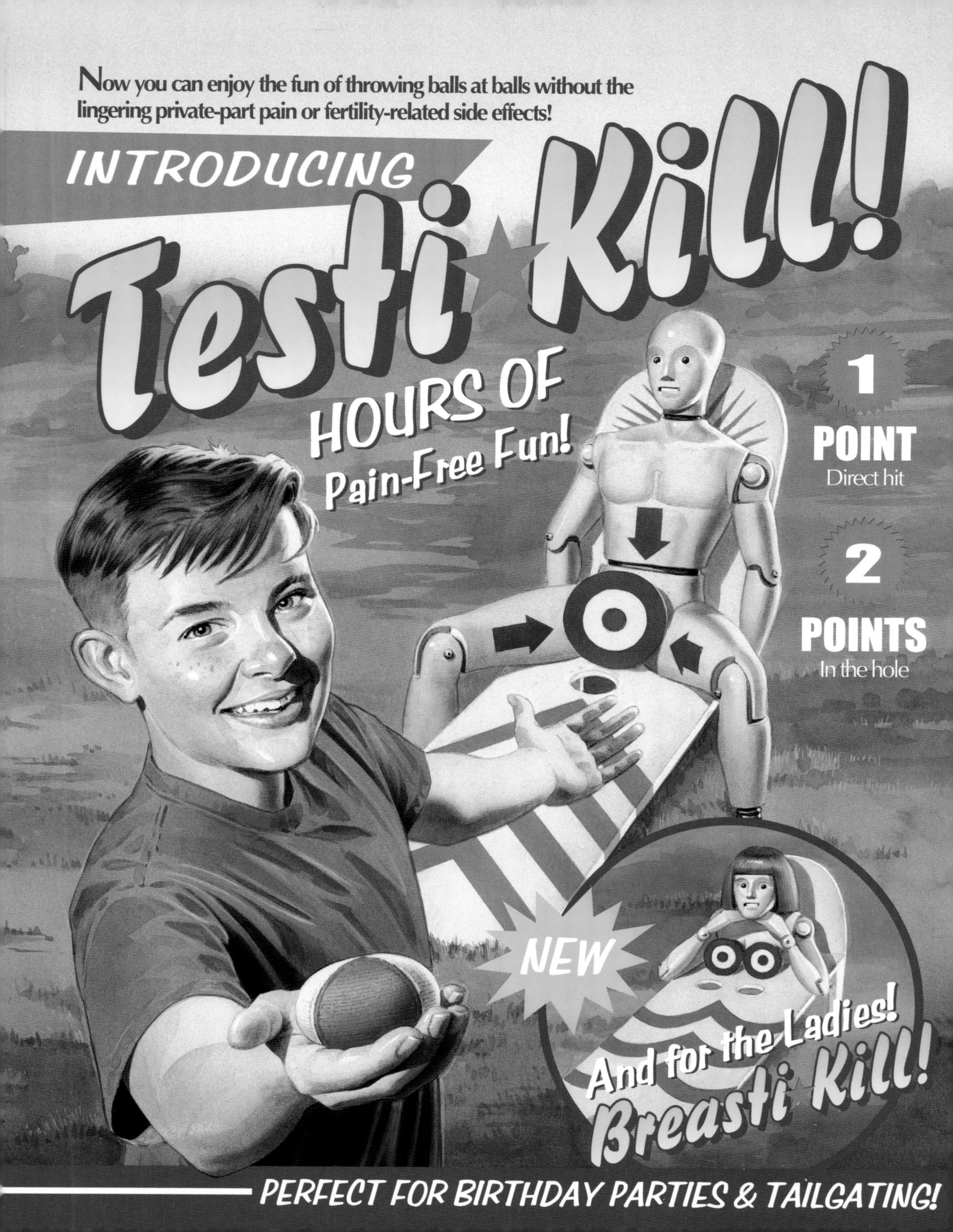

Now you can enjoy the fun of throwing balls at balls without the lingering private-part pain or fertility-related side effects!

INTRODUCING

# Testi★Kill!

HOURS OF
Pain-Free Fun!

1
POINT
Direct hit

2
POINTS
In the hole

NEW

And for the Ladies!
Breasti Kill!

PERFECT FOR BIRTHDAY PARTIES & TAILGATING!

PICK A FIGHT
WORTH PICKING

# PICK A FIGHT

"AS I EMERGED FROM THE CHANGING AREA LIKE A FRESHLY STUFFED SAUSAGE, I DIDN'T SEE THE TAILOR. INSTEAD, I WAS GREETED BY WHAT LOOKED LIKE A PRISON GANG LEADER COVERED IN TATTOOS, INCLUDING A WEIRD SET OF TALONS DIRECTLY ON TOP OF HIS HEAD."

**I**N EARLY 2013, while filming episode 231 of *Good Mythical Morning* (entitled "Killing Rhett's Beard"), we spun the "Wheel of Mythicality" at the close of the episode, just as we had done 230 times before. Since the rule of the wheel was to follow whatever prompt it stopped on, we were obligated to fulfill the request when it landed on "Slap Each Other."

**LINK** It's worth mentioning that we had never, up until that point, actually physically fought each other. There had been close calls—especially when we were kids—such as the time Rhett picked up a fresh cow patty with a stick and threw it at me, hitting me squarely in the chest. And we'd definitely had our fair share of heated arguments, most often about creative decisions, including our impassioned exchange about who would be the rear-end of the "Dope Zebra." Thankfully, neither of us had to after we decided to put actual dancers inside it.

Contrary to popular belief, we were not inside the zebra costume for our Dope Zebra video. It was an actual zebra.

To be honest, neither of us has ever been much of a true fighter—even during our UFC phase in college—so we're not really inclined to come to blows. Sure, we occasionally hit each other for entertainment purposes, most notably the time that I shot Rhett at extremely close range with a powerful foam dart gun during our "Epic Gun Battle" video, causing a nosebleed. But it was never personal, and it never escalated. When the wheel landed on the slap prompt that day, however, things would prove to be different.

Rhett wore his bloody nose like a badge of honor during our "Epic Gun Battle".

**RHETT** After deciding that we should slap each other at the same time, I prepared myself to give and receive a slap simultaneously. However, I had reason to believe that Link would slap me harder than I would slap him. He always pushes things a little too far. This is the guy who ate a worm's anus in eleventh-grade biology class to impress a girl; the guy who lost control of his Nissan pickup truck while fishtailing on a dirt road just weeks after getting his license, leaving the truck sitting on its side in a ditch and us lying one on top of the other.

Even with that mental preparation, I wasn't ready for the power of his slap. Maybe it was just an especially vulnerable time for me, considering I had trimmed my very bushy beard (hence the episode title), but as soon as Link slapped me—just as I was slapping him—I was convinced he had struck me significantly harder. I immediately retaliated like some provoked rabid coyote, slapping him again. He returned the favor, and I knew that we had just begun a real fight. A slap fight, yes, but a real fight. For a moment, I contemplated taking him down like we were inside the UFC Octagon, but I remembered that we were on camera, making a show, so I just let out an obviously fake laugh.

The initial, simultaneous slap.

Rhett feels that he was slapped too hard.

Rhett slaps in retaliation.

Link slaps in retaliation.

Rhett remembers he is on camera and fake laughs.

Immediate cut to outro.

**LINK** I admit I'm prone to getting a little carried away from time to time, but I don't think this was one of those instances. So, when Rhett slapped me a second time, I lost all perspective that we were on camera. For a second, I thought about balling up my fist and actually punching him in the face, but then I remembered that not only does he outweigh me by forty pounds, but Rhett receiving a black eye from me would probably have been difficult to explain to the Mythical Beasts. It also helped that I remembered that we weren't the only people in the small converted garage that was our "studio." Jason Inman, our only employee for the first few seasons of *GMM*, was sitting behind the camera. He had witnessed a number of our arguments during his employment, so I doubt he was surprised. But it was the very first day of work for Stevie Levine, now the executive producer of *Good Mythical Morning* and all things Rhett & Link. She was sitting about four feet away from us, just off-camera, watching her new bosses. She should probably tell it from her perspective.

**STEVIE** You know how when you're first getting to know someone, and there's this awkward tension whenever they do or say something unexpected? Your brain automatically puts everything through this polite filter, and you question if they were trying to be funny—in which case laughter was not only appropriate, but welcomed—or serious, and you've just really screwed things up by laughing at the wrong time? Have you ever had that feeling, but this time you're watching two adult male comedians with wives and children, who are now not just "someones," but your new bosses, repeatedly slapping each other? Just me? OK.

At the time, I made the choice to not laugh and assumed that this was not a comedic bit. I instead sat in awkward silence, wondering if a significant part of my job description was going to be breaking up fights between two man-children. Thankfully, before I had to step in and defuse the situation (and after no more than four slaps each), they took care of that themselves by calming down and talking through it. They also stopped to acknowledge that this must be a weird first day for me, and promised that this was not a normal thing. I didn't necessarily believe them at the time, but several years have passed and I have never seen them purposely hurt each other again. Let me rephrase that. I have seen them slap each other with an eel and an octopus and shock each other repeatedly with a stun cane, but I have not seen them purposely hurt each other out of anger. Either they no longer do it, or they do it on their own time.

**IT'S IMPOSSIBLE** to work as closely as we have—for as long as we have—without having some arguments. But as time has passed, we've gotten better at resolving our disagreements by simply being honest with each other. In fact, our practice of talking things out has actually helped our friendship grow stronger through conflict. If we had let things fester, we probably would have ended up slowly drifting apart—or eventually having an epic throw-down where someone got legitimately hurt. (Of course, if we caught it on camera, we'd post it because it would probably get a lot of views, especially if we called it "EPIC BFFF [BEST FRIEND FOREVER FIGHT] WARNING: BLOOD AND CURSING").

You might think that with as much practice as we have in resolving conflict between us, we would be relatively good at handling it with other people. Unfortunately, that has not proven to be the case. The reality is we're pretty bad at it—in completely different ways.

**LINK** While I've gotten to a place where I can calmly talk through issues I have with Rhett, I have a track record of not-so-calmly attempting to address conflict with strangers. I find myself in these situations more than I would like.

A couple of years ago, a guy honked his horn at me when I nearly backed my minivan into his sedan at a gas station. When I heard his honk, I looked at him in the rearview camera—that I had decidedly not been using up until that point—and saw him flailing his arms in a "Why would you do that, you minivan-driving idiot?" kind of gesture. Feeling that his hand motions

When we hired Stevie, we did not think it was necessary to disclose that one of her duties as executive producer of *GMM* would be to smell our sweaty underarms on camera.

Rhett slaps Link with an eel.

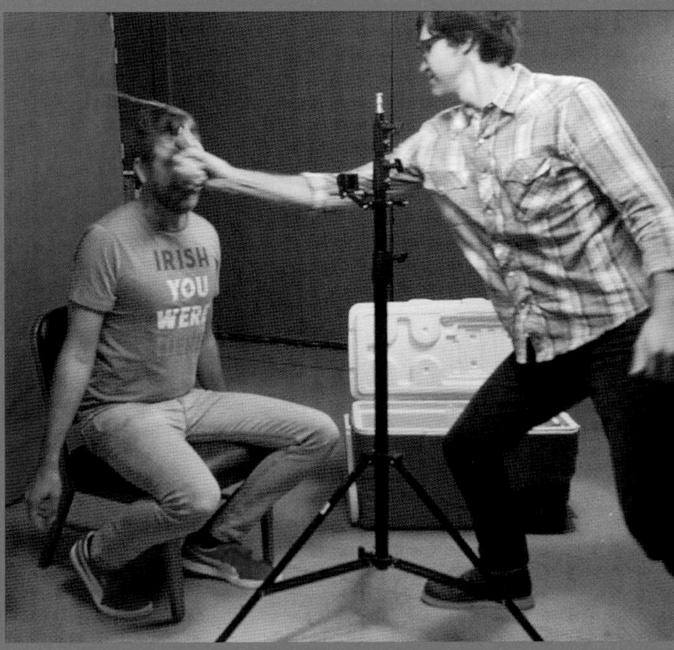


Link slaps Rhett with an octopus.

Link is much more impressed with himself and his minivan than his family is.

were excessive, I responded with my own gesture (not what you're thinking, but more of a "I know that was a dumb thing to do and I feel sorta stupid, but you are making too big of a deal out of it, dude" hand sign). This resulted in the angry man suddenly swerving around my van and peeling out of the parking lot in anger. At that point, I could have let it go. And I should have. But I didn't. I reached down with everything I had, and although I'm fully aware that pressing harder on your car horn does nothing to increase its volume, I leaned into it with my full weight, letting out a seven-second honk to exert my gas-station dominance.

Truthfully, I thought he was long gone and probably missed hearing my horn altogether. Turns out he wasn't, and turns out he didn't. The now-even-angrier man popped a U-ie in the street and rocketed back into the parking lot. He got out of his car, and bolted over to my wife Christy's passenger-side window. So I pushed the button and rolled her window down. She was thinking clearly and said nothing. I was not thinking clearly and proceeded to give him a piece of my mind (along with unintentional physical access to my family). He didn't assault us, but he did unleash an F-bomb-laden tirade on me in front of my wife and children. After contributing several new words to my kids' vocabulary, he closed his profane soliloquy with "One of these days, you're gonna get yours." All righty, then. Actually, I have no interest in ever "getting mine." I wasn't missing it. But what I did receive was the loud-and-clear message that I need to learn to choose to stay calm in the midst of conflict.

**RHETT** I've found myself erring on the opposite end of the spectrum from Link. Instead of too easily getting drawn into needless conflicts because I can't keep my cool, I all too often avoid necessary confrontation.

Because I'm a tall, slim guy, I have to get a lot of my clothes tailored to fit correctly. You may have noticed that there's a Big and Tall store, but have you ever seen just a Tall store? No, you haven't, and that's a problem for me. I typically buy shirts that are long enough for my giraffe-ish frame, and then have them altered. After moving to a new area of Los Angeles a few years ago, I had to find a new tailor who could reliably reduce my shirts to the required size. I took five new shirts to a place I found on Yelp and went through the normal process of having them pinned to my liking.

When I returned to get my shirts the next week, the tailor asked me if I wanted to try them on. This is where my tendency to avoid conflict went into effect. I said, "No, I'm sure they're fine," not only because I was in a hurry but also because I didn't want to experience that awkward moment where I had to tell her if she had done a poor job. Instead, I went home and tried them on—or, more accurately stated, tried to try them on. I have no idea what happened, but it was as if after I had left, she brought in a small boy and refit all my shirts for him. There was only one shirt that I was able to fully button, but I had to quickly remove it for fear of cutting off circulation to the lower half of my body.

She had ruined my shirts. I was fully justified in pointing out her mistake and even demanding that she pay to replace my clothes, but I was still extremely hesitant to go back and tell her. So, I waited a month. When I finally returned, the place was crowded. This was my worst fear. I had to confront her in front of an audience. She asked, "How can I help you?" I said, "Uh . . . there's a little problem with my shirts." When I called it a little problem, I wasn't implying—as I should have been—that all my shirts had been tailored to fit little people. I was minimizing

When buying traditionally fitting T-shirts, Rhett must often make a choice between one that is long enough but much too big—which he calls "Bell Syndrome" (left)—or a shirt that is tight enough for his fashion sense but much too short (right). This has been referred to as the Tall Man's Quandary.

what was actually a big problem. She said, "Come and try them on and show me." My penchant for avoiding conflict was about to make things even worse.

I walked into a small, curtained-off changing room, put on the one shirt I could still button, and walked out, hoping that she would simply look at me and see the error of her ways. But as I emerged from the changing area like a freshly stuffed sausage, I didn't see the tailor. Instead, I was greeted by what looked like a prison gang leader covered in tattoos, including a weird set of talons directly on top of his head. As soon as he saw me, he began yelling, "What are you doing back here, dude? My fourteen-year-old daughter is changing! Why are you invading her privacy?!" I saw his eyes look me up and down, and he made a face that seemed to say, *This sick freak likes to wear children's clothes.*

I could have told him that the tailor had instructed me to go back there, that she was the reason I looked like I had just stepped out of a Gap Kids fitting room, but I didn't. I just I said, "Oh, sorry," and walked back to the main area, defeated. The tailor eventually saw me in my boy clothes and knew something was wrong. She blamed it on the seamstress, and told me to leave my shirts there so she could "see what she could do with them." I don't know much about tailoring, but I was convinced that, unless she had the ability to cast a spell that would turn a youth-sized shirt into one that could fit an adult man, I was never going to wear those clothes again. With no idea what to do, I left my shirts there and never went back. I like to think that they eventually found a home with some children in need.

WE'RE CONVINCED THERE'S a healthy balance between the ways that the two of us naturally approach discord—somewhere between releasing seven-second honks and sheepishly accepting tiny shirts. Sometimes being Mythical means taking the risk of standing up for yourself or someone else, and sometimes it means choosing to rise above a middle-school shouting match. This Mythical medium of conflict resolution—a combination of confronting people when necessary while avoiding uncalled-for clashes—is something we're both striving for.

There's also a need for a similar balance in a Mythical friendship. Sometimes friends need to fight—or at least argue—in order to maintain the open and honest communication that's key to a deep friendship. On the other hand, a friendship that consists of one meltdown after another isn't much of a friendship. If we could learn to fight the right fights in the right way, both with friends and strangers, there's no doubt the world would be a more Mythical place.

We like to imagine a future in which no adult has to wear the suffocating clothing of Oompa Loompas, where car horns are used only in short, friendly bursts to greet other drivers, or to get someone to look up from *Clash of Clans* when the light turns green. This is a world where every time someone loses their cool on the highway and gives the one-finger salute, the recipient chooses not to return the favor by letting their own birdie fly, but instead keeps it in its cage and just smiles. This is a world in which a restaurant patron who finds a curly hair in his mashed potatoes, when asked by their waiter, "How is everything?" doesn't just respond with a knee-jerk "Good!" No, in this Mythical world, that restaurant goer would proudly point at the hair and say, "Actually, there's a pube in my potatoes." Even if he's wrong, he'll probably get a free potato.

# CREATIVE CONFRONTATIONS

**Fistfights are sooooooo last century. Throwing hands never accomplishes anything except possibly making you go viral on worldstarhiphop.com. The following is a list of alternative confrontations you can feel free to use to settle differences, along with some "signature moves" you can unleash to achieve victory in each arena.**

## 1 RAP BATTLE

SIGNATURE MOVE:
The Rabbit Reversal. In the movie *8 Mile*, Eminem's character, B. Rabbit, disarms his adversaries by making fun of himself before launching his own verbal assault. Not only does the Rabbit Reversal cannibalize your opponent's best material, it also endears you to your audience.

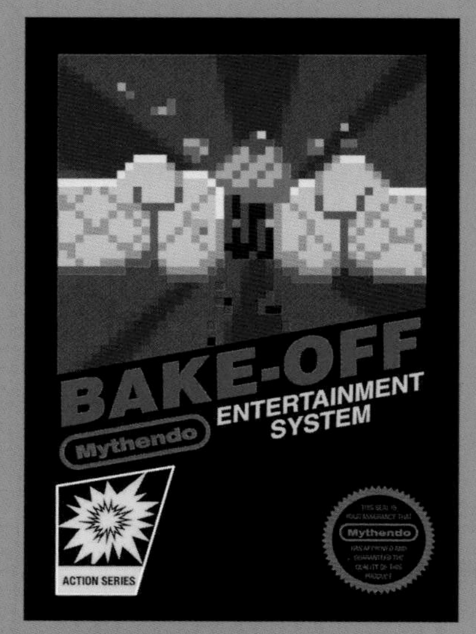


## 2 BAKE-OFF

SIGNATURE MOVE:
The Betty Crocker Special. In the current era of gluten-free soy quinoa, folks often forget that the silver bullets of the baking arena are and will always be butter and sugar. Too much butter and sugar might shorten your life, but they will guarantee bake-off victory.

## 3 STARING CONTEST

SIGNATURE MOVE:
The "Spy-ris." They key to winning a staring contest is to distract yourself from the taxing task of staring. Focus intently on breaking down the exact color combination that makes up your opponent's iris (the colorful part of their eye). Before you're able to figure it out, your challenger will blink.

## 4 A LASER TAG DUEL

SIGNATURE MOVE:
State the Obvious. Once you and your foe are all decked out in laser tag gear, point out the fact that you both look like dorks, and that this was a bad idea. The entire endeavor will quickly fizzle away at this point.

## 5

### AN ALMOST REAL FIGHT

SIGNATURE MOVE:
You Don't Want This.
Sometimes you'll find yourself in a situation where your opponent is committed to a physical altercation. Say, "You don't want this" and then follow it up with "No, YOU don't want THIS!" Repeat that phrase again and again until onlookers get bored. When your enemy loses their audience, they just might lose their nerve.

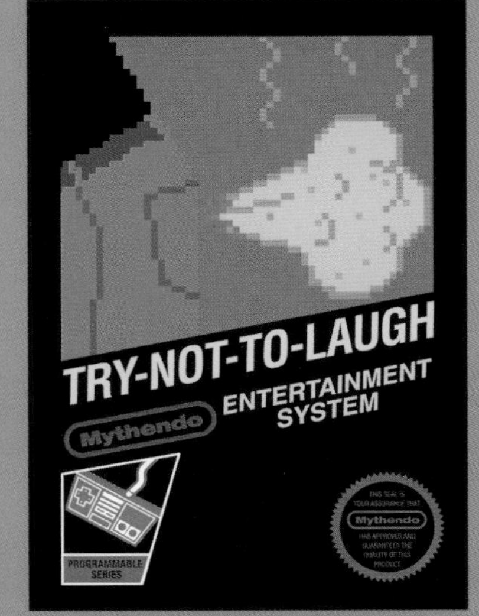


## 6

### TRY-NOT-TO-LAUGH CONTEST

SIGNATURE MOVE:
Fart. Your opponent will arm their defenses to deflect facial movements and sounds, leaving them defenseless against a well-timed toot.

## 7

### THUMB WAR

SIGNATURE MOVE:
The Fake Time-Out.
This is a controversial move considered unsportsmanlike in most countries, but it is wildly effective. In the middle of your thumb war, say, "Time out." Your opponent will let their guard down, at which point you will grab their thumb, pin it down, and remind them that there are no time-outs in thumb wars. This usually only works once.

## 8

### VIDEO-GAME FIGHT

SIGNATURE MOVE:
Signature Move.
No, this is not a typo.
The key to winning a video-game fight, regardless of platform, is playing defense until you have a chance to launch a signature move.
If that doesn't work, repeated leg sweeps are always an option, though you will (rightfully) be reprimanded for doing so.

## 9

### MILK CHUG CONTEST

SIGNATURE MOVE:
Widen the Portal.
The key to winning a milk chug is widening both your throat as well as the hole in the carton. Giving your opponent expired milk doesn't hurt either.

## 10

### HUG-IT-OUT

SIGNATURE MOVE:
The Creeper.
Just because you've suggested that a hug is the best way to settle a score, it doesn't mean you can't still win. A couple of seconds into your hug, whisper something cryptic into your opponent's ear, like "I know what your pillow smells like." You'll seem like a hero to everyone watching, but your adversary will feel defeated.

# ANGER ILLUSION

There are times when you find yourself in the midst of a confrontation, and if you don't stop and cool off, you're destined to get into trouble. We have provided the above image. If you stare at it long enough (slightly crossing your eyes helps), you'll calm down.

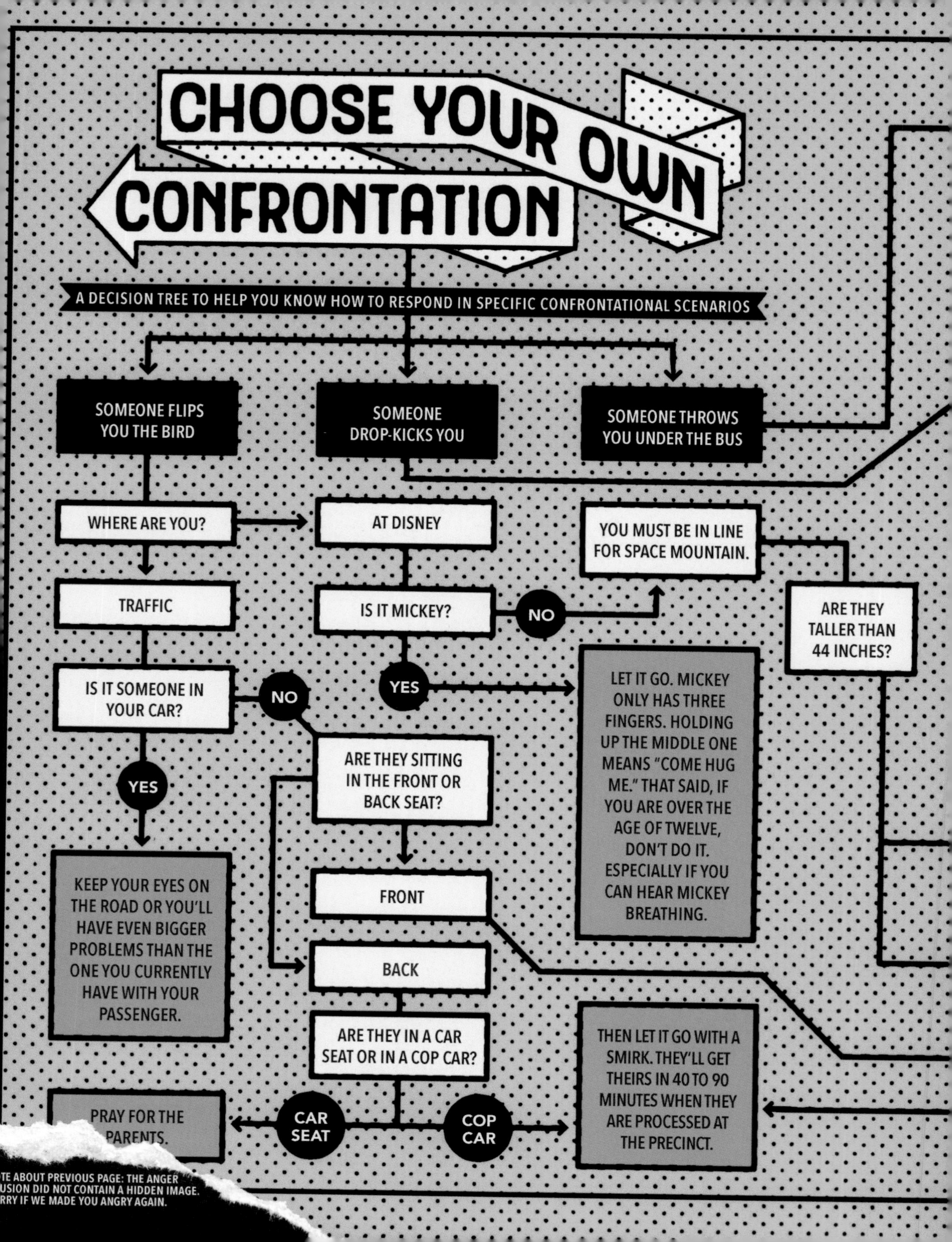

CHOOSE YOUR OWN CONFRONTATION
A DECISION TREE TO HELP YOU KNOW HOW TO RESPOND IN SPECIFIC CONFRONTATIONAL SCENARIOS
SOMEONE FLIPS YOU THE BIRD
SOMEONE DROP-KICKS YOU
SOMEONE THROWS YOU UNDER THE BUS
WHERE ARE YOU?
AT DISNEY
YOU MUST BE IN LINE FOR SPACE MOUNTAIN.
TRAFFIC
IS IT MICKEY?
NO
ARE THEY TALLER THAN 44 INCHES?
IS IT SOMEONE IN YOUR CAR?
NO
YES
LET IT GO. MICKEY ONLY HAS THREE FINGERS. HOLDING UP THE MIDDLE ONE MEANS "COME HUG ME." THAT SAID, IF YOU ARE OVER THE AGE OF TWELVE, DON'T DO IT. ESPECIALLY IF YOU CAN HEAR MICKEY BREATHING.
ARE THEY SITTING IN THE FRONT OR BACK SEAT?
YES
KEEP YOUR EYES ON THE ROAD OR YOU'LL HAVE EVEN BIGGER PROBLEMS THAN THE ONE YOU CURRENTLY HAVE WITH YOUR PASSENGER.
FRONT
BACK
ARE THEY IN A CAR SEAT OR IN A COP CAR?
THEN LET IT GO WITH A SMIRK. THEY'LL GET THEIRS IN 40 TO 90 MINUTES WHEN THEY ARE PROCESSED AT THE PRECINCT.
PRAY FOR THE PARENTS.
CAR SEAT
COP CAR
TE ABOUT PREVIOUS PAGE: THE ANGER
USION DID NOT CONTAIN A HIDDEN IMAGE.
RRY IF WE MADE YOU ANGRY AGAIN.

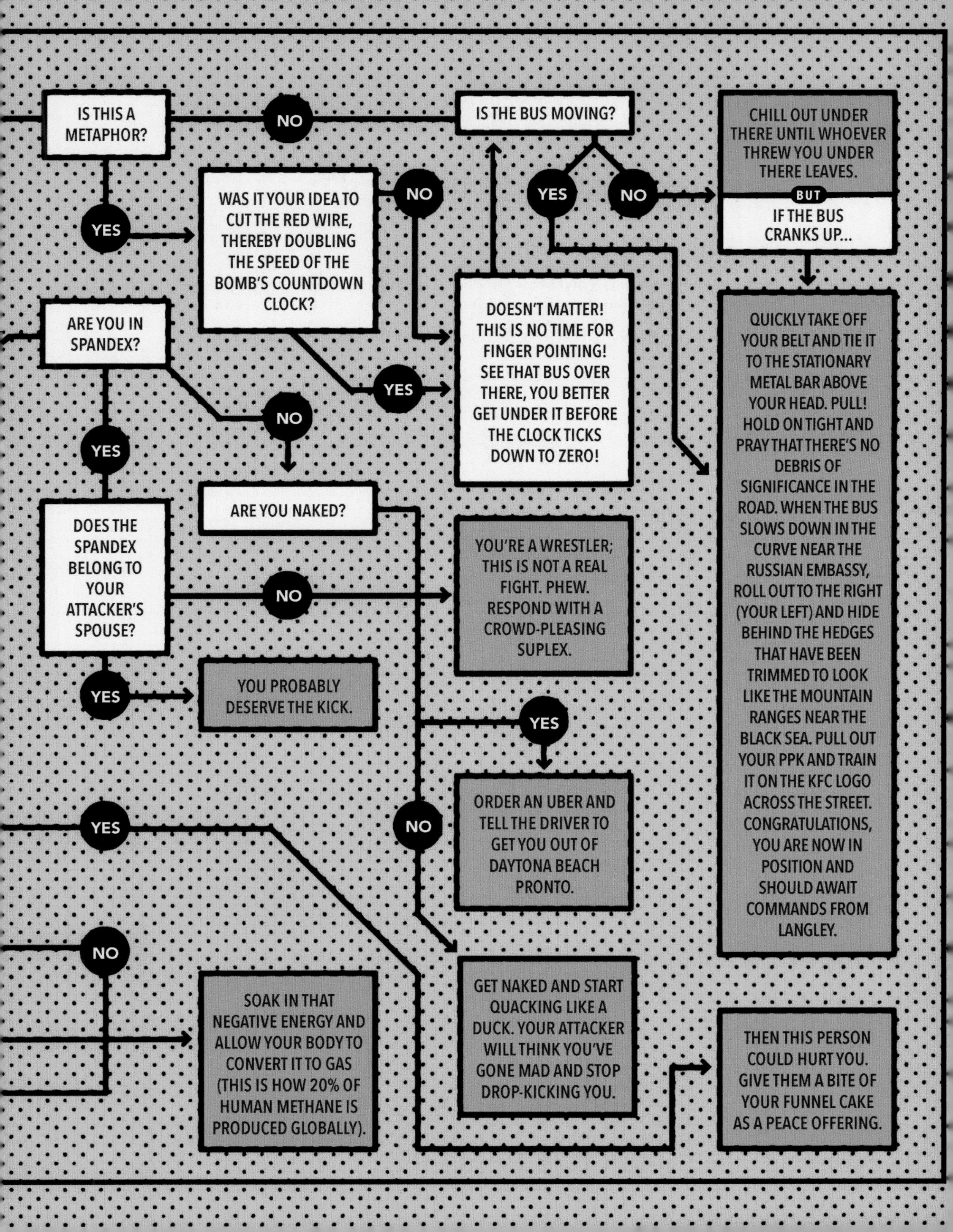
IS THIS A METAPHOR?
NO
YES
IS THE BUS MOVING?
YES
NO
CHILL OUT UNDER THERE UNTIL WHOEVER THREW YOU UNDER THERE LEAVES.
BUT
IF THE BUS CRANKS UP...
WAS IT YOUR IDEA TO CUT THE RED WIRE, THEREBY DOUBLING THE SPEED OF THE BOMB'S COUNTDOWN CLOCK?
NO
YES
DOESN'T MATTER! THIS IS NO TIME FOR FINGER POINTING! SEE THAT BUS OVER THERE, YOU BETTER GET UNDER IT BEFORE THE CLOCK TICKS DOWN TO ZERO!
QUICKLY TAKE OFF YOUR BELT AND TIE IT TO THE STATIONARY METAL BAR ABOVE YOUR HEAD. PULL! HOLD ON TIGHT AND PRAY THAT THERE'S NO DEBRIS OF SIGNIFICANCE IN THE ROAD. WHEN THE BUS SLOWS DOWN IN THE CURVE NEAR THE RUSSIAN EMBASSY, ROLL OUT TO THE RIGHT (YOUR LEFT) AND HIDE BEHIND THE HEDGES THAT HAVE BEEN TRIMMED TO LOOK LIKE THE MOUNTAIN RANGES NEAR THE BLACK SEA. PULL OUT YOUR PPK AND TRAIN IT ON THE KFC LOGO ACROSS THE STREET. CONGRATULATIONS, YOU ARE NOW IN POSITION AND SHOULD AWAIT COMMANDS FROM LANGLEY.
ARE YOU IN SPANDEX?
NO
YES
ARE YOU NAKED?
DOES THE SPANDEX BELONG TO YOUR ATTACKER'S SPOUSE?
NO
YOU'RE A WRESTLER; THIS IS NOT A REAL FIGHT. PHEW. RESPOND WITH A CROWD-PLEASING SUPLEX.
YES
YOU PROBABLY DESERVE THE KICK.
YES
ORDER AN UBER AND TELL THE DRIVER TO GET YOU OUT OF DAYTONA BEACH PRONTO.
NO
YES
NO
GET NAKED AND START QUACKING LIKE A DUCK. YOUR ATTACKER WILL THINK YOU'VE GONE MAD AND STOP DROP-KICKING YOU.
SOAK IN THAT NEGATIVE ENERGY AND ALLOW YOUR BODY TO CONVERT IT TO GAS (THIS IS HOW 20% OF HUMAN METHANE IS PRODUCED GLOBALLY).
THEN THIS PERSON COULD HURT YOU. GIVE THEM A BITE OF YOUR FUNNEL CAKE AS A PEACE OFFERING.

DINK IT
&
SINK IT

# EAT SOMETHING THAT SCARES YOU

"ONE OF THE REASONS I HAD A HARD TIME ENJOYING NEW FOODS WAS MY NANA'S OBSESSION WITH CHOKING. MY SWEET AND WELL-INTENTIONED NANA WOULD LITERALLY TELL ME TO CHEW EVERY BITE THIRTY TIMES IN ORDER TO RID FOOD OF ITS NASTY HABIT OF PLUGGING A WINDPIPE."

Link discovered that a pig anus can be easily adapted into a musical instrument.

**LINK** I recently rewatched the video of me eating pig anus with Rhett on the "Will It Soup?" episode of *GMM*. I have to be honest, as I watched myself happily stick my finger through a cylindrical piece of "panus," as I regretfully called it, and then later hum through it as though it were a kazoo, I thought to myself, Man, I'm proud of that guy. My kids will watch this when they're my age and say, "You know what? I'm the person I am today because of the man my dad was when he ate that pig anus."

**RHETT** I don't know if the adult versions of Link's kids will be proud or disturbed when they watch him play the panus flute, but what I do know is that we have eaten a lot of crazy stuff on *GMM*. We've consumed pig brains, spiders, live mealworms, gnats, leeches, cat food, duck tongue, cod milt (don't Google that), congealed pork blood, a fermented fertilized duck egg, fish eyes, clay, soap, suntan lotion, baby shampoo, dung beetles, pine needles, scorpions, the testicles of at least three animals (I say three, because while we've definitely eaten guinea pig and bull testicles, we ate some insects whole and I'm guessing some of them had some testicle-y parts), and more.

Eating this questionable fare hasn't always ended well, especially for Link. After swallowing a whole Carolina Reaper—certified at that time to be the hottest pepper in the world—Link

Link has deposited more food into his custom barf bucket than into his own stomach.

spent the rest of the day in the fetal position. He has gagged, dry heaved, and vomited so many times while trying to get these seemingly inedible items down that a fan of the show made him a custom barf bucket. (When I complained that I felt left out, somebody sent me my own bucket as well.) Despite the pain and discomfort that our culinary adventures have brought upon us, we still believe that pushing our palates to the brink has added Mythicality to our lives.

**LINK** I was about the furthest thing from an adventurous eater when I was a kid. My mom fed me approximately ten meals on a rotation. If it couldn't be made in a countertop electric skillet, it wasn't in the rotation. Several varieties of Hamburger Helper made up approximately 50 percent of the menu (I'm still amazed at the many ways hamburger can be helped). The other five meals were fried chicken tenders, chicken-fried steak, Stove Top Stuffing–stuffed chicken, beef stir fry, and my mom's pièce de résistance: fried bone-in pork chops. These pork chops were the only thing she was willing to serve to guests.

**RHETT** I remember those. I thought I was repeatedly winning some improbable dietary lottery, just happening to show up only on nights when Sue was making her famous pork chops.

**LINK** Nope. You were just getting "guest chops," along with mashed potatoes and garden peas, the vegetables my mom served exclusively alongside her proteins. Peas were the only green things I ate until I was an adult, with the exception of the short-lived Hi-C Ecto Cooler and apple-flavored Jolly Ranchers.

Link's nana was always wary of him choking, which explains why she held him in such a way as to be ready to perform the Heimlich maneuver at all times.

One of the reasons I had a hard time enjoying new foods was my nana's obsession with choking. My sweet and well-intentioned nana would literally tell me to chew every bite thirty times in order to rid food of its nasty habit of plugging a windpipe. I took her advice to heart, and to jaw. Whenever possible, I opted for soft, safe, fried meats and mushy vegetables. These foods were easy to swallow on their own, but I still puréed them in my mouth by counting exactly thirty crushing chomps for every bite. This was about survival. And thus, the combination of my mama's limited menu and my nana's chewing regimen left me with little motivation to sample new foods.

**RHETT** I noticed Link's chewing habits from the early days of our friendship. He chewed a lot. He even chewed stuff that didn't require chewing. I swear I once saw him chewing chocolate milk. I'm legitimately convinced that he has done the chewing of ten average men during his lifetime. And these aren't simple chews. These are intense, jaw-popping, room-reverberating mastications that have led me to believe he's going to wear out his teeth like an old circus elephant on his seventh set of molars. Eventually, he'll just end up smacking away thirty times on every sip of his Ensure meal-replacement shakes.

Ain't no party like a pizza party.

I bring a completely different philosophy to food. I have some genetic quirk that gives me an impulse to fully consume each and every item on a plate in front of me. If you put an old, worn-out, thrift-store wallet next to a side of mac and cheese, I will find a way to get that wallet down. Not only that, but I eat with an inexplicable urgency, as if my plate could be taken from me at any moment. I promise I was never denied food as a child, and my parents never used a stopwatch at the dinner table. I've just always had a need to feed with speed. And chewing? Chewing is for losers. Once it's in my mouth, it's swallowing time. You could probably take the contents of my stomach after a meal and basically re-create the meal itself in its original form. I'm not saying it's good or healthy. It's just the way it is.

**LINK** My approach to food has changed drastically since Rhett and I began working together. Over time, he has worn me down with incessant complaints about how my picky eating is childish and prevents him from enjoying certain cuisines. I've also gotten tired of being interrogated each time I express hesitation toward a particular food. He won't accept answers like "I just don't like it." He demands details.

Here's how our conversations often go:

LINK (to server): I'll take the house salad, but no cucumbers or tomatoes.

*The server leaves.*

RHETT (shaking his head): What about cucumbers tastes bad?

L: The cucumber part.

R: But what exactly tastes bad about the cucumber part?

L: The cucumber-taste part.

R: And what about tomatoes? What's wrong with tomatoes?

L: The texture. It has the mouthfeel of a poison fruit, like something you shouldn't eat.

R: Well, you still shoulda ordered cucumbers and tomatoes. I could put them on my salad.

L: Why don't you ask for extra cucumbers and tomatoes?

R: Because I don't want them that much. I'm just willing to eat extra if the opportunity presents itself.

As you can imagine, this gets old, and Rhett has slowly worn my food restrictions down over time. But the main reason I've changed my approach to food is that the Mythical Beasts get some sick joy from watching me try to consume unconventional foods, even though it usually involves me repeatedly spewing these foods into a bucket. I can't say that I enjoy consuming nasty delicacies (it doesn't help that they are often just boiled for safety and not seasoned), but I also can't deny that my desire to give the people what they want on *GMM* has helped me evolve as an eater. I am much more willing to try different foods in my normal "not doing it for the camera" life. Fact is, once you've eaten pig anus, cucumbers and tomatoes don't seem that scary anymore. I've even gotten to a place where I can occasionally get something down that Rhett spits into his bucket.

BRINGING A SENSE of adventure to your meals and taking the risk of overcoming your food fears is an important step in leading a Mythical life. You don't have to go as far as we have in your food conquests. We're thinking more about the food you hate because you had one bad experience with it in kindergarten. Or maybe you've never tried it at all. We recently had dinner with an adult male friend who had never tried shrimp. What? How does that happen? There are so many shrimp out there, either swimming in the ocean, spilling out of buffets, or sitting on random trays brought around at parties, you would think that most people would end up getting shrimp in their mouths accidentally. But no, he had never tried it. Until he did. And he liked it. "It's kinda like crab!" he said.

Aside from helping you discover that you actually might love a food you've been afraid of, there are tons of other reasons why you should take the Mythical step of expanding your meal rotation to include more than Cheerios, PB&J, and chicken fingers (in addition to the fact that repeating those three meals exclusively will likely give you late-onset diabetes, which could make you go blind and lose your feet):

**Being the person who ate something makes you inherently more interesting than the person who turned something down.** Declining to eat something doesn't make a memory; it doesn't create a story. When we are sitting side by side on the porch of a Floridian retirement center in the year 2060, we won't lean over to each other and say, "You remember that time we didn't eat pig anus?"

**Eating something exotic gives you an opportunity to make a personal connection.** When you're on a first date and your potential bae suggests the sushi boat for two, you don't want to be the person who says, "I don't like sushi." You also don't want to be the person who says, "I don't like boats," which would just be strange. You want to be the person who boards the sushi boat, says, "Ahoy, matey!" and sails it right into a committed and healthy long-term relationship.

**Eating crazy foods can save your life.** What happens if you accidentally touch a poisonous frog while studying abroad in Venezuela, and a local shaman insists that you ingest a foul-tasting magic elixir in order to survive? Turning it down because you don't like the taste (or the texture) of foul-tasting magic elixir could result in your death. Not cool.

Finally, **pickiness isn't great for the apocalypse.** At any moment, our world could become a Mad Max–like desert landscape filled with leather-clad guitarists strapped to rusted-out school buses. If you're lucky enough to stumble upon a dead pig during these dark times, and all that's left is the anus . . . you get the picture.

Rhett McLaughlin's
Mythical
Monster Truck
Spit Bucket

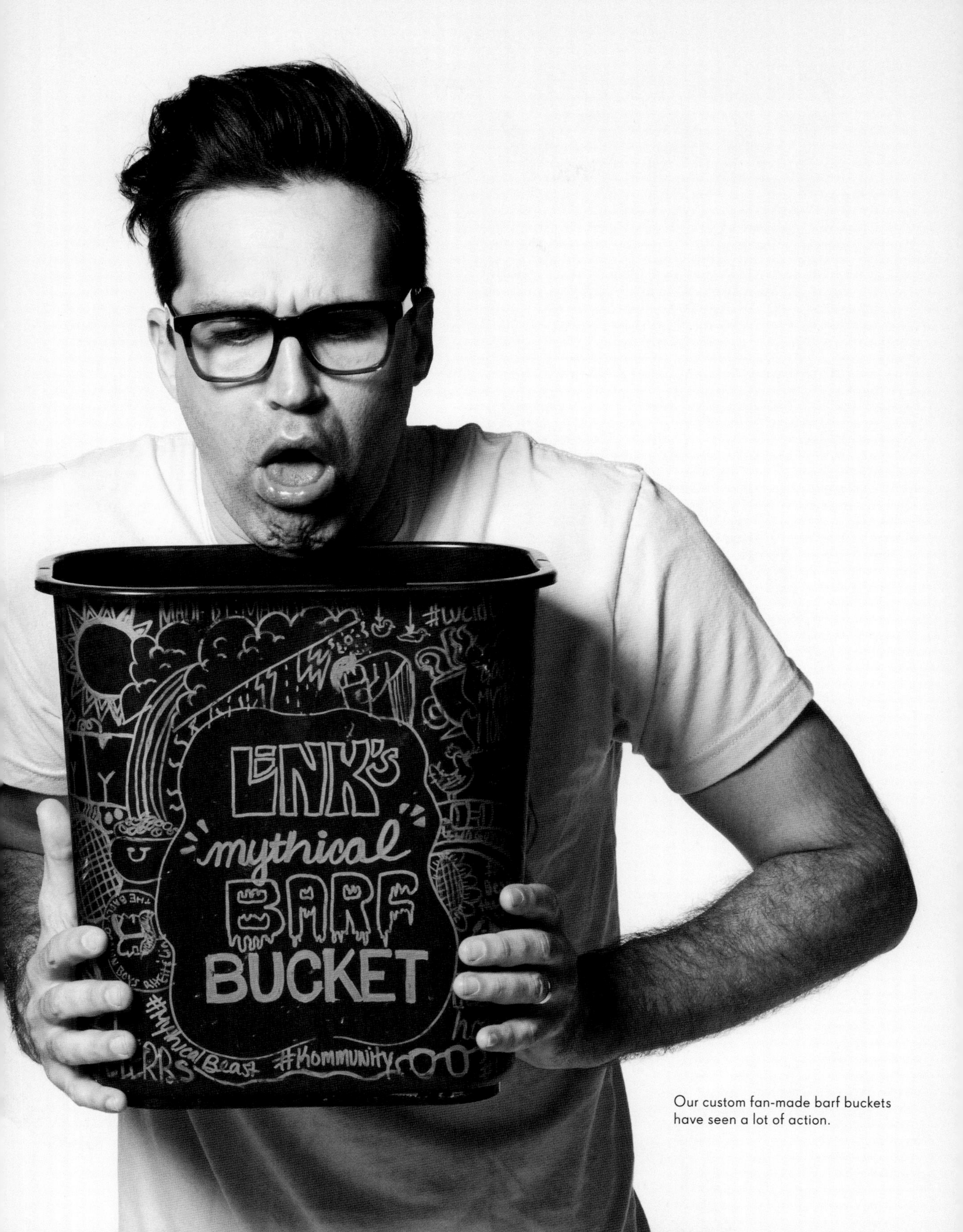


Our custom fan-made barf buckets have seen a lot of action.

# WHERE IS THE TASTY ZONE?

After eating so many weird things, we've developed a theory on what makes a particular food gross—especially when it comes to animal parts. Most meat eaters consider a chicken leg tasty, while they think a chicken liver is somehow nasty. It turns out that there is a "tasty zone" for animal parts that captures a balance between similarity to ourselves and essentiality to survival. Stated simply, if an animal is either too dissimilar to humans (insects) or too similar (chimpanzees), we find the thought of eating them gross. Also, the more essential the body part for that animal's survival, the more gross it is to eat. Still don't get it? Check out the graph below for a definitive illustration of the tasty zone. Plot your next meal on this chart to determine if you should think it's nasty or tasty.

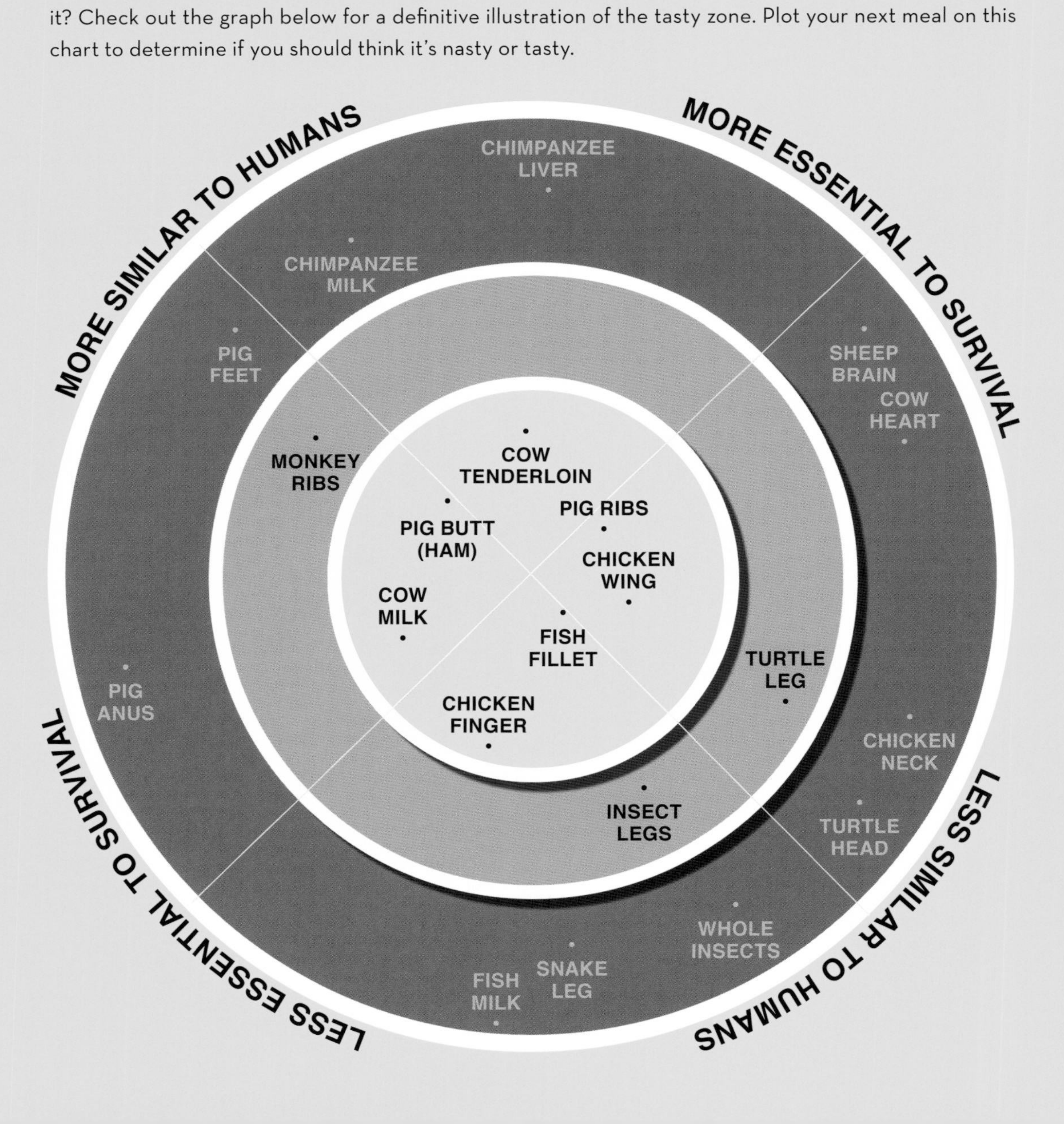

# OUR PROCESS FOR EATING SOMETHING NASTY

ONCE YOU'VE DETERMINED THAT YOU'RE GOING TO EAT SOMETHING THAT FALLS OUTSIDE THE TASTY ZONE AND IS TRULY NASTY, YOU CAN'T JUST START EATING IT. NO—IF YOU DON'T HAVE A PROCESS, YOU'RE VERY LIKELY TO END UP RALPHING THAT CHICKEN HEART RIGHT INTO YOUR CUSTOM BARF BUCKET. WE'VE BY NO MEANS PERFECTED IT, BUT WE HAVE DEVELOPED A DETAILED PROCESS FOR GETTING NASTY FOODS TO PASS THROUGH OUR DIGESTIVE SYSTEM WITHOUT BEING REJECTED.

**Willpower:** You must make a definitive decision to eat this nasty thing. There is no room for waffling. This is not a waffle.

**Smell Inhibition:** Some 80 percent of taste is smell, so you can remove most of the nastiness of food if you disengage your nose. This is the one case where being a mouth breather is not only acceptable, but of great benefit.

**Self-Deception:** Convince yourself that you are in a different setting, like a fancy party where you are trying to fit in with rich people who like to eat gross delicacies like fish eggs, or you have been taken prisoner in a remote jungle by a cannibalistic tribe, and the chief says, "You must eat this pudding made from mud and all the village elders' saliva, or we will eat you." If your reputation or life is at stake, you're gonna eat it.

**Donkey Lipping:** We have found that it is helpful to explore a nasty food with your lips prior to eating it—especially when blindfolded. While we've never actually seen a donkey do this with its food, we can assure you that it's a great way to ease into consuming nastiness.

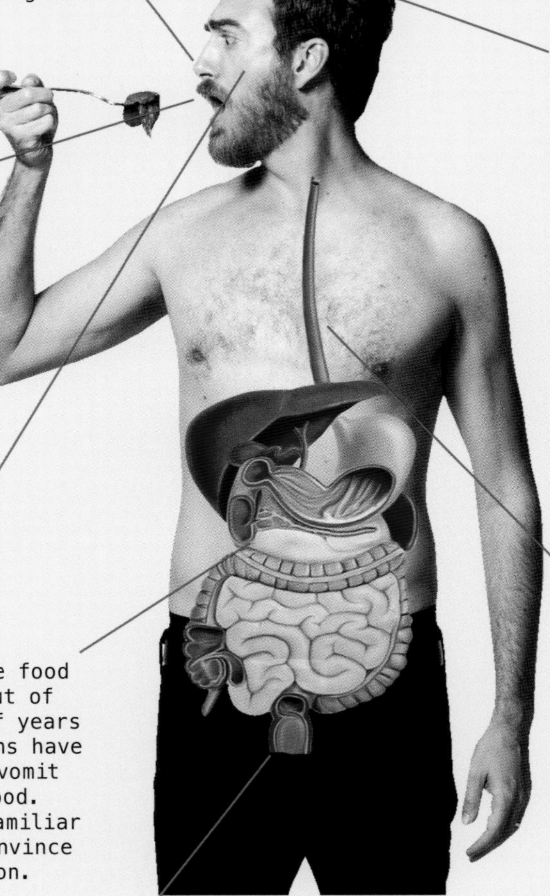

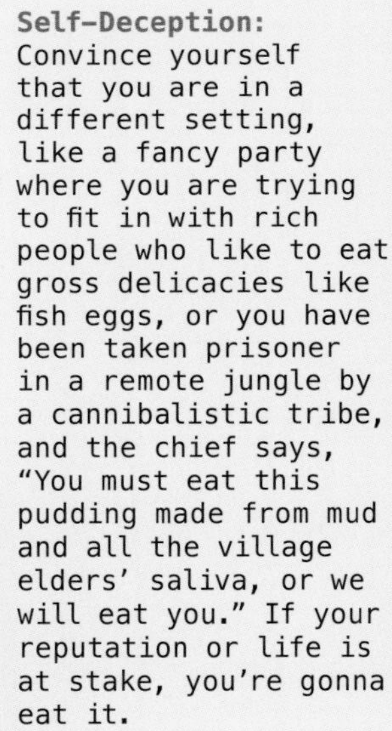

**Chipmunking:** Once you have gotten the nasty food into your mouth, there is no better way to induce instant gagging than going for an early swallow. Instead, place the undesirable chow in your cheek, slowly working out small amounts to chew and swallow. By the way, we have seen chipmunks do this.

**Self-Flagellation:** The most difficult stage is swallowing. We have found it useful (well, Rhett has) to beat our chests like gorillas and yell in order to convince our bodies to swallow particularly nasty food. This is not recommended in restaurant settings.

**Chaser:** Swallowing the food doesn't mean you're out of the woods. Millions of years of survival adaptations have attuned your body to vomit up unfamiliar, foul food. Following up with a familiar food or liquid can convince your stomach to hold on.

**The Great Escape:** You want the nasty food to exit your body like you would leave a community-theatre play—quickly and quietly. Don't tax your body with more unwelcome foods until you have passed this one nasty thing into the abyss (the abyss is the toilet, in case you aren't following).

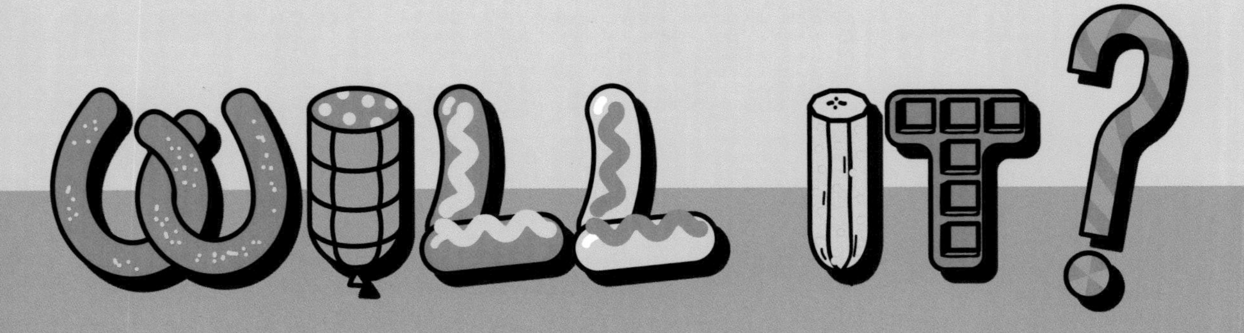

We have a longstanding tradition on *GMM* of asking the question "Will It?" in which we attempt to combine two foods that have likely never been brought together before. Of course, we weren't the first to do this. In fact, some of history's most loved foods are a result of brave people stepping out and asking, "Will It?"

## WILL IT SANDWICH?

### Julia David Chandler–peanut butter and jelly sandwich

In 1901, Ms. Chandler published the first recipe for PB&J in the unnecessarily formal-sounding publication *The Boston Cooking School Magazine of Culinary Science and Domestic Economics.* She wrote: "For variety, try making little sandwiches, or bread fingers, of three very thin layers of bread and two of filling, one of peanut paste, whatever brand you prefer, and currant or crab apple jelly for the other. The combination is delicious and so far as I know, original." Bravo, Julia David Chandler. Also, how come nobody eats crab apple jelly anymore?

## WILL IT BREAKFAST?

### Tia Sophia's Restaurant–the breakfast burrito

Folks in New Mexico had been eating eggs and bacon wrapped in tortillas long before the owners of Tia Sophia's branded theirs as a "breakfast burrito" in 1975. However, sometimes that little extra bit of branding is what allows a great idea to grow wings and become a handful of happiness for boys and girls around the world.

## WILL IT DESSERT?

### Frank Wisner–the root beer float

One night in 1893, Frank Wisner was gazing out his window in Cripple Creek, Colorado, and was so taken by the view of the snow on nearby Cow Mountain that he decided to re-create the scene in his drink by dropping a scoop of ice cream into his root beer. Thus the root beer float was born in the most romantic "Will It?" way possible. Side note: the root beer float was originally called a "Black Cow Mountain," later shortened to "Black Cow" by the Cripple Creek children, and later changed to root beer float so people wouldn't think it had cow in it.

## WILL IT LATE-NIGHT?

### Jeno Paulucci–the pizza roll

The "King of Frozen Food" got his start packaging Chinese food for grocery-store mass consumption in the 1950s. In true "Will It?" pioneer spirit, however, Jeno's legacy stems from an experiment that fused his Italian heritage with the machine that made his egg rolls. The result was the legendary pizza roll, the late-night snack and sleepover staple for generations to come. Sadly, when Jeno sold his company to Pillsbury, they rebranded his product as Totino's, but he still lives on in every pizza roll (to clarify, he is not actually inside any pizza rolls).

## WILL IT ETHICALLY QUESTIONABLE SNACK?

### Rob Nelson–Big League Chew

When Rob Nelson was nearing the end of his baseball-playing career at the dawn of the '80s, he met a kid who liked to pretend he was a big-league ballplayer by chewing on black licorice and then spitting out the dark juice. Nelson thought it would be a great idea to apply the same principle to bubble gum and, long story short, he invented Big League Chew, the gum that made every baseball and softball player swell with the confidence of a big-league chewing-tobacco addict. It would be tough to adequately explain just how cool Big League Chew was in the late '80s and early '90s. Somewhere, the inventor of candy cigarettes is crying into three fingers of scotch, wondering where he went wrong.

## WILL IT WILLETT?

### William Willett (pronounced "Will-it") Jr.

We would be remiss if we wrote a section about "Will It?" pioneers and didn't include someone from the Willett whiskey family, a mainstay in Bardstown, Kentucky, for hundreds of years. We picked William Junior (born in 1743) because the Willett family website says that he operated an "ordinary," which was a tavern that doubled as an all-inclusive inn for travelers and their horses. William would be saddened to learn that hotels no longer allow horses, but he can't learn because he's dead.

CONFIDANCE

# UNLEASH A SIGNATURE DANCE MOVE

"THERE HE WAS: MY GANGLY BEST FRIEND, KICKING HIS LEGS IN ALL DIRECTIONS, SPINNING LIKE AN ICE SKATER WHO HAD BEEN INJECTED WITH ADRENALINE. I HAD NO IDEA WHAT HE WAS DOING, BUT IT WAS WORKING. WE WERE GONNA WIN THIS THING."

**A LOT OF PEOPLE** experience a sudden anxiety when they learn that an event they are attending may involve dancing. For them, the thought of attempting to gyrate their midsection or move their limbs to music in a semi-recognizable pattern is a straight-up nightmare. We're convinced that they're just thinking about it all wrong. Dancing remains one of the purest forms of self-expression, and that makes it a unique opportunity to be Mythical.

**RHETT** In seventh grade, the powers that be at Buies Creek School announced that we would be having a lip-sync contest at that year's seventh-and-eighth-grade dance. Link and I were both obsessed with DJ Jazzy Jeff and the Fresh Prince (aka Will Smith), having memorized every word of all their songs, so we knew we would be performing one of their tracks. It may not strike you as terribly strategic for two guys to lip-sync a song from a group consisting of one DJ and one rapper—seeing as how only one guy is doing something you can actually sync your lips to—but Link had a plan.

While their latest album, *And in This Corner*, had plenty of songs to choose from—including the popular single "I Think I Can Beat Mike Tyson," Link convinced me that we should perform "Jazzy's Groove," a song featuring Will rapping his best friend's praises. Sure, there were a couple of small speaking parts for Jeff, but there were also long periods of uninterrupted record scratching. "Why limit ourselves to lip-syncing when we could incorporate scratch-syncing," Link argued. I reluctantly agreed. I would rap as the Fresh Prince, and Link would man a fake, cardboard-box DJ booth, bringing the record-spinning heat as DJ Jazzy Jeff himself.

**LINK** I could tell that Rhett had his doubts about my plan. The contest would be judged by the level of applause from our peers—much like our favorite TV talent show at the time, *Showtime at the Apollo*. Our reputations were on the line, and for some reason, he worried about my ability to capture the crowd by just rubbing my hands on top of a three-foot-tall-box.

**RHETT** The song began. The rap kicked in, and judging by the looks on the acne-laden faces staring at me, I was off to a strong start. I had practiced hard and hit each word perfectly, spitting out lines like "Jeff's about to give an incredible display. And unequivocally prove that he's the best DJ." But with those lyrics, I was really setting the bar high for Link—and his box.

Then, the first record-scratching break came. I turned to Link, who gave me a reassuring nod, then looked down and went to work. As he caressed the cardboard in time with the music, I surveyed the crowd. It was obvious that this was not going to hold up. He was losing the audience fast. But Link was so engrossed in his box that he had no idea that it wasn't working. That's when I began to dance. Unfortunately, I had planned absolutely no dance moves. So I winged it.

I began with a very basic version of the Running Man, and then checked the crowd. We still had at least ten seconds before I would begin rapping again, and they seemed to be thinking, "OK, yeah . . . he's doing the Running Man. Big deal." And so, without any forethought or calculation, I amended the Running Man on the spot, adding an outward leg kick. Some eyebrows raised, and we had the crowd on our side again. The rapping picked up once more, and I hit every lyric without missing a beat. Of course, I knew that Mr. Box Scratcher was soon due for another round, so I entered the next DJ break completely ready. I reintroduced my Modified Running Man, this time trying my outward leg kick in both directions, and even throwing in a complete 360-degree turn. Everybody was into it.

Rhett's Modified Running Man, with outward-leg kick accents.

This was our best attempt at dressing like rappers, because, you know...rappers wear hats over their beanies.

**LINK** It was at this point that I—head down in the middle of another perfect depiction of the complex finger stylings of the world's best DJ—heard the crowd react with clapping and a few shouts of "Woot!" I knew it. My plan had worked. These sheltered middle-schoolers had never seen anyone execute box-top record scratching at this level. To soak in the admiration, I looked up. There he was: my gangly best friend, kicking his legs in all directions, spinning like an ice skater who had been injected with adrenaline. I had no idea what he was doing, but it was working. We were gonna win this thing. Even though Rhett's weird dance was taking the pressure off of me, I still continued my amazing DJ pantomiming to the very end.

**RHETT** When the song ended, everyone cheered—just as loudly as they did for our classmate Lynwood Campbell after he performed "The Choice Is Yours" by Black Sheep. We tied. But it was still a huge victory. I left the dance that night with a newfound confidence in my ability to invent a completely original dance out of nowhere.

**LINK** My personal peak in original dance creation occurred in college at a '70s-themed party. These parties were incredibly popular at colleges in the late '90s, because you could still easily go to a thrift store and score a pair of bell bottoms and a shirt with a butterfly collar. A number of partygoers were dancing, most of them doing some lame version of the repeated "disco point," which is often what people default to during '70s music. No one was really making a statement. This was my chance. I approached the DJ, who was actually just a dude at the CD player who didn't want to dance, placed my hand on his shoulder, and said, "Gimme some 'Brick House.'" If you happen to not be familiar with the funky masterpiece that is the Commodores' "Brick House," I feel sorry for you. All you need to know, though, is that it's a song celebrating the fullness of a woman's body, going so far as to compare it to an actual structure made of bricks (the only structure that the Big Bad Wolf couldn't blow down). Walter "Clyde" Orange's lead vocals paint a poetic picture with lines such as "The lady's stacked and that's a fact, ain't holding nothing back." In other words, it's the perfect song for a 145-pound male college student in extremely tight pants to get down to.

I walked to the middle of the dance floor and thought to myself, I'm going to give these people something completely original. As the music started, I gave myself over to the rhythm as if I were being puppeteered by the drums and bass. I was bending, bouncing, and wiggling in ways I didn't think my body could handle. Halfway through the song, everyone else just stopped dancing. They got out of my way and watched me explore the far reaches of musical body movement. I eventually settled into a dance in which I pictured a gate in front of me, the kind you'd see at the exit for a parking garage. I would take a step over this imaginary gate, duck back under it, then proceed with a brisk pelvic thrust. It was more than a dance. It felt like an out-of-body experience. When the music was over, a girl approached me and asked, "What was . . . that?" I responded with, "Oh, that? Just a little somethin'." I had unleashed a signature dance move.

Link let the music possess him and created a spontaneous original dance for a crowd of mesmerized onlookers.

**WE'VE NEVER REALLY** been fans of predetermined dances. We resist falling into a conga line, and we've both been known to exit the dance floor if the DJ has the audacity to play "The Electric Slide." Sure, we respect people who have the ability to perfect a specific style of dance, but there's just something more Mythical about a dance that is all your own. Improvised dances also have a much easier entry point. You just need to know how to move.

Next time the beat drops and you're presented with an opportunity to dance, don't migrate to the sides of the room. Instead, as the woman from C&C Music Factory (not the woman from the music videos, but the other woman who actually did the singing) sang, "Let the rhythm move you!" She also said, "Come on and sweat! Swweee-eeeeat!" You don't necessarily have to sweat. But go out there and take a chance. Here are some things to remember as you unleash your dance:

**No one will know if you screw up.** Since you're not following a template, there are no mistakes. If you hyperextend your knee in the middle of an especially aggressive pop or lock, causing you to slowly limp off the dance floor, it doesn't matter. It can still be part of your dance. Michael Jackson included tons of zombie-limp dancing in "Thriller," and it's the greatest music video of all time.

**You may end up actually creating a popular dance.** Every dance that we now consider a "real" dance was once just someone's decision to move their body in a certain way. Drake obviously ad-libs his way through all of his music videos, which is why most of his dancing looks like he's just brushing some lint off his pants or putting a loaf of bread into a grocery basket. But that hasn't stopped people everywhere from trying to mimic his moves. It's not as hard as you think.

**Don't get too locked in.** If your dance move is too simple and repetitive, like twirling your hands around in little circles for an entire song, you're going to scare people and lose friends. Mix it up and keep people guessing. Use your arms, legs, neck, and don't forget the pelvis. The pelvis is the dancing linchpin. If you pull it out of your dance, the whole thing falls apart.

**Just let go and don't look back.** Above all, let your dance happen. Don't be afraid to look stupid. Remember that the people standing in the corner watching you dance just wish they could be out there doing what you're doing. You're the one introducing the world to a new Mythical dance.

# CONFI-DANCE

***When you are on the dance floor, the look on your face must communicate that you know what you're doing—even if you most certainly do not. Dancing an original dance is not the time for grimaces or flashes of regret. You've got to own it. Make the same face that is required for sneaking into a second movie at the theater. If you look like you're supposed to be doing it, no one will question you. Don't believe us? Check out these photo pairs. In the first picture our expressions reflect our actual level of dance expertise. The only thing that changes in the second photo is confidence.***

## HOW TO CREATE AND COORDINATE A

# SHOWSTOPPING DANCE CIRCLE

**Up to this point, this chapter has been all about the ways that you can own the dance floor as a performer. However, not everyone will fulfill their destiny as dancers. The ceiling is much higher as a producer or promoter, meaning some folks would be better served to essentially take over the dance floor by orchestrating the atmosphere. For those of you who possess the rare combination of a puppet master's personality and limited rhythm, we would like to offer up the five steps to producing a perfect dance circle:**

**1 Target a Track** A great dance circle starts with a great song. For years, Michael Jackson's "Billie Jean" was an automatic circle starter. There's a clear reason for this. The best dance-circle songs have more than 100 beats per minute and almost always contain obscure lyrics that are difficult to understand. In "Billie Jean," Michael says, "Who will dance on the floor in the round" or something very much like that. Unclear lyrics help the audience to focus on the dancing. Find a modern song that you don't quite understand the meaning of with a tempo over 100 bpm, and you'll be in business.

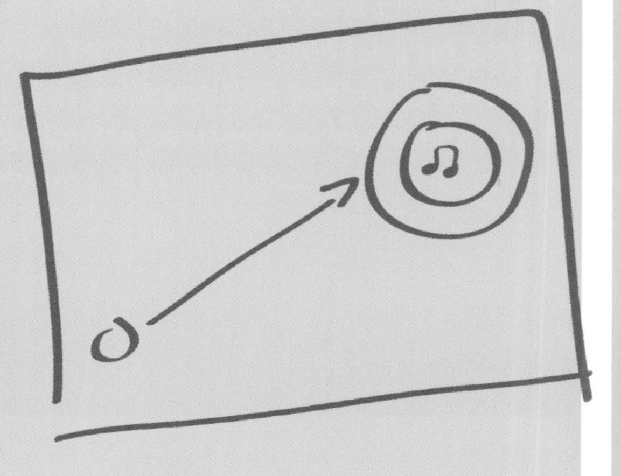

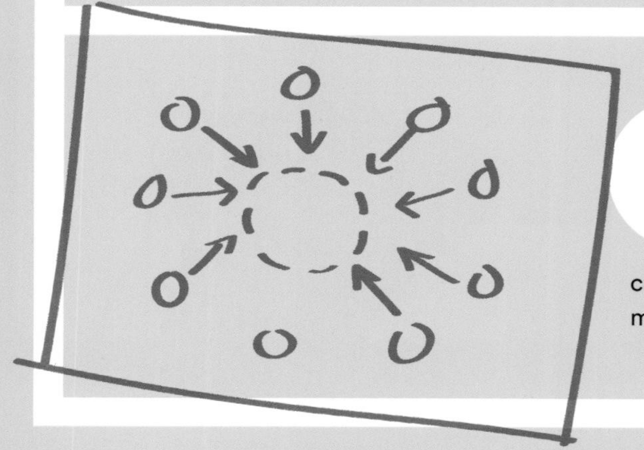

**2 Circle the Wagons** When your track gets dropped, find a great dancer on the floor and begin to circle him or her rapidly, protecting your star from the crowd like you're the Secret Service at a presidential meet-and-greet.

## 3 Make Them Believe the Hype

As you establish your perimeter, begin to bring special attention to your first dancer. It can be helpful to shout something like "Go, Janet; go, Janet; go, go, go, Janet," especially if your dancer's name is Janet. Make the crowd want Janet to go.

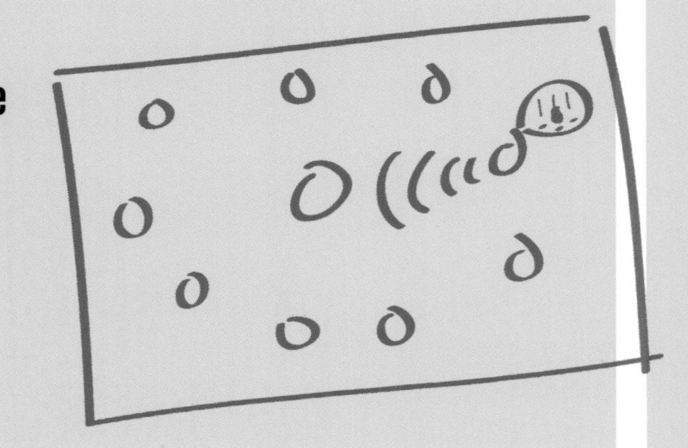

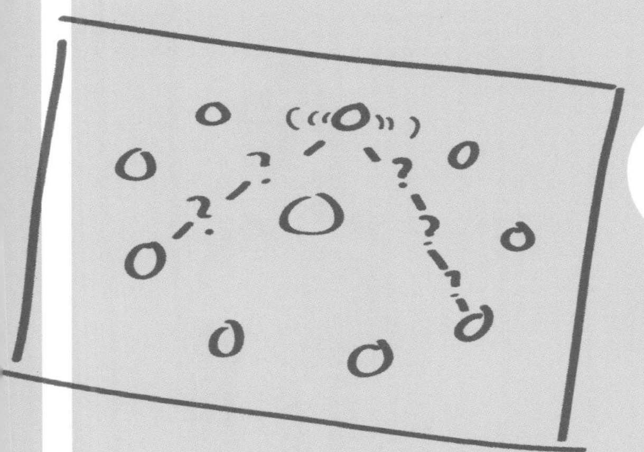

## 4 Scout the Perimeter

Keep an eye out for your next dancer. Your first dancer is always an alpha-dancer, but to keep the crowd guessing, your next entry should be a diamond in the rough—someone unexpected who looks to possess more flavor than he/she lets on in his/her daily life.

## 5 Give 'em the Hook

Most dance circles end early because they grow stale and predictable. Two or three dancers, addicted to the momentary love of the crowd, keep jumping back into the circle and, given that they used their best moves in their first appearance, they quickly underperform. For this reason, you must curate your circle by pulling dancers out after no more than thirty seconds. It's your job to make sure that there are new flavors constantly being added to the mix.

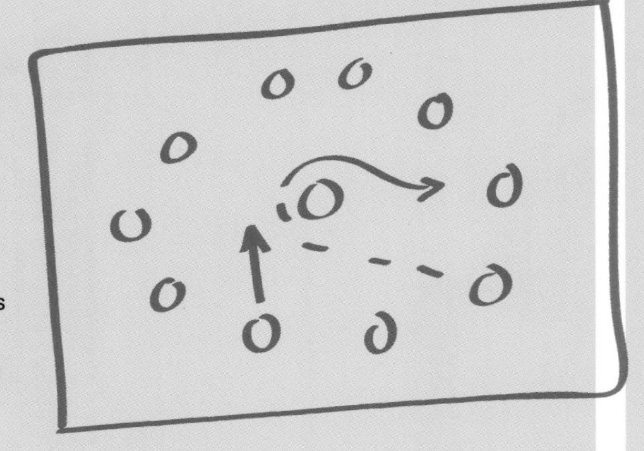

# A VISUAL GUIDE TO SLOW DANCING

Slow dancing is an art. Unfortunately, most partygoers consider it to be an afterthought or, worse, a three-minute break from the "real" dancing. Such a shame. There are as many different slow dances as there are fast dances, and like Tai Chi, they can take entire lifetimes to master. Enjoy a glimpse into the world of sophisticated slow dancing.

ROOM FOR THE HOLY GHOST

GETTING CHEEKY

GETTING CHEEKIER

TENTATIVE BUMP 'N' GRIND

TOOK ONE DANCE CLASS

CRY IT OUT

LONDON BRIDGE

MY FACE IS UP HERE

STIFF ARM

COMMITMENT ISSUES

RIDE THE PONY

SLEEPY TIME

DO YOU EVEN SQUAT, BRO?

BABY KOALA

BABY KANGAROO

A LIL
DIRT
DONT HURT

# GET YOUR HANDS DIRTY

"IN ORDER TO MAKE IT THROUGH THAT FIRST DAY, I PRETENDED THAT I WAS AN ARCHAEOLOGIST EXCAVATING AN IMPORTANT MAYAN RUIN, SEEKING TO DISCOVER CLUES ABOUT AN ANCIENT PEOPLE. HOWEVER, IT WAS HARD TO MAINTAIN THAT ILLUSION EACH TIME I CRAWLED THROUGH A SECTION OF DIRT THAT REEKED OF CONSTRUCTION-WORKER URINE."

GROWING UP IN rural North Carolina, we were taught the value of a good, firm handshake. To achieve one, you need to first establish a properly set grip, getting that webbing between your thumb and index finger—we like to call it the "hand crotch"—in full contact with the same area of the other shaker's hand. Hand-crotch-to-hand-crotch contact is essential. Also, you must look the other person in the eyes the entire time. People who break eye contact midshake can't be trusted. They are the kinds of people who are definitely hiding something, like a collection of weird, faceless dolls in their attic. If you want to be respected, you give a confident handshake.

Besides the grip and eyes, there remains an additional piece of data you can gather from a handshake: the softness of the hands. While this is something that people have much less control over, you can still draw some important conclusions from it. In Buies Creek, we would often shake a hand with thick, muscle-bound fingers covered in skin that felt like a pair of alligator boots. It was obvious that this was the hand of a working man, someone who made a living by the sweat of his brow.

Living in Los Angeles, it's easy to go for years without shaking a hand like that, because this is a town full of people making their living not with their hands but with their faces and mouths. If/when the long-anticipated massive earthquake hits Southern California, this city of pretty-faced, soft-handed people won't stand a chance.

Of course, we're talking as if this doesn't apply to us, but our hands are just as soft as a voice-over artist lounging poolside in Palm Springs. At this point, our "manual labor" consists mostly of mounting abstract oil paintings with names like *Translucent Eggs No. 7* to the walls of our houses in the locations our wives have approved. We don't even mow our own grass. It's pathetic, we know. Thankfully, before we became softies who get paid to flap our pie holes, we each had the chance to learn what real work was.

**LINK** Seeing as how we grew up literally surrounded by tobacco fields, it was nearly unavoidable that at least one of us would end up falling into the gravitational pull of North Carolina's economic epicenter. Three of my nana's unibrowed brothers were tobacco farmers, and each summer they needed seasonal help to process their crop. During the summer of 1994, I had just turned sixteen, and I was enjoying the newfound freedom afforded by my driver's license. I'd gladly accept any excuse to drive anywhere. Even to work. When my uncle Johnny offered me a job on the farm, I pictured myself zooming down all those back roads, a "hardworkin' man" with my tanned elbow hanging out the driver's-side window of my red 1987 Nissan pickup (featuring chrome wheels and a Brooks & Dunn front plate). The scene looked epic. I accepted the job.

I learned that I'd be "barning" tobacco, which sounded easy enough, but I failed to account for several factors. First and foremost was the crippling heat. Even though we started each day at dawn in order to minimize our time in the blistering North Carolina summer sun, our clothes were soaked through with sweat less than an hour after we started. If you've never spent much time outdoors in the southern United States during the summer months, just imagine what it would be like to constantly be in a bathroom with a hot shower running. Everyone walks around with a shiny film of perspiration on their faces like they're all auditioning for a role alongside Matthew McConaughey in an Old South period piece. It adds a grueling element to any outdoor activity.

# THE PERFECT HANDSHAKE

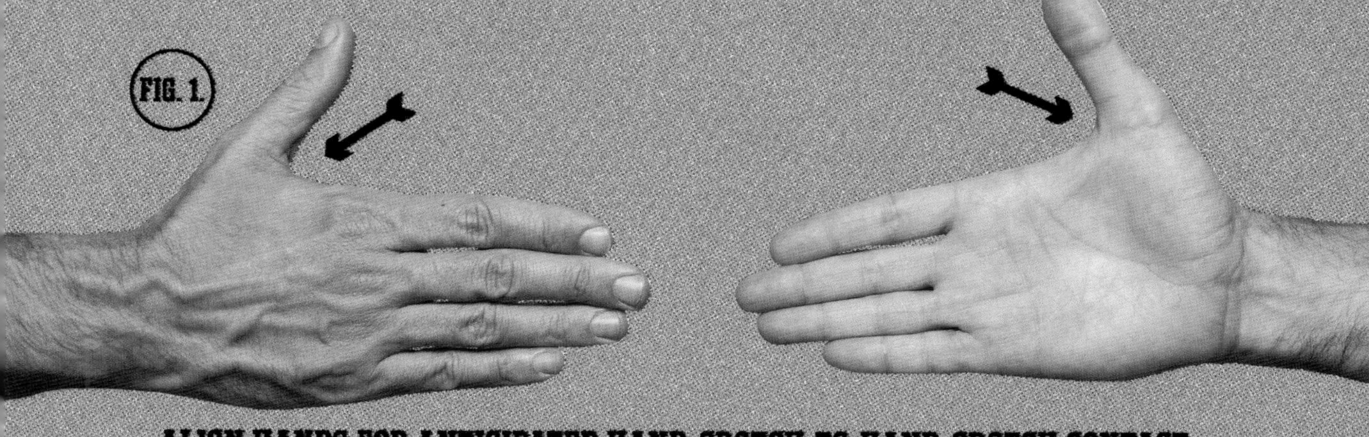


ALIGN HANDS FOR ANTICIPATED HAND-CROTCH-TO-HAND-CROTCH CONTACT.

MAKE SOLID HAND-CROTCH-TO-HAND-CROTCH CONTACT.

GRASP TIGHTLY TO SECURE HAND-CROTCH-TO-HAND-CROTCH CONTACT.

Link loved his red Nissan. It was the perfect vehicle for backing into large piles of dirt.

My job was to stack tobacco into a large metal rack, and then help guide the full racks into a metal "barn" (it was really more of a box), where the tobacco would dry into its familiar brown and brittle state. That was it. Over and over and over again. It was the most monotonous job I'd ever had, and the repetition of stacking and stowing tobacco lulled me into a semiconscious state. I would end up standing there motionless for minutes at a time, neglecting my simple duties. My uncle Johnny would say, "He's having another brain fart." I would snap back into the moment, grab the rack, and do my part. A few more minutes would pass and I would fall right back into my state of cranial flatulence. That summer, I earned the nickname "Mr. Brain Fart," and it was well deserved.

Barning was far from the worst part of the job, however. One day, the majority of the tobacco that we were handling was wet from an overnight rain. Later that afternoon, I began to feel ill. The next morning I woke up feeling even worse. It turns out that my skin had absorbed the nicotine from the wet tobacco and I was suffering from a condition called green tobacco sickness. It was absolutely awful. When I wasn't lying in bed with a splitting headache, I was in the bathroom playing eenie meenie miney mo between orifices. I decided that this would be my last summer of working tobacco. I had done my required part as a North Carolina native, contributing to the distribution of more cigarettes around the world.

**RHETT** I too was given a chance to temporarily try my hand at callus-inducing work before I eventually settled into my cushy Internetainment job. Frankie Hamilton, the father of one of our close friends, Trent, owned a residential real estate construction company. The same summer that Link was toiling in tobacco, Trent was planning to work for his dad and asked me if

I wanted to join him. This seemed like the sweetest deal possible. I knew Trent well enough to guess that he wasn't going to needlessly overexert himself for the family business. Furthermore, his dad was well regarded as a wealthy man, so it naturally followed that I was going to be raking in cash like a sixteen-year-old Scrooge McDuck.

The reality of my circumstances came crashing down on me when Frankie informed me that I would be making just $6/hour, and I would not be working alongside Trent. He had set aside a very important job for me. I would be the sole individual responsible for cleaning out the crawl spaces of newly constructed homes.

I remember kneeling down and peering into my first crawl space, completely unaware of what horrors were lurking in the blackness. I folded up my 6′5″ frame (I had not yet reached my wholly unnecessary height of 6′7″) and crawled on my belly, a flashlight in one hand and a trash bag in the other. I quickly learned that construction workers viewed the open foundation of a home as a veritable dumpster—and occasional toilet—until it was covered with subflooring. Every few feet or so I would discover a new surprise. It might be a crumpled-up Big Mac carton covered in ants enjoying Special Sauce remnants, or if I was lucky, it was a RC Cola bottle half full of what looked to be RC Cola but was actually dark, putrid tobacco spit. It was lovely.

In order to make it through that first day, I pretended that I was an archaeologist excavating an important Mayan ruin, seeking to discover clues about an ancient people. However, it was hard to maintain that illusion each time I crawled through a section of dirt that reeked of construction-worker urine (it has its own distinct scent: Busch Light and pressure-treated lumber). That summer, I would return home each evening to nurse another knot on my head and hop in the shower to release the cavalcade of dust boogers that had accumulated in my nostrils.

At 16, Rhett was old enough for a summer job but not too old to have number candles on his birthday cake.

The following summer, Frankie promised me the opportunity to explore a more legitimately constructive part of the construction business. With a completely straight face, he informed me and Trent that he wanted us to build a house. Given that I had barely ever swung a hammer, I figured he'd either had a stroke or was talking about a doghouse. But no, he wanted us to frame an actual home that a human family would later occupy. He said, "Mr. Fred will help y'all."

Mr. Fred was a sixty-five-year-old retired friend of Frankie's who helped out with various jobs in order to stay not actually retired. Every day, he wore a blue short-sleeved shirt that said "Fred" on it and smoked at least one pack of cigarettes. I was really hoping he knew how to construct a home.

Thankfully, some qualified people had laid the foundation, floor joists, and subflooring, so our job was limited to framing the house. On the first day, Mr. Fred lit a cigarette and said, "Lemme show you how to build a wall." Before he finished his cigarette, he had deftly nailed together a series of eight-foot-long two-by-fours, sixteen inches on-center. He then asked us to stand the wall up on some marks he'd made on the subfloor, and proceeded to quickly nail the wall into place. He commanded, "Let go." The wall stood there on its own. This was going to be a breeze.

"Now y'all do it." Mr. Fred lit another cigarette, walked off into the yard, and sat down under a tree. Approximately one hour later, our wall was complete, but still lying on its side waiting to be set upright and nailed into place. Mr. Fred moseyed on over, tossed aside another expended cigarette, stepped up onto the foundation, and said flatly, "Took ya long enough." He then leaned in to inspect our work. He pointed at one of the many nails sticking out from our wall, making it look like a strange cactus, the result of our nail-gun ineptitude. "Don't do that," he said. He then ordered, "OK, stand 'er up." Trent and I reached down to proudly see our work materialize as an actual wall, but when we lifted, it wouldn't budge. Mr. Fred shook his head

Nothing says true friendship like eating cereal off of each other's hands.

and said, "Y'all nailed the damn thing to the floor." He then lit another cigarette and went back to his tree, leaving me and Trent to solve the problem ourselves.

After a few weeks of being forced to deal with our own blunders, Trent and I were semi-respectable home builders. Sure, we continued to make mistakes, like the time we misread the blueprints and accidentally made one of the bedroom closets a mere twelve inches deep, but we pulled it off. We framed an entire house. Every time I think about some poor soul in western Harnett County having to hang their shirts sideways in their ridiculously shallow closet, I feel a sense of pride knowing that I can build a house. Sort of.

I'm grateful that Frankie asked us to do something so far above our capabilities that summer. I think he wanted his son to get a small taste of manual labor, knowing that a couple of summers on a construction site would be enough to motivate him to get a college degree and not have to make a living by the sweat of his brow. It worked. But there was more to it than that.

GETTING OUR HANDS dirty, even if it was only for a few short summers in high school, has helped us approach our current jobs with more curiosity and appreciation. Those hot summers remind us how lucky we are to do what we do today. When we happen to get our hands dirty these days, it's not because we're handling tobacco or hammering a nail. It's usually because we're doing something like dipping our hands in honey, nuts, and Cheerios, and then interlocking our fingers and putting our fists into a bowl of milk so we can enjoy "Honey-Nut Cheerio Hand Cereal." We may work hard, but it's not hard work. Without those summer jobs, we might not have that perspective.

Plus, we actually learned some useful skills during those summers. We hope that tobacco-barning knowledge won't be necessary at any point in the future, but when that earthquake hits and all the soft-handed people's homes collapse, Rhett may actually be able to help rebuild the city of Los Angeles (as long as everyone is OK living in two-bedroom ranch-style homes with one extremely shallow closet).

Our short stints at "real" jobs also serve as a reminder that there are millions of individuals out there roughening up their hands and breaking their backs every day. We wouldn't have houses or, uh, cigarettes, without them. It's enough to make us want to listen to the song from the classic country group Alabama called "Forty Hour Week (For a Livin')." Do yourself a favor and Google it, and then watch the music video. It features every member of the band portraying a blue-collar worker, as well as some out-of-place dance numbers. In fact, you could have just listened to that song instead of reading this chapter, but it's too late now.

THIS IS NOT WHAT I

# WANTED

TO DO THIS SUMMER... BUT I LEARNED A LOT

# "MY WORST SUMMER JOB"

## BY THE *MYTHICAL* CREW

Like us, most members of the *Mythical* Crew have worked at least one terrible yet character-building summer job. Here are their descriptions of those minimum-wage experiences, along with what each crummy job taught them.

### JEN

I delivered newspapers every Wednesday and Friday. But I was no ordinary papergirl. I didn't ride a bike. I rode on roller blades. The worst part was that when it would rain, driveways would get very slippery. I crawled up and down many driveways to stuff a sopping-wet newspaper into someone's mailbox. For $2.50/hour.

The job definitely taught me accountability. I knew I had to make it up those driveways because people were counting on me and my killer roller blades for their local news.

**EDDIE** I was a "stock associate" at Old Navy. I'd get up at 5 a.m., ride my bike to the mall, and unload boxes and boxes of Performance Fleece and $1 flip-flops for four hours. Then for the next four hours, I'd stand next to the fitting room to make sure people went in and came out with the same number of khakis. To make things fun during breaks, my manager would put on a DVD of season 2 of *Friends* to keep morale up. I hate *Friends*. Chandler's voice literally began haunting my dreams. So I quit.

I learned that a job isn't going to be cool just because your title has the word "associate" in it.

### CASEY

When I was fourteen, I operated the Dragon Train at Heritage Square Amusement Park. I had to clean up a lot of kid vomit. I never understood it. It was a slow train . . . on a circle track. Sure, it was shaped like a dragon, but come on.

I learned that great bonds can be made over crappy jobs, and that well-made amusement-park rides have vomit drain holes.

### LIZZIE

I worked for a cash-for-gold company that collects human teeth from dentists and sells them for their precious metals. This is a real thing. I met a woman in a parking deck and rifled through a bucket of teeth in the trunk of her Mercedes. I quit later that week. I am thrilled to be alive.

I learned you should trust your gut. If something seems shady, it probably is—and if you find yourself buying teeth in the alley behind a Yoshinoya, it definitely is.

### STEVIE

I worked at Build-A-Bear from sixteen through my freshman year of college. I had to endure a lot of kid slobber, but the worst part was when adult couples would come in to make a bear. There's a part in the process where you hand a little cloth heart to the bear maker and ask them to make a wish and kiss the heart before sticking it inside the bear. For some reason, every couple saw this as their opportunity to say something totally inappropriate and then proceed to make out less than a foot away from me. Adult slobber. The worst.

I learned to stop offering adult couples the little cloth heart.

### MORGAN

I performed "general maintenance" at a summer camp. Turns out general maintenance includes: daily cleaning of the outhouses and emptying the rotting kitchen trash that was stored in an airtight outdoor shed. It was a long summer.

I learned that you should get "specific" details before accepting a job with "general" in the title.

### ALEX

My summer after graduating college I got a job as a grader for elementary school standardized math tests. Each week, we were given only one question that we would have to evaluate for thousands of different kids over and over. And I despise math.

I did learn some math though.

### KEVIN

One summer I worked at a print shop, where I made copies of blueprints alongside two eighty-year-old women who chain-smoked all day long. Eight bucks an hour was meager compensation for all those paper cuts and secondhand smoke. But there was an amazing Carl's Jr. across the street.

I learned how to make copies of blueprints. Haven't copied a blueprint since, but if the day ever comes, I'll be prepared.

# CHARACTER BUILDING

## ... THE BOARD GAME

**GAIN CHARACTER**

**5** You sit next to someone on a plane who brought their own fish sandwich.
**18** Your mom starts playing the recorder competitively.
**22** You go fly-fishing with someone who does celebrity impressions.
**31** You take a road trip with people who do CrossFit.
**56** You express a dog's anal glands.
**66** You babysit identical twins that bite.
**74** You're falsely accused of public urination and sent to a Siberian prison.
**97** You are forced to re-take "Intro to Slam Poetry."

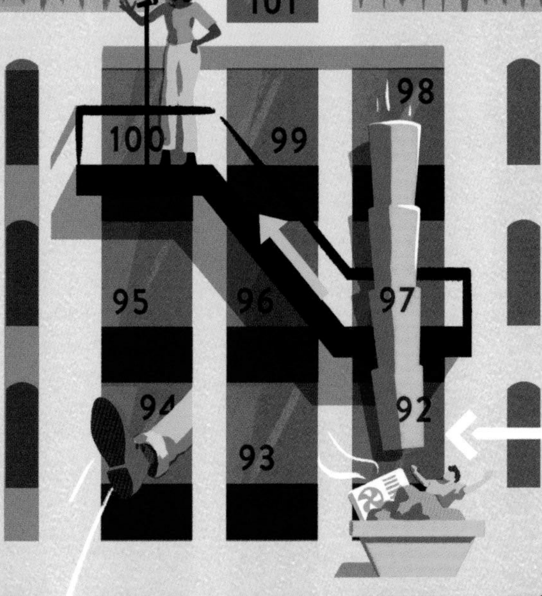

**LOSE CHARACTER**

**40** You get cold at the fair but remembered to bring a lightweight jacket.
**57** You eat an entire pint of ice cream but have a super fast metabolism.
**61** Your cupcake bakery is fully funded on Kickstarter.
**76** You inherit $3 million from a relative you didn't love.
**85** Your significant other becomes a massage therapist.
**90** You discover you are a master sleep-painter.
**94** Your parents get a hot tub.
**98** Your dorm room has air conditioning.

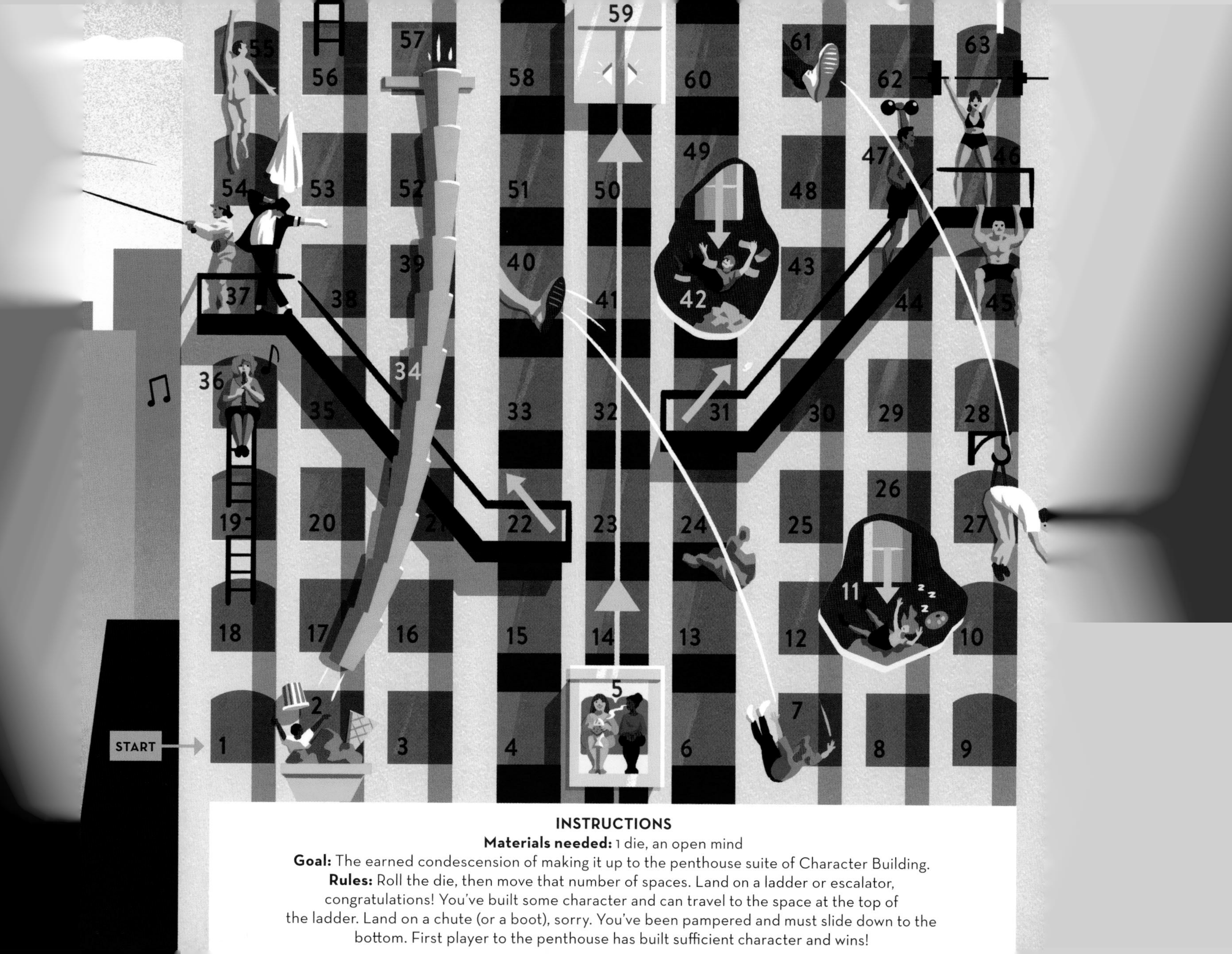


**INSTRUCTIONS**

**Materials needed:** 1 die, an open mind

**Goal:** The earned condescension of making it up to the penthouse suite of Character Building.

**Rules:** Roll the die, then move that number of spaces. Land on a ladder or escalator, congratulations! You've built some character and can travel to the space at the top of the ladder. Land on a chute (or a boot), sorry. You've been pampered and must slide down to the bottom. First player to the penthouse has built sufficient character and wins!

ELEPHANT
JUICE

# SAY "I LOVE YOU" LIKE IT'S NEVER BEEN SAID

"IT WAS TIME FOR OUR FIRST OFFICIAL DATE, AND I CONSIDERED THE DETAILS CAREFULLY. I WANTED TO COMMUNICATE THAT I WAS A MAN OF MEANS WITH IMPECCABLE TASTE IN RESTAURANTS. SO, I TOOK HER TO OUTBACK STEAKHOUSE."

**IN THIS CHAPTER,** we'll be talking about the efforts we undertook to convince our wives to marry us. While using terms like "our wives" and "marry us" might seem to suggest that we are in some kind of two-man, two-woman polygamous arrangement (known as the "Squarriage" in some circles), that is not the case. It is just an unfortunate by-product of using the collective "we" voice to talk about our marriages. We will begin speaking individually about our wives soon, and hopefully it will clear up any confusion. In the meantime, we will use the term "wifes" to refer to our wives. It's incorrect English, but it helps to establish that we are speaking jointly about two distinct individuals. If you don't like it, you are free to mark out the *f* and replace it with a *v*, although it will lower the value of this book by 7 percent.

Early on in our career, we made the decision to limit how often we put our families on camera. Sure, we used our kids if we needed a baby for something (both Link's daughter Lily and Rhett's son Locke were in our first Internet video, "Pimp My Stroller," and we once used all of them as weights in a video called "KID DUMBBELLS!"), but it has not been a regular thing. Our wifes, Jessie (Rhett's) and Christy (Link's), never expressed a desire to be in the spotlight, and we learned early on just how heartless a place the YouTube comments section could be, especially toward women. So we saw very little reason to parade them in front of our audience. As a result, our wifes have remained somewhat shrouded in mystery. Until now.

Jessie and Christy made a rare (and covert) cameo as deranged, ice-cream-sandwich-loving zombies in our "I'm on Vacation" music video.

We've decided to pull the curtain back a bit in order to talk about romance, because we think it's possible to fall in love in a Mythical way. While we personally think we did some pretty Mythical things during the process of wooing our wifes, we're not the best ones to judge that. So, we have asked Jessie and Christy to contribute their perspectives throughout this chapter in order for you to know the truth. This may have been a bad idea, and it could go horribly wrong (for us), but here we go.

**RHETT** Even though Jessie's father was my dentist growing up, I had no idea she existed. It wasn't until my junior year in college, during a trip back home, that I met her. From our very first conversation, I was mesmerized. She was unlike any girl I had ever met. Sure, she wasn't the only girl in North Carolina who was funny, intelligent, talented, and beautiful. But I felt an instant, intense connection with her. It was like we had been preparing to meet our entire lives, only to be perfectly in sync when we finally did.

Then she told me she was a senior in high school. *What the?! Mission compromised! Abort! Abort!* screamed the voice in my head. Despite my connection with her, I was not about to date a high-schooler. So I didn't. Kind of.

**JESSIE** If your definition of "not dating" includes asking a girl to go to concerts, restaurants, and on hikes with you; calling her at 11 p.m. the night before Valentine's Day to see if she wants to go to a Valentine's banquet together; and doing everything in your power to make her like you (except opening doors for her . . . that would cross the line); then yes, we were not dating. The good thing about not dating Rhett, though, was that I could freely not date other guys as well, which I did. But he had my heart, and I couldn't get that tall, almost scarily skinny boy out of my head.

This is what it looks like to be in a relationship that is not technically a relationship.

When I was with him, the world came alive. He once created a whole brochure about the New Zealand holiday Waitangi Day. We happened to be going out on one of our non-dates that night, and he thought we should commemorate the day with pizza, coffee, and a stroll through the aisles of Super Kmart (it was a small town and a simpler time). He was both utterly silly and staggeringly smart, which is a pretty dynamic combo. After hanging out with him one night I floated into my house and reported to my mom, "He's a beautiful person." She had never heard me talk about a boy like this before.

**LINK** The first time I saw Christy, she was standing in line waiting for the roller rink to open. I remember she was making all her friends laugh. Plus, she was gorgeous. I had to meet her. When you're in third grade, a great way to tell a girl you think she's "the one" is to intentionally trip her while she's roller skating. So that's what I did. Except I wasn't in third grade, I was a sophomore in college.

**CHRISTY** It was a college social. I remember arriving early at Jellybeans Super Skate Center because of how nervous I was that I couldn't actually skate. I was wearing my usual preppy-style outfit: a white collar button-up with an orange J.Crew sweater neatly tied over the shoulders, and pearl earrings. I noticed a guy with bleach-blond, spiked hair and huge wide-leg jeans making his way down the line. He definitely wasn't my type, but when he looked at me and I got one glimpse of his eyes, I knew a conversation needed to be started immediately.

I said something about how anxious I was about skating for the first time. He offered to give me lessons, and he assured me that they would be successful. Then he walked back to the end of the line.

The night Link fell for Christy.

After a couple of songs, Link found me in the rink and we started the "lessons." He would skate up and offer some quick advice, skate off, and then return a few minutes later to check on me. Only later did I learn that there were two other girls that he was "checking on" as well. And then, in the middle of one of these checkups, Link thought it would be funny to insert his wheels in my wheels to make me fall. Which I did. But as he was making his quick getaway, I grabbed the cuff of his wide-leg jeans and pulled him down with me. Of the three girls getting skating lessons that night, I won.

Oh, to be young and in love (and not wear sunscreen).

**RHETT** Jessie spent the summer before her freshman year in college as a camp counselor in the mountains of North Carolina, while I was in eastern Europe working at an English teaching camp. In order to lay the foundation for an actual romantic relationship in the fall, I developed a complex plan of correspondence.

In the late '90s, it wasn't unusual for people to get their first email address when they entered college, so Jessie didn't have an account. However, her seventy-five-year-old grandmother, whom we called Gaga, did (AOL, of course). Throughout that summer, I would find an Internet café in whatever town I found myself in and write Gaga an email. The first paragraph would be addressed to Gaga. Then, I would write, "OK, Gaga, this next part is for Jessie." Gaga would then print the email out and snail-mail it to Jessie in the mountains. Jessie would handwrite a letter in response, and mail it to me in Europe. This was our correspondence for the summer of 1999. It was like those letters from Ken Burns's Civil War documentary, just without the war.

**JESSIE** Let me just say that camp-counseloring, while it may not be hand-to-hand combat, is no walk in the park. I was dealing with a cabin full of prepubescent girls, and I'm not sure I was fully equipped to handle all of their shenanigans. Getting a letter from Rhett (via my Gaga) was surprising, magical, and comforting. He was on a completely different continent and yet still found a way to connect with me in the rural mountains of North Carolina—and he was winning me over.

**LINK** Christy attended Meredith College, a private women's school that was basically across the street from my school, NC State. Meredith was surrounded by towering walls topped with ominous wrought-iron demons, and a deep moat filled with the blood of fallen suitors. OK, there were no demons and no blood in the moats. Or moats at all. But Meredith did have walls—and a gate, with a guard on duty all night. I took it as a challenge. And an opportunity to prove my love for Christy on Valentine's Day.

**CHRISTY** At this point, we had officially been dating for a little over a year. Back on our first Valentine's Day date, Link brought me a lovely peach white-tipped rose and took me out to lunch. I don't remember very much about that lunch date, but I did have another Valentine's date that night, with a guy named Andrew. I do remember that date; it was great.

**LINK** If you're going to take someone out for Valentine's Day, do not make it a lunch date. You're just inviting someone else to swoop in for dinner. So, one year later, things were getting more serious, and I wanted to make Valentine's Day Mythical. Lionel Richie's "Stuck on You" was "our song" so I asked myself, *What would Lionel do?* Then I went to CVS Pharmacy and bought a couple hundred square yellow Post-it notes.

I scaled the wall of Meredith just before daybreak. Then I climbed on the hood of her car and started postin'. I'd spent the previous hour meticulously cutting each note into the shape of a heart. Now I was just desperately hoping no one else drove a 1989 blue Honda Accord with a dream catcher hanging from the mirror. I arranged the notes in a huge heart-shaped configuration, wrote a note on the last one, and then disappeared into the night. Take that, Andrew.

Post-it notes can be almost as romantic as rose petals (and much more sticky).

**CHRISTY** That morning, I walked out to the parking lot to head to work and found my car covered in heart-shaped Post-it notes. One said, "I'm Stuck on You." It was so creative and sweet! I was late to work because it took a while to pull all of them off, but I didn't mind at all. In fact, I've kept those hearts for over seventeen years. I also still have my sticker collection from third grade. It's a very special sticker collection.

**RHETT** Once Jessie was on campus that fall, my efforts to convince her to be my girlfriend went into full effect. It was time for our first official date, and I considered the details carefully. I wanted to communicate that I was a man of means with impeccable taste in restaurants. So, I took her to Outback Steakhouse. As far as I was concerned, Outback was a top-tier restaurant. They served prime cuts of meat and had a signature appetizer, and the servers wore collared shirts with cool pins all over them. In my twenty-year-old mind, Outback said, "I'm serious about the potential of this relationship, and I think the Australians really know how to cook meat."

**JESSIE** I remember the pink shirt and black capris that I wore that night—because it was a big deal. He had sent me an actual invitation in the mail to go out with him on an official date, with "yes" and "no" boxes to check. In an unprecedented move, he even went so far as to open the car door for me, but he didn't simply walk around to his side of the car and get in. He grabbed a random pair of enormous aviator sunglasses that were leftover in his car from some discarded costume and began to do an impression of a police officer . . . questioning me . . . in a flirty way.

I laughed at first, because it was funny. But then he kept going, and I started to sweat a little. I had no idea how to respond. He was actually, unabashedly flirting with me for the first time, but he was pretending to be a police officer while doing it. I couldn't decide if it was really charming or really creepy, and those aviators fell firmly outside the proper sunglasses-to-head ratio. But I had to give him one thing: he had guts.

Link and Christy's relationship that summer depended entirely on the reliability of the US Postal Service and a Type 1 Normal Bias cassette tape.

**LINK** Christy and I spent the summer after our junior year of college on opposite coasts. She was in Santa Cruz, California, and I was taking summer classes in Raleigh. But I wanted to develop a strategy to keep us connected. I called it the Link and Christy Long-Distance Walkie-Talkie (or the LCLDWT, if you're in to unpronounceable acronyms). Since actual long-distance walkie-talkies (that is, cell phones) weren't widely used yet, I utilized advanced mixtape technology (that is, cassettes). Think of it as an audio-only vlog made on a handheld cassette recorder.

I'd carry it in my pocket and capture snippets of my day, interject my thoughts and commentary for Christy, and of course throw in some Lionel Richie. Then I'd mail it across the continent. She'd add on to the same tape and mail it back to me. Since we only spoke on the phone around once a week, getting that tape in the mail was really a thrill.

**CHRISTY** I loved Link's idea of the LCLDWT. He recorded the first installment for my flight to California. This was a big deal because it was my first time ever on a plane. Yep, I was a junior in college and I had never been on an airplane. But hey, at least I could roller skate by this point. I pressed Play as the plane was taxiing the runway and Link guided me through the process of takeoff. He probably kept me from having a panic attack that morning. It was seriously the sweetest thing. And all of the passengers around me enjoyed it too. (I didn't have headphones, so I took a risk and played it for everyone to listen in.)

We shared our summers with each other on that tape. I would sit on the beach, press Record and just tell him about my day. I couldn't wait to mail it off after adding my installment, because he literally couldn't add to the conversation until he received the tape. And when he mailed it back to me, I would run to the beach to listen to what he'd recorded (no longer with strangers listening in).

**RHETT** It didn't take me long to realize that I wanted to spend the rest of my life with Jessie. Of course, she was a college freshman with her whole life ahead of her, and she had the ability to date whomever she pleased. I had to up my game and prove that I was worth committing to, so I decided to get creative. Over the course of that year, I dug deep into the depths of my personal reservoir of Mythicality, unleashing a series of tactics to communicate just how hard I was falling for Jessie.

**JESSIE** And communicate he did. We talked on the phone, sure, but this was in the days of yore, when phones were connected to walls and texting wasn't a thing. I got lots of emails with lots of words, and words are my favorite. Rhett also continued to work that snail mail. He sent me a fake letter from a fake teacher in the music (my major) department complete with the official letterhead. He sent me an article about myself written by "Harry D. Reporta." He wrote a heartwarming fairy tale that had an uncanny resemblance to our relationship. He also re-

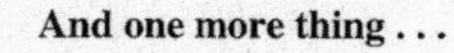

**And one more thing . . .**

*Rhett James McLaughlin*

cordially invites

*Jessica Nicole Lane*

to spend an evening with him on
the night of Saturday,
the 28th day of August
(and if that's not possible, well, then the
night before will do just fine, and if
that's not possible, Rhett will figure
something else out, he guesses).

MEMO

DATE: 01/28/2000
TO: JESSIE LANE
CC: HER FAMILY
FROM: RHETT
RE: HIS ROLE DURING THIS TIME

It is to be noted that starting at his arrival today at Granville Towers to pick up Jessie that Rhett McLaughlin, her boyfriend of three months, will baby her because she is sick and treat her nice like sugar and spice because that is exactly what she did when he was ailing just a few days ago with the flu, which, by the way, would've naturally killed him if it hadn't been for Jessie's intervention and care.

RJM/RJM

ABOVE: These were the days before Tinder. RIGHT: Rhett regularly communicated through unusual means, including physical memos that he mailed to Jessie. Weird? Yes. Effective? Yes.

ally loved the free clip art you could add to your Word documents to spice them up. Let's just say I received lots of typed letters with dogs holding a sign with my name on it and teddy bears hugging hearts. They were the emojis of the '90s.

When you're in love, you do things like celebrate five months of dating by creating incredibly sappy, custom notes.

**RHETT** By the following summer, things were getting very serious. Jessie was going to Los Angeles for a couple of months to work with the homeless and inner-city youth, and I selfishly wanted to make sure she kept thinking about me. There was no video chat, and I didn't want to distract her from her work by calling her constantly, so I made a doll of myself—kind of like a Flat Stanley—and gave it to her before she left.

**JESSIE** Genius move. Since Rhett couldn't be there in person, he sent a surrogate. I would carry "Baby Rhett" around with me, which must have acted as a huge deterrent to any other dudes who might have been interested. They would see that either (a) I was taken or (b) I was a weirdo who carried a homemade doll around with her.

**RHETT** Even though Jessie's parents' dog ate the Rhett doll shortly after she returned home, my plan to remain on her mind and in her heart worked. At least it seemed to, because when I asked her to marry me a week after she got back, she said yes. And while the fact that I proposed to her when she was only nineteen years old seems completely insane to me now (it was—we don't recommend getting engaged as a teenager), we are extremely fortunate that it has worked out well for us, and that we've been happily married for sixteen years.

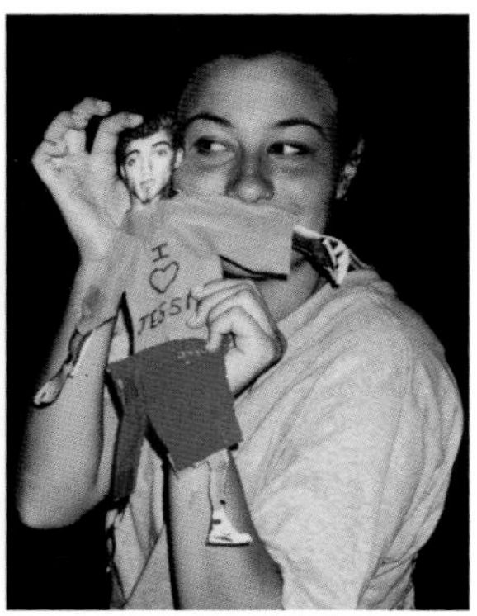

Baby Rhett kept Jessie company during her time in Los Angeles, and she kept him all summer until she replaced him with the real thing upon her return.

**JESSIE** Did Rhett mention that you shouldn't get engaged at nineteen?

**LINK** A week before Christy came home from her summer in Santa Cruz, I went to visit her parents. I called them the night before and casually asked them if they minded if I dropped in. It was a two-hour detour to "drop in" on them. And I had never done it before. They knew something was up.

I was in the backyard with her dad grilling burgers when I asked for his blessing to marry his daughter. He stared at me, then pointed toward the house. "I think you better ask that woman spying on us through the kitchen window."

Once I got her mom and dad's blessing, I told them they had to keep it secret for at least a couple of weeks. That's how long it was going to take for me to get the engagement ring. They agreed, and the next morning we all headed to the airport to pick up Christy.

**CHRISTY** I was so excited to be back at home, to see my parents, my sister, and Link. We drove back to Kinston, my hometown, and the only thing that I missed more than them was Bojangles. After a wonderful reunion with some famous fried chicken and sweet Bo Berry Biscuits we headed home for the evening. That night, Link and I spent hours outside, walking around my neighborhood catching up and talking about our summers. It felt so comfortable to be together again. But then I noticed the vibe shifted a bit. Link got super serious; no laughing, no joking. And he said the three words.

**LINK** I had this idea at the time (admittedly, it was pretty overzealous) that I wasn't going to tell my girlfriend that I loved her until I absolutely knew that I wanted to marry her. I actually explained this to Christy pretty early in our dating relationship. I've always been pretty good at making conversations weird.

**CHRISTY** I did think it was kinda weird, but when you really like (or even love) someone, you tend to frequently miscategorize "kinda weird" as "kinda cute." So that night in my front yard, I knew what those three words meant. *Oh boy, here we go. He's going to propose!* So, he said he loved me, then he slowly got down on one knee. There was only one issue. One small, ring-shaped issue. Link didn't have a ring.

His proposal turned into an odd run-on sentence: "Christy . . . will you . . . marry me even though I don't have a ring my mom has a friend who runs a jewelry store and I'm going to get one from her very soon I just need, like, two weeks or so. Maybe less. I was supposed to wait to ask you but I just couldn't."

I said yes as soon as he let me get a word in edgewise. I didn't care at all. I was in love.

Their engagement photo involved a "trust catch" where Christy plummeted thirty feet from the tree canopy above.

Honestly, I don't believe that you have to have a ring in order to propose to someone, get engaged, or get married. But let's say you are planning to get a ring in "two weeks or so." Then I would highly recommend that you wait until after that point to propose. That's a superior order of operations. Trust me, I know—I have a math degree. And now I also have a diamond ring (it took him a little less than two weeks to get it).

AS YOU CAN SEE, we made a few missteps as we tried to convince our wifes that we were worth committing to. A Bloomin' Onion is not exactly a wise choice on a first date, and proposals should typically involve rings unless you've both discussed that rings don't matter. Despite our shortcomings, we still made some pretty Mythical efforts in those early days when we were trying to show our love.

We're not suggesting that you should follow in our footsteps exactly. In fact, if you decided to do any of the specific things that we did, it would actually cancel out the Mythicality because they wouldn't be original. When you're deciding what to do to show someone you love them, you don't want it to be something you read in a book or saw in a movie. You want it to be the kind of thing that is so Mythical that it *should be* in a movie. You really can't go wrong. If you go big and it backfires, you'll have a funny story to tell the rest of your life. If it works, you'll have an amazing memory to share with the person you made it with.

A word of caution is necessary, though. Some of the most cringeworthy videos ever uploaded to the Internet feature someone going to great lengths to communicate their love—whether it be asking someone to the prom with a horribly off-key serenade, or a marriage proposal involving BASE jumping into a stadium and pulling out the ring while on the Jumbotron—only to have their would-be date or partner publicly reject them. It's not Mythical to be that out of touch with your love interest.

Honestly, reflecting on the Mythical lengths we went to in those days of young love reveals a deficit of Mythicality that we've brought to our marriages as we've aged. Today, we direct a very large percentage of our creative energy toward our audience. Unfortunately, we think this has resulted in us neglecting to bring that same creativity to romancing our wifes. Here's to you, wifes, and a commitment to Mythically romancing you in the years to come.

SEE HOW YOU SCORE!

# love-line MATCH-UP

*The following is a list of romantic love lines from great poets, writers, and musicians from historical and modern times. See if you can match up the romantic scribes with their romantic lines.*

1) "Could be an organ donor, the way I gave up my heart."
2) "I love you like a fat kid love cake."
3) "When you breathe I want to be the air for you."
4) "I had rather hear my dog bark at a crow than a man swear he loves me."
5) "You can run, you can hide, but you can't escape my love."
6) "Your looks are laughable, un-photographable, yet you're my favorite work of art."
7) "Love is sharing your popcorn."
8) "I'll drown my beliefs to have your babies."
9) "When I look at you, I'm home."
10) "If you wanna be my lover, you gotta get with my friends."

A) Radiohead, "True Love Waits"

B) Charles M. Schulz, *Peanuts*

C) Enrique Iglesias, "Escape"

D) Spice Girls, "Wannabe"

E) 50 Cent, "21 Questions"

F) Dory, *Finding Nemo*

G) Shakespeare, *Much Ado About Nothing*

H) OutKast, "Happy Valentine's Day"

I) Rodgers/Hart, "My Funny Valentine"

J) Bon Jovi, "I'll Be There for You"

Answers: 1. H, 2. E, 3. J, 4. G, 5. C, 6. I, 7. B, 8. A, 9. F, 10. D

INVENTIONEERER

# INVENT SOMETHING RIDICULOUS

"LIKE SOME SORT OF MAGICIAN, MATTHEW ENZOR SHOWED UP ON THE DAY OF THE REVEAL WITH A FULLY FUNCTIONING APPARATUS THAT HE CALLED THE 'SCISSOR SPOON.'"

**IN FOURTH GRADE** we were given the opportunity to compete in the nationwide invention contest known as Invent America. It was our chance to show our school, and potentially the entire country, the extent of our creative genius. We both took the contest very seriously, carrying a secret hope that if we came up with the right idea, we could bypass school and become self-made child millionaires who lived in kid mansions with entire rooms devoted to our favorite candies. Naturally, we would let the other guy—the one with the inferior invention idea—stay in the guesthouse, which would be a smaller version of the big house. It was all planned out.

Re-creating the U-Comb was all that was required to determine that it was a truly horrible idea.

**RHETT** I don't recall the exact name of my invention, but it was essentially a large U-shaped comb that you could run across your head in order to comb all your hair in one direction—forward, backward, or even sideways. We had been instructed to invent something that met a particular need or solved a problem. I guess I thought that some people might need to comb all their hair in the same direction in two seconds or less.

While I'm sure this concept strikes you as revolutionary, my product was actually beset with challenges. Knowing that it was advisable to develop a model of my idea—or better yet, a fully functional prototype—I took two nonmatching combs from my house, ran a lighter up and down the length of them to soften the plastic, and bent them into a curved shape. I then joined the two combs together with duct tape, which left a two-inch wide section in the middle that was essentially combless. This comb-free zone was not ideal. Another issue with my U-comb was, well, trying to comb with it. If you kept it low enough to touch your head, it would rake right over your ears when you moved it forward or backward. If you were a fan of the sideways comb, it would inadvertently comb your eyebrows as it moved from side to side. Despite these inherent limitations, I figured the kinks would be worked out once it went into mass production. Unfortunately, the judges didn't see it that way. To my surprise and disappointment, I didn't win my class.

**LINK** My invention tackled a much more practical issue than unidirectional hair combing: having to wear sunglasses while driving. I'm not entirely sure why I thought this was a huge problem. As an adult, I actually think it's pretty cool to wear sunglasses while driving. But as a child, I apparently thought it was such a huge inconvenience that it warranted the invention of a retractable sheet of tinting. When a button was pressed, it would slide out from within the roof of the car and cover the entire windshield, forever eliminating the need to take the extra four seconds to don a pair of shades before pulling away.

I called my product the SunShield. I knew I wasn't capable of building a full-size prototype, so I created a 3-D diorama that fit entirely inside of a shoebox. My car was made from red construction paper, and my SunShield was a piece of black construction paper that I would slide from the roof down to the windshield. Each time I slid the black paper in place, I thought of all the millions of pairs of sunglasses that would now have to be discarded because of my landmark invention. No doubt I was destined to win the class. But I forgot to account for Matthew Enzor.

Link's genius idea: The Sunshield, brought to life in a captivating diorama complete with a sunglassed sun.

Like some sort of magician, Matthew Enzor showed up on the day of the reveal with a fully functioning apparatus that he called the "Scissor Spoon." It was a spoon split in half that operated like a pair of scissors, and according to Matthew, was "especially useful for the consumption of garden peas." I knew I was beat as soon as I saw him demonstrating it in class. He even brought in the freaking peas! He explained later that his dad, Benny, had made the prototype using some special tools at his job. I thought that was a little unfair, but I couldn't deny the genius of the idea. Matthew won the class contest, and my dreams of hearing the sounds of SunShields retracting into cars all across the nation were dashed.

WHILE WE NEVER got to move into that childhood mansion, we are grateful that we ultimately stumbled into a career that allows us to conceptualize buttloads of weird inventions. *Good Mythical Morning*, in particular, has been the birthplace of a series of ridiculous ideas. We've included a few of our favorites on pages 152–53. You probably won't find any of our inventions on the shelves at Target next year. Maybe Big Lots if we're lucky. Fortunately, we don't have to make a living selling our stupid contraptions. But conceptualizing something ridiculous is a Mythical thing to do.

Often, it doesn't even require making anything—just imagining. During many of our "Will It?" food episodes on *GMM*, we've come up with restaurant ideas that should never actually

Mythical Mall

## PATENT PENDING*
# GOOD MYTHICAL INVENTIONS!

## THE CONCHO PONCERT

It's been proven that there is a 74 percent chance that you will have a drink spilled on you if you attend a Kenny Chesney concert. With the **Concho Poncert,** this is no longer a problem, but rather something you can actually look forward to. Protect your clothes and use the attached drinking tube to enjoy the spilled beverage yourself!

**GMM101A** Concho Poncert ~~$300.00~~ **$81.93**

## *DUAL-ACTION* WATER-TASTING APPARATUS

Sharing a drink with your friend using two straws is so 1950s, and who wants to risk spreading a global pandemic by drinking after the other person? Thankfully there's the **Dual-Action Water-Tasting Apparatus** (not to be confused with the Dual-Action Juice-Tasting Apparatus).

**GMM124A** Dual-Action Water-Tasting Apparatus **$19.99**

## THE SMELL-O-VATOR

Smelling one thing while eating another can be a delightful or horrifying experience, and the only way to do it reliably is with the **Smell-O-Vator!** It may look like an upside-down visor with a hole cut out for the mouth, but it's so much more.

**GMM276A** The Smell-O-Vator **$21.99**

# THE BLOW COOKER

Microwaves are expensive and scary. Hair dryers are safe and familiar. With the **Blow Cooker**, a four-part system consisting of a Hula-Hoop, multiple hair dryers, soda bottles, and a lazy Susan, you can cook a chicken with hot, steady air. Spinning required. **WARNING: The Blow Cooker has never even gotten close to cooking a chicken to a temperature recommended by the USDA.**

GMM360A
The Blow Cooker
**$34.99**

# POOL PANTS

The best way to stay cool is to stay in the pool. Actual pools are expensive and full of strangers' urine. **Stay out of the public pool and in your own private Pool Pants!**

GMM488A Pool Pants **$122.21**

# THE SPIRT

MULTI-COLOR!

Shopping for clothes that fit perfectly can be a time-consuming process. Those days are over thanks to the **Spirt**, a spray-on shirt made entirely from Silly String. Extremely breathable, lightweight, and multicolored. A buddy is required if you want to have back coverage.

GMM397A The Spirt ~~$99.95~~ **$3.95**

welcome any actual patrons—like the mall food court dumpling eatery that offers a free extra dumpling with every order, Take a Dumpling on Us. (Of course, if you're a restaurant investor reading this and you want to take a chance on Take a Dumpling on Us, let's talk.)

While playing the classic board game Operation on the show, we discussed a potential version of the game called Operation with Steaks, where instead of pulling strange plastic items out of the man's body, players would pull out actual pieces of steak. It's a meal and a game! Although we discussed this idea publicly on the Internet, no Hasbro representatives have contacted us. Why? Because it was a horrible idea. But it led to a Mythical conversation.

Although we've never had one of our stupid ideas become a well-known and useful product for the public at large, there's a precedent for dumb ideas taking the world by storm. Think about the Snuggie. Neither of us has ever actually seen a person wearing one unironically. But as evidenced by the hundreds of millions of dollars in sales it has generated, lots of people have decided to spend their hard-earned money on that ludicrous blanket costume that seems like something we would have joked about on *GMM*. The Flowbee is no different. It's a vacuum cleaner hooked up to hair clippers, the kind of thing that a demented (but resourceful) parent would create to punish their children. That didn't stop more than 2 million people from buying one during the '90s, because apparently sucking your hair up into a tube and chopping it off at a specified length is a pretty awesome way to cut hair.

Who knows? Maybe someday one of our misguided brainchildren will blossom into a successful business of its own. Our greatest hope at the moment is our grandiose idea of creating a BBQ sauce that doubles as cologne. There have been BBQ-scented colognes—and possibly cologne-scented BBQ sauces—but no one has pulled off the delicate balance of taste and smell in a non-staining, sprayable liquid that won't poison the user. Until that day, we're going to have to place our trust in you. We're hoping that some Mythical Beasts out there will be inspired by this chapter to formulate their own preposterous ideas.

"But I'm not creative," you might say. We're not buying it. The ability to invent isn't something you either have or don't. There may be some people who are more prolific at generating ideas, but creativity is a process that comes naturally to every person. Inventing something is less about forcing out an idea and more about simply letting your brain work the way it naturally does. If you let your thoughts form without second-guessing yourself, you'll find that you've got your own set of bizarre inventions waiting to emerge. And, if we're any indication, the bar is pretty low. Look at us wearing the Smell-O-Vator one more time, and remember that we are proud of that.

Go forth and invent. Just promise us that you'll invite us over to your massive house to see the candy-filled rooms when your invention becomes the next Scissor Spoon.

**Snubee (or Flowggie)**

**Mythical Museum of Art**

Purchased with funds from Friends of the Mythical Museum of Art (i.e., Rhett and Link). Well, not really purchased because it was just made for this book. Also, it's not really our art. It's just some images of a Snuggie and a Flowbee tiled into a pattern.

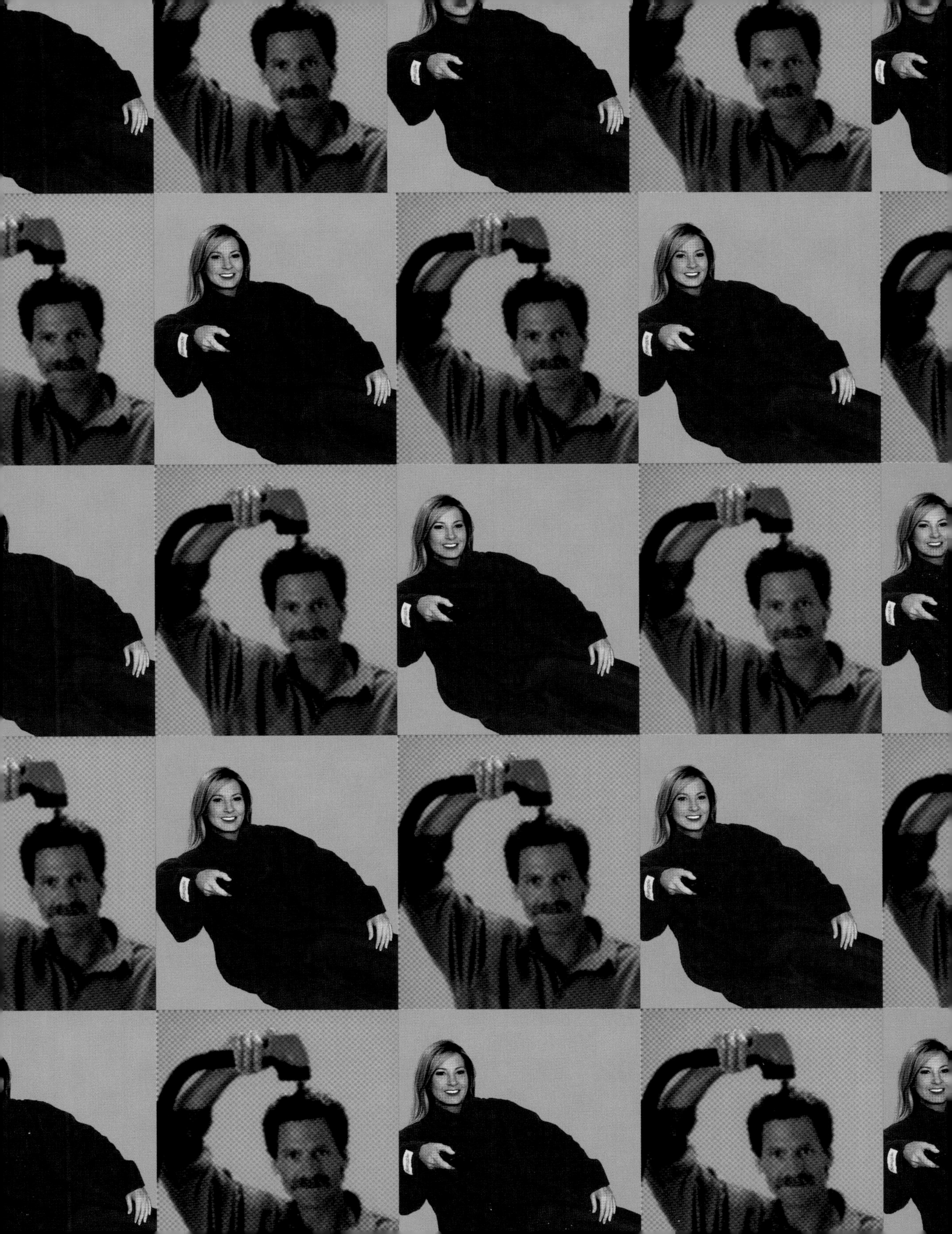

MYTHICAL BEASTS' INVENTIONS
INTRODUCING THE LOW HEEL!
stop feeling freakishly tall around your short friends!
absolutely NO foot pain included!*
heel is placed in the front so you can be stylish with no added height!
AVAILABLE IN 4 STYLES!
the LOW-TOP
the TIPPY TOE
the STILLE-TOES
the ORIGINAL FLOP
* while no foot pain is included in the box, some foot pain may occur naturally with use
©2017 HANNAH ENGLAND
Hannah England
Ivy Hrg
The Conveyer Sneakers!
Rhett!
Control the Speed!
Solar panel on backpack.
You'll never have to walk again!
There are Side Conveyer belts to turn left and right!
Swith to turn on and off.
Goes down to Shoes
battery box
Conveyer belt
Close up
Conveyer
yeah!
Cool!
amazing
wow!
Woohoo!
awesome!
The Hammock Ride
Michał Czapnik

Kyle Aulenback

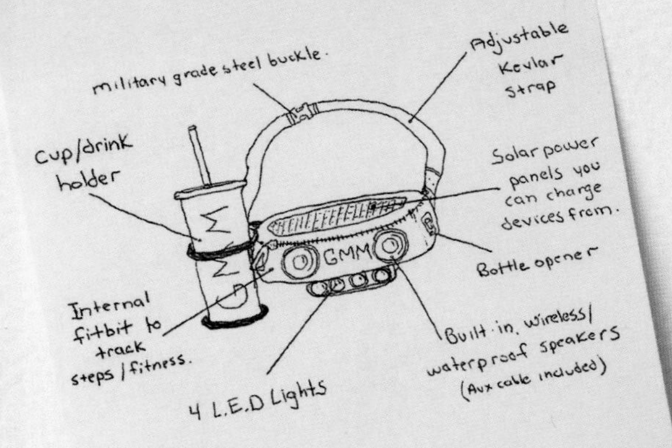


Liam Ellison

(AND FAMILY, LAKIN, KRISTY & GRANT)

COOL
Why go to the groomers when you can do it at home, brush, trim, shampoo, toothbrush, massage, and flea away all in one brush!
Brush Buddy
Groom away with Brush Buddy!!!
2 buttons
shampoo
flea away
Be the first to get the Brush Buddy!
Any furry companion can enjoy the Brush Buddy

Nutsa Koreli

Michele Cronin

PLAYBACK PILLOW
P.M.
A.M.
Watch your dreams the next morning!


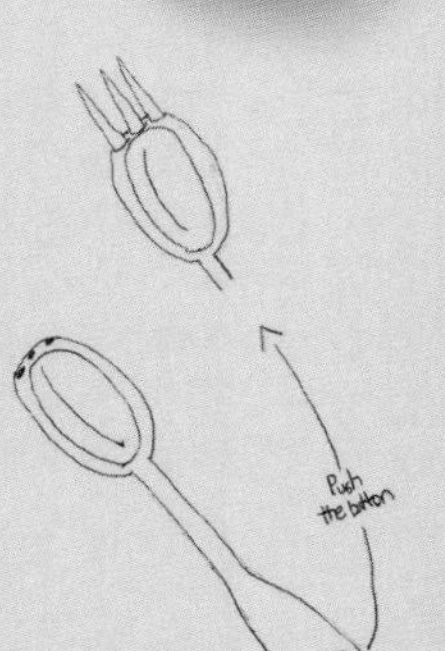


John Underwood

# BEST WORST INVENTIONS

In 2010, *Time* published a list entitled "The 50 Worst Inventions." We took issue with this list for several reasons, starting with the unspeakable inclusion of some amazingly weird and creative inventions (like "Honegar," a mixture of honey and apple cider vinegar and developed by a man with one of the greatest inventor names of all time, Dr. DeForest C. Jarvis). Then there was also the issue of some pop-culture cheap shots, like the criticism levied against the Segway. We get it; the Segway didn't revolutionize personal transportation—but one of the fifty worst inventions of all time? Come on. Have you tried the Beef Bacon Ranch Quesadilla at Chili's? Anyhow, our biggest gripe with the *Time* list is that it exists at all, because we believe strongly that there is no such thing as a bad invention. To prove it, we've provided counterarguments for five of the entries.

## 1 FAKE PONYTAILS

This is one of the most underappreciated fashion accessories of the last century. When paired with a single dangly earring and a business suit, a fake ponytail is guaranteed to grant you access to virtually any event—even if you didn't RSVP. You don't even need to feather your bangs (but it doesn't hurt).

## 2 SMELL-O-VISION

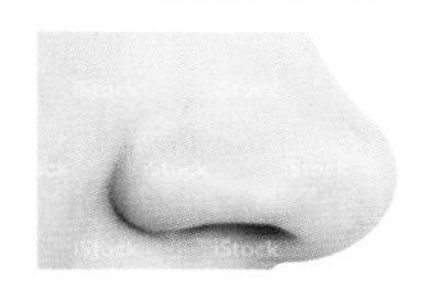

*Time* describes Smell-O-Vision as a failed gimmick. The idea was to outfit theaters with special vents, which would allow filmmakers to incorporate distinct smells into their storytelling. Only one Smell-O-Vision movie was ever made: *The Scent of Mystery*. That's a shame. To understand the potential for Smell-O-Vision, simply bake a dish of ratatouille—and then watch *Ratatouille*, making sure to hold the ratatouille up to your nose each time it appears on screen. It will blow your mind.

## 3 PONTIAC AZTEK

The Aztek is often decried as one of the ugliest cars ever made, but we believe that the design was simply way ahead of its time. Sure, the intergalactically angular design might have looked out of place when compared to the Dodge Neons of its day, but the Aztek exterior has aged a lot better than, say, the Geo Metro. Bonus fun fact: the Aztek was part of the prize package for Richard Hatch, the winner of the first season of *Survivor*. Good enough for the Hatch, good enough for us.

## 4 THE COMFORT WIPE

The Comfort Wipe looks eerily similar to the slightly flexible plastic stick that non-athletic people use to throw tennis balls to their dogs. But this is an extended butt wiper. Any product that allows you to maintain at least twelve inches of hand-to-butt clearance while wiping should be celebrated.

## 5 THE BABY CAGE

Gotta be honest, this one is tough to defend. In the early twentieth century, big-city nannies found a solution for taking care of babies in cramped apartments: hanging a wire cage outside their windows and putting the baby in there. It sounds horrible and abusive, and might have the worst branding of any product ever. However, when compared with the option of leaving a baby to fend for itself in an apartment where every surface was covered in asbestos and lead paint, a fresh-air escape pod (better branding) seems like a lifesaver.

## BONUS SECTION AN ODE TO THE BEST/WORST INVENTION ON THE ROAD—THE SPYDER, AKA THE REVERSE TRIKE MOTORBIKE

You've seen it on the road, and there's no doubt that it's raised some questions. Is that a motorcycle? Are ATVs allowed on the highway? Why does that thing look like a Kawasaki Ninja mated with a golf cart? Over the last ten years there has not been a single invention more deserving of the title "Best/Worst Invention." There's one way to take each and every ounce of badassery out of riding a motorcycle: put two training wheels on the front. But. We must admit that every person we ever saw riding one looked incredibly happy. Ridiculous, but happy. And if we're being honest, we'd gladly accept an offer to ride a pair of them around town while running errands for our wives. Of course, we would wear blacked-out, face-covering helmets—both for protection and anonymity.

REWIND
AND
BE KIND

# GIVE THROWBACK THANKS

"SHE EMERGED FROM HER OFFICE AS A SILHOUETTE,
BACKLIT BY THE SUN—IT MAKES A GREAT SCENE—
AND REMEMBERED US AS SOON AS SHE SAW OUR FACES."

**AS WE EXPLAINED** earlier, Ms. Locklear played a huge role in kick-starting our friendship when she punished us for defacing our desks. Plus, she was instrumental in establishing this whole Mythical theme, seeing as how she made us color those mythical beasts. But Ms. Locklear isn't just Mythical because she was present for the beginning of our friendship. She's Mythical because she cared about her students and sparked our curiosity and creativity—even as first-graders. Oh, and it didn't hurt that she was hot. We had as big a crush on her as was possible for prepubescent boys. While the rest of the world had Heather Locklear to drool over, we had Lenora Locklear. Also, it's worth noting that Van Halen's "Hot for Teacher" came out the same year we met Ms. Locklear. Coincidence? We think not.

We lost touch with Ms. Locklear after elementary school, but she was never far from our hearts. So, in 2006, we decided it would be cool to find her and tell her how much she meant to us twenty-three years later. We could have just looked her up online and called her, but what's the fun in that? Instead, we chose to use only word of mouth, and we made a feature-length documentary about the process, appropriately titled *Looking for Ms. Locklear.* (It's available online, and you should watch it, if for no other reason than to see Rhett with a chinstrap and Link without glasses. Spoiler alert: We found her. Obviously. Who wants to watch a movie called *Looking for Ms. Locklear* that doesn't include finding Ms. Locklear?)

After talking to dozens of people over a period of weeks, riding around in the bed of a pickup

Our class photo with Ms. Locklear. Can you spot us?

From our documentary *Looking for Ms. Locklear*. We looked for Ms. Locklear in a lot of places, including this field. She wasn't there.

truck selling puppies door-to-door, playing music at a Native American cultural festival, and attending a congressional hearing, we finally found ourselves face-to-face with then Principal Locklear. She emerged from her office as a silhouette, backlit by the sun—it makes a great scene—and remembered us as soon as she saw our faces. We had the chance to sit down with Ms. Locklear and tell her how significant she was to us. There was laughter. There were tears. It was Mythical.

And Ms. Locklear thought it was pretty cool too.

Ms. Lenora Locklear

**MS. LOCKLEAR** I was a first-grade teacher at Buies Creek Elementary for ten years, so there were many children whom I had taught. Years later, when two men walked into my office at school, I immediately knew who they were! Rhett McLaughlin and Link Neal! It had been more than twenty years. What a wonderful feeling to reunite with these once first-grade students of mine who were now grown men. They shared their timeline of school, college, family, and friendship since my first-grade class. Their journey to find me, and their thanking me in person, was a beautiful reminder that I had influenced the lives of not only Rhett and Link, but many students during my thirty-five years in education.

With Ms. Locklear at the film premiere, where she was significantly easier to find.

RECENTLY, WHILE REFLECTING on our afternoon with Ms. Locklear in 2006, we thought, "That was amazing. We need to do that again." Not go looking for Ms. Locklear again—which would be a little weird—but rather re-create the experience of thanking people from our past without warning. We want that elixir of surprise, nostalgia, and gratitude to be something that happens more than just once a decade (and also something that doesn't necessarily require us to make a documentary).

But thanking people can be difficult. There are some times when it comes more easily than others, like when someone holds a door open for you, or lets you cut in front of them at the TSA line when you're late for a flight, or sacrifices themselves by pushing you out of the way and taking a dollop of pigeon crap right on the head (this may seem unlikely but you can't prove it's never happened). In these moments, it would almost be unnatural not to say thank you.

However, when someone does more than just a solitary act of kindness, such as pigeon defecation interception (PDI), and invests time and effort into helping you through a difficult circumstance or teaching you something invaluable, it can be difficult to find the right time to express your gratitude. And the longer you wait, the tougher it gets. Thanking someone from your past requires taking the risk of being vulnerable, but it makes a real difference in the life of whomever you choose to thank. This risk/reward is exactly why it's a Mythical thing to do.

Of course, it's best to thank someone in person. If they're the person who pointed out the horrible halitosis that had been plaguing each of your relationships for years, you can lean in very close to them and use a very breathy voice to show them that your stank breath is really gone. If you're thanking a New Orleans voodoo psychic for reading your palms and then convincing you to break up with your loser boyfriend, you can burn a picture of your ex in front of the priestess, and then give her a chicken-foot necklace (they are widely available online at very reasonable prices).

Unfortunately, arranging these types of meetings can be impractical. And so, in an effort to bring more gratitude into the world, we humbly propose a simple concept that allows you to show gratitude with a tool you use every day: Throwback Thanks—#TBT

We know what you're thinking: #TBT already exists. It stands for "Throwback Thursday," a day when we carefully curate snapshots from the past to remind our online friends how cute we used to be. A select brave few of us occasionally share an embarrassing picture or two from our more socially awkward days, but really that's just undercover narcissism, as we are hoping that someone out there will find us more endearing because of our willingness to release a picture with our best friend in which we wear matching purple shirts with gorillas on them at the North Carolina Zoo. (And you can seem even more endearing when you re-create said picture as adults.)

After all these years, Link is still smiling cheesily, and Rhett is still trying to be cool.

You're right. #TBT is taken. And seeing as how we once fought an online war with two different morning TV news shows (*Good Morning Memphis* and *Good Morning Maryland*) for the sole use of #GMM (we won), we can respect that a hashtag's meaning is somewhat sacred. So, instead of trying to change the definition of #TBT, why don't we just expand it?

Let's make #TBT mean more than us just showcasing ourselves to the world. Start seeing Thursdays as an opportunity to throw some thanks to someone who deserves it. If you'd like to stick with the traditionally visually driven nature of #TBT, include a picture.

Once you get going, it's pretty easy to jog your memory and generate a list of people who deserve some Throwback Thanks. We've written some thank-you notes of our own that might help to get you started. You may not have had experiences as strange as ours, but there's no doubt you've got more than a handful of people who have helped you in some way that deserves a shout-out. Make their day Mythical by putting yourself out there and saying thank you.

Benny Enzor: Thank you for not being self-conscious about being in a band with a bunch of teenagers when you were in your forties and thanks for letting us play all those weird songs that you wrote in the 70s that sounded like Eagles B-sides.

THROWBACK THANK YOU

TRENT HAMILTON: THANKS FOR AGREEING TO BE OUR FIRST DRUMMER EVEN THOUGH (A) YOU DIDN'T YET OWN A DRUM KIT OR (B) KNOW HOW TO PLAY DRUMS.

throwback thanks

Dick Bowser: Thank you for nearly choking on a piece of meat at a Myrtle Beach Steakhouse. We literally think about you everytime we eat meat, and throw in a few extra chews for you.

T T Y B

THROWBACK THANK YOU

MRS. ENNIS: THANK YOU FOR NOT REALIZING THAT THE GUY ON THE TAPE THAT RHETT BROUGHT INTO YOUR US HISTORY CLASS TO PLAY FOR EXTRA CREDIT WAS ACTUALLY JUST RHETT DOING A TERRIBLE BRITISH ACCENT.

THROWBACK THANK YOU

OLD MAN WITH A SHOTGUN AT PIG FARM: THANK YOU FOR NOT SHOOTING DIRECTLY AT US, BUT JUST OVER OUR HEADS, WHEN YOU WERE CHASING US OFF OF YOUR FARM AFTER WE GOT THE IDEA TO LEAVE THE HIGH SCHOOL FOOTBALL GAME ONE FRIDAY NIGHT AND ATTEMPT TO RIDE PIGS WITH MICHAEL JUBY.

THROWBACK THANK YOU

Michael Juby: Thank you for being willing to leave the football game to attempt to ride pigs with us.

THROWBACK THANK YOU

Heather Wilson: Thank you for grabbing Link's hair in one hand and slapping him with the other in eighth grade. He can't remember what he said but he's been trying not to say anything stupid since then (to varying degrees of success.)

THROWBACK THANK YOU

throwback . . .
merci
dzięki
tack
dík
thanks
bedankt
ευχαριστώ
gracias
obrigado
grazie
arigato
danke

BLEACHERS NEXT TO THE HARNETT CENTRAL BASKETBALL BENCH: THANKS FOR BREAKING RHETT'S BIG TOE WHEN HE THREW A TANTRUM AND KICKED YOU AFTER MISSING A FLURRY OF THREE-POINTERS AGAINST WESTERN HARNETT.

BIG BIRD: THANK YOU FOR ALLOWING RHETT TO DRESS AS YOU FOR HALLOWEEN AS A PRESCHOOLER. YOU HELPED HIM BELIEVE THAT BEING FREAKISHLY TALL DOESN'T NECESSARILY MAKE YOU A FREAK.

throwback thank you

Garfield-shaped phone: thank you for being the conduit for those couple of extremely awkward conversations Link had with Lesli before she decided to dump him for Tyler Hamilton.

THROW BACK THANK YOU

Hurricane Fran: Thank you for not throwing a tree on us our freshman year when we cluelessly rode our bikes around NC State's campus saying "Man! It sure is windy out here tonight."

throwback thank you

Todd Smith and Mark Valentine: Thank you for challenging us to watch all 384 minutes of Lonesome Dove in one sitting. Our urologists have traced our current conditions back to this and would like to speak with you.

THROWBACK THANK YOU

NC highway patrolman: Thank you for helping us clear the debris from the interstate that flew out of the back of Link's truck. And thank you for the added touch of issuing a citation that literally said "failure to secure load" on it.

Throwback THANK YOU

Our friend Jared who worked at Baskin Robbins: Thanks for all those "free samples" that were the size of normal ice cream cones, man. You really put your job at risk for us.

THROWBACK THANK YOU

CHEWING TOBACCO: THANK YOU FOR HAVING SUCH SOBERING WARNINGS PRINTED ON YOUR PACKAGING AS WELL AS FOR TASTING ABSOLUTELY AWFUL. YOU MADE US VOMIT AS SIXTEEN-YEAR-OLDS AND THEN VOW TO NEVER TRY YOU AGAIN.

throwback thank you

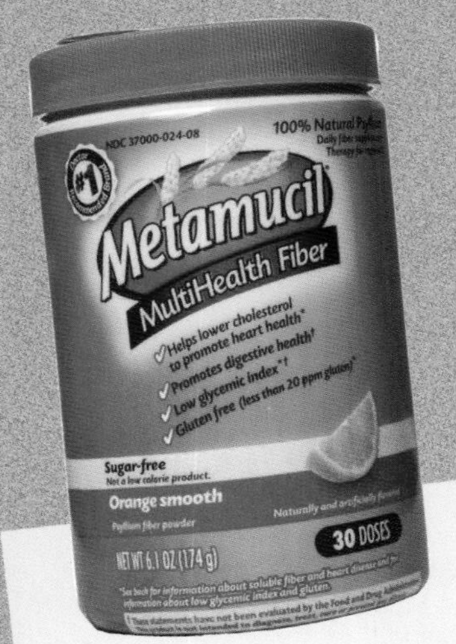


BRIAN RATLEDGE: THANK YOU FOR TELLING US ABOUT FIBER SUPPLEMENTS. WE'RE LIKE CLOCKWORK NOW.

College roommate Gregg: Thanks for refusing to ever wear a belt. That night you ran out of our dorm and didn't stop until your pants fell all the way down and made you fall on your face was priceless.

COLLEGE ROOMMATE TIM: THANKS FOR FINALLY CLEANING UP ALL YOUR HALLOWEEN CANDY. OH WAIT, THAT WASN'T YOU. THAT WAS THE GIANT RAT WHO STUFFED IT ALL INSIDE OUR COUCH WHERE HE HAD MADE A NEST FOR HIMSELF.

Shirtless college professor: Thanks for not acknowledging Link when he bent over in the locker room and accidentally pressed his bare buttcheeks against your back.

The Dunn Daily Record: Thank you for featuring us on your June 26, 2009 cover, alongside "Erwin Woman Murdered, Teen Charged" and "Sampson Horse Farm in Trouble Again."

PHARMACIST AT ELLIOT'S IN DOWNTOWN FUQUAY: THANKS FOR TAKING A BREAK FILLING PRESCRIPTIONS TO HOLD THE MIKE FROM FOR OUR "EPIC RAP BATTLE" VIDEO BEHIND YOUR STORE.

# The Daily Record

ANGIER BENSON BUIES CREEK DUNN ERWIN FALCON GODWIN LILLINGTON LINDEN NEWTON GROVE

## Erwin Woman Murdered; Teen Charged

## Enter The World Of Internetainers

## Benson To Celebrate 89 Years Of Southern Gospel

## Sampson Horse Farm In Trouble Again

TIME JUMPER

# VISIT THE FUTURE

"TODAY'S EPISODE IS ABOUT THE TWO OF US STRETCHING OURSELVES INTO INFINITELY SMALL STRINGS ACROSS THE ENTIRE UNIVERSE, AND THEN WINDING OURSELVES AROUND A VINTAGE FISHING ROD AND REEL FROM YOUR TIME AND BEING USED AS FISHING LINE."

IN CHAPTER 2, "Get Lost," we suggested that a Mythical approach to life is to simply pick a direction and go, instead of getting overly bogged down in attempting to plan every detail of your future. That sense of adventure and risk-taking is at the heart of Mythicality. However, there are times when knowing something about the future can help you take better-informed risks. If your cousin builds a Ferris wheel in his backyard, there is a reasonable expectation that someone will die on it. Turning down his repeated offers to take a ride doesn't mean you're not Mythical. It means you're smart.

Most of the time, we can only make educated guesses about the future. But there are some instances in which we can know the future definitively. This chapter is one of those times. You're going to have a difficult time believing us, but this chapter was (or will be) written in the year 2075. We are not at liberty to explain the particulars of how we accomplished this, and we would risk irrevocably altering your time stream if we were to introduce time-travel technology in this book. All we can tell you is that time travel involves getting inside what looks like a Pontiac Aztek. So, if you're currently driving one, hold on to it. Its value will increase dramatically in the future.

**HELLO FROM 2075.** We hope we can be of help to you, dear Mythical Beast from the past. We would love to take the time to outline your future in great detail, but that would be a direct violation of the Universal Time Travel Act of 2064. So instead, we will be focusing on telling you what our lives have been like over the years. If you are reading the physical version of this book, you may have noticed that this chapter is employing a different font. That font is Futura, not because we think that's funny, but because coincidentally, Futura actually became the font of the future.

In the year 2075, we are both ninety-seven years old. Before you begin to picture two frail, elderly men, you must know that ninety-seven is no longer considered old. Thanks to exponential advancements in human longevity, we are basically middle-aged. Nobody knows for sure, but we won't be surprised to make it to two hundred. As you can see from the picture, we look remarkably similar to how we looked when we wrote the rest of this book, thanks to a number of extremely effective skin-regeneration treatments. Sadly, the one thing that has not yet been discovered is a solution to male pattern baldness.

Over the past decades, we have stopped and restarted *Good Mythical Morning* a number of times. Every ten years or so, we get burned out, and then, when a new technology comes along, we start it back up. Our current version of the show is something you would barely recognize. You see, in the future, about 70 percent of the world's population is permanently connected to what you might call the Internet. This is done using a subdermal wireless system installed at birth. (Some parents refuse the implant, leaving these children to later wear something that looks strikingly similar to a Bluetooth earpiece. It is still not cool.) While you would guess that this network has a catchy name like the "Hive," it's just called the Interwebz. (Yes, with a *z*. The *z* is a thing again.) Everyone on the Interwebz is constantly giving/taking information from it, and we can no longer distinguish it from our own original thoughts and memories. It sounds scary, but trust us, you will think it's awesome when you can instantly access not just the recipe for gluten-free, lab-grown beef stroganoff but, bet-

Touching your friend's face is very common in pictures in 2075. Bomber and jean jackets are also back in style.

ter yet, the sensi-memory of what it is like to have just eaten gluten-free, lab-grown beef stroganoff without actually having to eat it.

*GMM* consists of a fifteen-minute period every weekday where "subscribers" simply tune in to our minds. Around the year 2060 or so, after years of being accused of it by commenters, we actually ran out of stuff to do on the show. So, we don't "do" anything and no one "watches." People find it much more entertaining to experience us thinking about things that are physically impossible. And we probably shouldn't admit this, but two years ago we purchased a creativity bot named LL Cool Bot that generates the thoughts for us. Today's episode is about the two of us stretching ourselves into infinitely small strings across the entire universe, and then winding ourselves around a vintage fishing rod and reel from your time and being used as fishing line. We are then taken on a deep-sea fishing trip where no one catches anything. This may sound strange to you now, but this is absolutely hilarious in the year 2075. It was the bot's idea. LL was worth the money.

Logos in the future are shinier.

Even with our trusty creativity bot, it's hard to keep up with competition in the future. There are an overwhelming number of entertainment options, and people can create nearly any experience using simulation software that is indistinguishable from reality. All it takes is a little well-written code for people to enjoy a version of *GMM* with two Links or two Rhetts, or an actual Rhett-Link fusion, Rhink. These knockoff versions of the show tend to be even more popular than ours—we are personally fond of *Bad Mythical Morning* (a gory version of *GMM*)—and it's impossible to stop their proliferation.

The 2050s were a golden age for *GMM*, thanks in large part to developments in protein-arranging nanotech that allowed every food imaginable to be created. We were able to push our "Will It?" episodes further than we ever imagined. Our most viewed episode is from 2054, in which we asked "Will it still taste good if it drives into my mouth?" We arranged various foods into small remote-controlled vessels and had them directed into our mouths. Link had to be airlifted to the ER when the "Macaroni 'n' Golf Cart" was lodged in his throat and could not back out because we forgot to enable reverse.

We're still best friends, although there was a rough patch. In 2045, the government finally figured out how to accurately digitize thoughts. Shortly after that, a law was passed that allowed intelligence agencies to monitor and record thoughts for the "greater good." (Don't worry. Twenty years later, this finally backfired, and thought monitoring is now illegal.) But there was one interesting by-product of these mental databases: services that could evaluate your mind, and then perfectly match you with the most compatible mate, best friend, business partner, or whatever you were seeking. Because all the Mythical Beasts insisted, we put our names in the mix to see who our ideal best friends would be. They were hoping against hope that out of the 10 billion people in the world, we'd be a perfect best-friend match for each other. We weren't.

Link matched up with a guy named Alejandro from Guadalajara, and Rhett matched up with Siphon (a horse implanted with a human consciousness). We agreed to meet Alejandro and Siphon for the fun of it, thinking that it would be a good idea for a *GMM* episode, but we underestimated the impact of being face-to-face with the person (or manimal) you are most compatible with in the entire world. When Link met Alejandro, there was an instant connection. Without planning it, they had each brought the other a cereal variety pack as a gift. After a long embrace, they sat down and worked their way through the cereals, smiling and laughing like old friends.

When Rhett met Siphon, the horse lowered himself onto one knee, inviting Rhett to mount him. Even though he had very little experience with horses, Rhett hopped right up on Siphon's back (without a saddle) and they began to ride. That first day, they lost track of time and rode all the way through the night and ended up in Vegas, where they enjoyed the "Tournament of Kings" horseback show (Siphon's favorite) at the Excalibur casino.

These connections with Alejandro and Siphon were so overwhelmingly strong that we collectively decided to do what we never thought we would. We took a break from being best friends. The Great Best Friend Break lasted three years, from 2048 to 2050. During that time, Link and Alejandro began their own Internet show called *Linkejandro*. The show was a huge hit, mostly due to a very catchy theme song in which "Link-e-jan-dro" was sung to the tune of Fleetwood Mac's "Go Your Own Way."

A shirtless Link having the time of his life with his best friend, Alejandro (and some other dude), in 2048.

Rhett and his soulmate, Siphon, caught in a candid moment of joy in 2049.

Meanwhile, Rhett decided to leave Internetainment behind, and he and Siphon began to trot across the Earth. Rhett quit grooming himself, and his hair and beard grew until they eventually formed a large single dreadlock that dragged the ground and attracted flies. There was a critically acclaimed documentary made about them entitled *Man and Man-Horse*.

In late 2050, as fate would have it, both Rhett and Siphon and Link and Alejandro traveled to an active volcano in Indonesia. Link barely recognized his old best friend, but once we began talking, the memories came flooding back. We decided right then and there to form a "Super Best Friend Group" of the four of us. Link suggested that Alejandro take a ride on Siphon. Siphon reluctantly agreed. As soon as Alejandro was on Siphon's back, you could almost taste the incompatibility. Siphon became instantly enraged, bucking and twisting, trying to eject Alejandro from his back. In his fury, he didn't realize he was approaching the rim of the volcano, and before we had a chance to stop them, Siphon and Alejandro fell over the edge and into the molten rock, bursting into flames. It was very sad but it looked awesome.

After that we traveled back to Los Angeles. We were best friends again, and we rarely speak about Alejandro or Siphon.

There's so much more we could tell you, but the Aztek is running out of gas and we've got to return to our time. We probably shouldn't do this, but because we care about you so much, we're willing to violate the UTTA of 2064. These are the most important things we can tell you about the future:

1. In 2024, McDonald's finally and officially phased out the McRib. It was literally available at zero locations. They threatened it many times, but 2024 is the year that it became officially official. Get it while it's hot.

2. In 2036, an asteroid was heading directly toward Earth, and scientists determined that the impact would be catastrophic. All the governments of the world collaborated in order to get every human on the planet to face the same direction and simultaneously sneeze in order to move the planet out of the way. Just as everyone was about to sneeze, Bruce Willis came out of retirement, took a private shuttle to the asteroid, and blew it up, sacrificing himself and saving the world.

3. In 2043, a massive flu pandemic took the world by storm. Millions and millions of healthy people fell victim to the disease. It turns out that the key to survival was deceptively simple. All you had to do to fight off the virus was—

HUH. I GUESS we got cut off. Probably wasn't that important.

Anyhow, we trust you gained some clarity about your own future based on ours. We sincerely hope that we have not ruined your present by making you long for the day when you can have food driven into your mouth. If you feel like the details of our future conquests weren't helpful to you personally, we can at least offer you some encouragement that learning to anticipate your own future can be a great way to accomplish it. If you want to land a Mythical job one day—say, for example, be a software developer responsible for the massively popular, immersive experience known as *Bad Mythical Morning*—it would be helpful to think about what things would have to be true about you in the future if this were to be the case. First of all, you'd be someone who understood how to write code, which means that sometime between now and then, you've got to learn code. That may sound overly simplistic, but it's actually a remarkably powerful way to begin working toward a goal. When you finally develop *BMM*, just know that we will expect royalties.

# THE TIME WE SHOWED MATT DAMON THE FUTURE

This is the actual Matt Damon.

*Back to the Future II* was a huge movie for our generation, and when October 21, 2015—the day that Marty McFly traveled to in the movie to save his future family—rolled around, the Internet exploded with lists fact-checking what the movie predicted right and wrong about the future. For example:

**RIGHT**
Hands-free video games
Wireless payments
Fingerprint-recognition software
Video glasses

**WRONG**
Flying cars
Dog-walking robots
Hoverboards (real ones, not the lame ones with the wheels)
Size-adjusting and auto-drying clothes

People love movies that predict the future, and you may have noticed that Matt Damon went on a future-films bender in the mid 2010s. This was no accident. In fact, it was our fault. More specifically, our future-selves' fault.

In the year 2062, we made a mistake. On the fiftieth anniversary of the beginning of GMM, we decided to go back in time to the beginning in 2012 and fix a few things from season one that have always bugged us: our set, a few jokes here and there, Rhett's whole look—but we incorrectly set the coordinates on our time machine and crash-landed in Matt Damon's backyard. Matt instantly recognized our time machine for what it was, and, being the curious man that he is/was, he had lots of questions. Long story short, we agreed to tell him about the future as long as he promised not to tell anyone and therefore alter the future for everyone else. Matt agreed, but after hearing about the future, he was so excited about the future of space travel that he wanted to share some teasers with his fans.

As guys who, by 2062, had spent half a century sharing nearly everything with their fans, we understood Matt's need and cut him a deal. He could share everything he had learned about space travel as long as he presented the accurate version of the future in a "fictional" movie. Furthermore, he also had to make two movies with false depictions of future space travel so that the public didn't get too close to the truth.

Being the reasonable man that he is, Matt agreed, and every year for the next three years, he starred in a film about space travel. Two of them are fictional and one of them will prove to be totally accurate:

***Elysium* (2013)**—Earth devolves into chaos and all the rich people move to an idyllic space station.

***Interstellar* (2014)**—Humanity is being destroyed by blight and space travelers must head through a black hole to find a habitable planet in order to save the human race.

***The Martian* (2015)**—Obviously, this film is the one that's true. In fact, Matt Damon is actually on his way to Mars right now as you read this. The Matt Damon people see in movies and in Hollywood is actually a high-res hologram the likes of which only the CIA had access to in 2017.

# SELFIES IN 100,000 YEARS

In 2013, artist and researcher Nickolay Lamm and computational genomics wiz Dr. Alan Kwan offered up their predictions for what humans might look like in 100,000 years. Their models predicted a number of interesting features, including:

- Big foreheads to accommodate larger brains
- Big eyes that are able to see in the dark
- Imperceptible sensory-enhancement implants
- Larger nostrils for off-planet breathing

While we have to applaud the efforts of these men of science, we are naturally obligated to pop their fantasy bubble with a needle of reality. To be clear, we are not claiming that our time machine has ventured 100,000 years into the future, but we're also not claiming it hasn't. If we had traveled that far into the future, we might have been able to produce the following photographs of our immortal future selves with explanations of each feature.

**Hair crops: Our heads are farms that grow crops. And our hair can be planted as we see fit. We are self-sustaining. Rhett grows beans. Link grows cereal.**

**Smart nostrils: Currently, it's necessary to smell a particularly nostalgic smell to trigger a memory. Smart Nostrils eliminate this need using a microcomputer that fools your nasal passages into thinking you're smelling whichever smell you choose from your past. The only downside is that nose size is increased by 40%.**

**Standardized ears: Everybody has the same ears because they are the perfect size and shape to balance utility and attractiveness.**

**Bionic eyes: Companies are already developing bionic eyes that combine retinal implants with external eyeglass-mounted cameras. Can you imagine 100,000 years from now?**

**Motorized jaws: Mouths of the future feature strong, robotic jaws and teeth, allowing for incredible chewing (and talking) speeds. Talking with your mouth full is not recommended, though. At these extreme speeds, food particles can be projected great distances during intense conversation.**

**Google Goozle: For too long, Adam's apples have served little purpose beyond a perceived indication of masculinity. In the future, Google sees this as a business opportunity and creates a biomechanical wonder, the Google Goozle, which allows users to Google something by pressing their Goozle.**

**Detachable heads: Our heads are all free-floating because the experiences we have in our subconscious are so much more vibrant than what we do on Earth. Also we have the ability to place our heads on a variety of bodies depending on whether we want to fly, dive, disappear, and so on.**

NOT
QUITE A
STAL
KER

# BECOME A SUPERFAN

"I LOOKED OVER AT LINK, AND HIS EYES WERE ALSO WET. THIS WAS THE MAN WHOSE VOICE HAD FILLED OUR EARS COUNTLESS TIMES, HIS MUSIC SERVING AS A GLUE THAT BONDED US TOGETHER AS FRIENDS, AND WE WERE SEEING HIM IN THE FLESH."

ANYONE WHO WATCHES more than a handful of our videos learns pretty quickly that the two of us are different. Our dissimilarities run deeper than one of us being freakishly tall and the other wearing glasses, or one of us preferring collared shirts with questionable color combinations and the other having a penchant for tight graphic tees. We tend to approach problems in distinct ways, and we often have different perspectives on a given topic. (For example, we are on opposite sides of the longstanding cake-versus-pie debate.) Despite our personality differences, we've found that we tend to be entertained by the same things. If one of us likes a movie, TV show, or band, chances are the other will as well. This shared appreciation for entertainment reaches a pinnacle when it comes to one artist in particular.

At one point in the '90s, Rhett was a little bit country and a little bit Bob Saget from *Full House*.

**RHETT** In middle school, I was digging through some old cassette tapes of my dad's, and stumbled upon a gem entitled *Marlboro Country Music*. It was exactly what it sounds like: a collection of country music hits compiled and sponsored by the good people at Marlboro cigarettes. Seeing as the tape was released in 1986 and we were in North Carolina, the fact that a cigarette company would sponsor a country music album didn't seem odd to us at all. In retrospect, it's surprising that this wasn't done more often.

Thankfully, the album didn't have Marlboro's intended effect of getting us to start smoking, but it did introduce an equally powerful addiction. One track was entitled "Okie from Muskogee" by a man named Merle Haggard. It was enthralling. The music was unlike any country music I'd ever heard. And the lyrics . . . the lyrics were golden, featuring pontifications such as "We don't let our hair grow long and shaggy" and "Leather boots are still in style for manly footwear." This was the work of a genius. And seeing as how I was currently sporting the "Rudolph," I agreed with his sentiments about hairstyles for men. I was hooked.

I immediately called Link and told him I had discovered something special. When he arrived, I cued up the song and pressed Play. We sat there in silence and listened to the entire song. When it was over, Link said, "Play it again."

**LINK** I remember feeling like I had discovered a portal to another world. After hearing that one song, we committed to spending what little allowance we had on Merle's music. I asked my mom to take us to the Sam Goody music store at the mall, where we pillaged the Merle Haggard section, filling our arms with bunches of cassette tapes in those massive plastic cases designed to prevent shoplifting. Once we arrived home, we put tape after tape into my stereo and listened to songs about doing prison time in San Quentin, living as a hobo on a train, working overtime to be able to buy Christmas presents for the children, and drowning the memory of a woman in 190-proof whiskey. Of course, we couldn't actually relate to any of what Merle was singing about, but we desperately wanted to.

Eventually, we became intimately familiar with the majority of Merle's songs (he released about six hundred of them during his career). We would sit together in one of our rooms and just sing along, doing our best to capture Merle's iconic twang, hitting every gravelly dip and yodeling falsetto of his voice. And although the image of two teenage boys sitting in a room next to a stereo, singing old country songs with lyrics like "There they say he met up with some women dressed in yellow and scarlet. Their warm lips like a honeycomb, dripped with honey" might seem awkward to you, we never thought about that. We were lost in the Merle zone. In large part, our ability to harmonize with each other came from those Merle sessions, when I began to try to mimic the notes of his background singers.

In high school, Rhett started to compile mixtapes by packing as much Merle onto a single long-play cassette as he could. He would carefully craft these tapes, giving them names like *Merle: Wall to Wall* and writing an iconic introduction on the lined cover. Rhett would offer these mixtapes to me as tokens of our shared love of Merle. One of his mixtapes was called *Merle: 45 Minutes of Pleasure.* While that was definitely a questionable title, I didn't question it at the time because he was right. Listening to Merle for forty-five minutes was one of the most pleasurable things I could think of.

Who in their right mind would say no to forty-five minutes of pleasure?

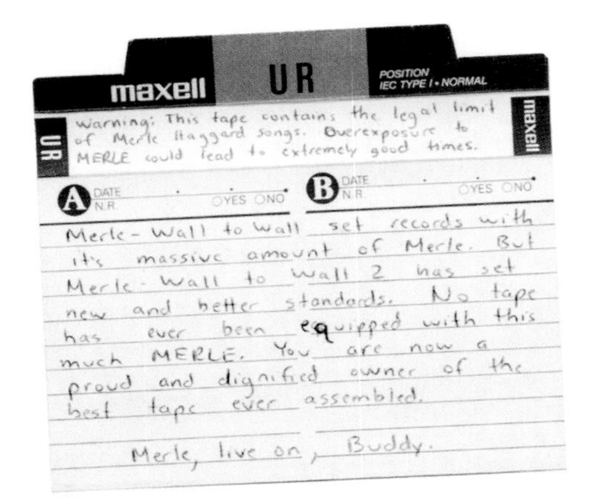

maxell UR POSITION IEC TYPE I • NORMAL

Warning: This tape contains the legal limit of Merle Haggard songs. Overexposure to MERLE could lead to extremely good times.

A DATE N.R. YES NO B DATE N.R. YES NO

Merle - Wall to Wall set records with it's massive amount of Merle. But Merle - Wall to Wall 2 has set new and better standards. No tape has ever been equipped with this much MERLE. You are now a proud and dignified owner of the best tape ever assembled.

Merle, live on, Buddy.

Rhett's custom liner notes for the *Merle: Wall to Wall 2* mixtape he gifted Link.

**RHETT** Having so thoroughly immersed ourselves in Merle's music, we jumped at the chance to see him perform live in the fall of 1994 in Myrtle Beach, South Carolina. Instead of inviting anyone along with us, we knew that this first real-life Merle experience should be reserved just for the two of us. When we entered the venue, we immediately noticed that we seemed to be the only sixteen-year-old boys who had come to see him, apart from a few teenagers who had been dragged out by their parents. We sat down and waited for him to emerge.

When Merle moseyed out onstage in a black suit and his signature short-brim hat, my eyes welled up with tears. I looked over at Link, and his eyes were also wet. This was the man whose voice had filled our ears countless times, his music serving as a glue that bonded us together as friends, and we were seeing him in the flesh. As he worked his way through his massive arsenal of hits, we found ourselves unable to sing along. There was something too sacred about hearing him in person. And even though his voice didn't have quite the same powerful tone as it did on the tapes we'd memorized, it was a magical night.

Posing with white shorts in front of the most important bus we had ever seen.

In hot pursuit of Merle's tour bus.

When the concert was over, we didn't want it to end. So instead of driving home, we walked around to the back of the building and found Merle's tour bus. We took turns posing in front of it as if it were the Eiffel Tower. Then—like a couple of stalkers—we stood, taking pictures of Merle's family through the windows. I don't know what we were expecting. Maybe we secretly hoped that Merle would stop on his way to the bus, see us, and say, "Hey boys, I can tell y'all are my biggest fans. Wanna come see the inside of my bus and meet my family?"

Merle eventually exited the building and walked the short distance to the bus, stopping quickly to acknowledge the fans who had gathered, which, besides us, consisted exclusively of people over forty. He didn't single us out or even make eye contact. But we were determined.

The bus pulled out, and without thinking, we hopped in Link's Nissan pickup and began following it. We figured that the bus might stop in town at a hotel, at which point we'd get our chance to commune with Merle. But after navigating through town, the bus got on the highway. Helpless, we continued to trail it.

Link said, "Well, somebody on that bus has got to stop and use the bathroom sooner or later." So, we kept on, not pausing to consider that tour buses had bathrooms. After following Merle for over an hour, we started to get scared. We were North Carolina boys, frightened by the possibility of running out of gas somewhere in the middle of South Carolina, where we'd be captured by locals and forced to denounce our state and swear allegiance to their flag. Reluctantly, we turned back.

**LINK** We may have missed our opportunity to meet Merle, but our obsession with him continued to grow. During our junior year in Mrs. Royal's English class, we were tasked with writing senior term papers, which would contribute substantially to our final grade. Mrs. Royal informed us that our papers could be about anything we desired, as long as it was a genuine topic of interest and something we could write about compellingly. Of course, we both chose Merle Haggard as our subject. When Mrs. Royal explained that no two students could have the same topic, we selected two different aspects of Merle Haggard and pleaded with her to let us proceed. She relented. My paper was entitled "Merle Haggard's Depiction of the Western Culture in the Late Sixties" and Rhett's was "Merle Haggard's Musical Commentary on the Prisoner Experience in Correctional Facilities." While other students saw their term papers as obligatory school assignments, we relished the opportunity to research and report on the man who had changed our lives. We both got A's.

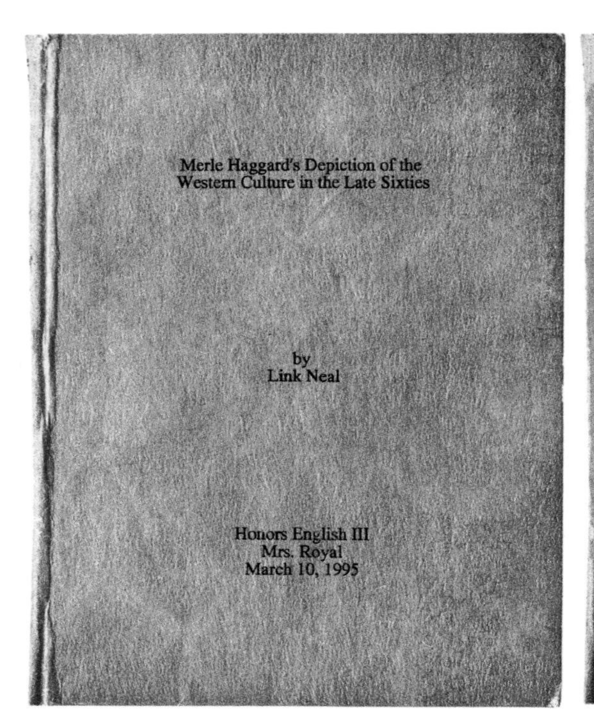


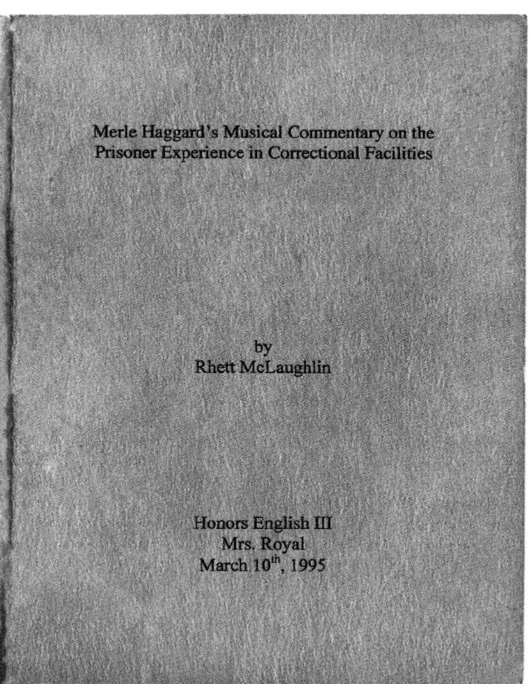


Our scholarly and sophisticated senior English class term papers.

**RHETT** That same year, I was taking an advanced math class that required a graphing calculator—specifically, the TI-82. While I could have been learning to better prepare myself for the four years of calculus to follow in engineering school, I instead spent 90 percent of the time in my advanced math class writing a Merle-themed "choose your own adventure" game in the calculator's BASIC program editor. The goal of the game was to bust Merle out of San Quentin (the prison he actually did time in). After navigating through a series of pitfalls to reach the prison, you had to incapacitate his large and intimidating cellmate before rescuing Merle. If you succeeded, you were rewarded by being able to travel with Merle to his home on Lake Shasta where you could fish with him forever. I've since lost that calculator, which contained the only version of the game that existed. I consider it one of my finest creative accomplishments.

**LINK** Our admiration for Merle and his music carried over into adulthood. Over the years, I have been collecting all of Merle's original vinyl records to fill our "Merle wall," which we've had in every office we've ever occupied together. That's no easy task, since Merle released 49 country albums during his career, and that number goes over 100 when you include gospel, Christmas, live, collaboration, and compilation albums. Whenever we have moved into a new space (five total since 2007), the first and most important question is "Which wall will be the Merle wall?" Once that is established, we move on to other less important issues like "How do we get the electricity turned on?"

The Merle wall.

**RHETT** We had always dreamed of meeting Merle in person, but we had never really taken any steps to make it happen (beyond chasing his bus into South Carolina). But thanks to our thoughtful wifes, everything changed in 2013. One evening, they surprised us with tickets to a Merle concert in Beverly Hills at the Saban Theater the very next night. Then, they informed us that they had pulled some strings and arranged a backstage meeting with Merle. Our hearts began to race. Before I knew it, I was tearing up. We were not emotionally prepared to meet our hero, and it was happening in less than twenty-four hours.

The next day, we couldn't focus on anything else. We stressed out about what we should wear. Would Merle judge us because our jeans were so tight? Should we dress like two up-and-coming country singers? We wanted to impress him. My stomach was churning all day, and I visited the restroom no fewer than four times. My body was evacuating everything, making sure I was totally cleansed in preparation for our rendezvous with Merle.

We decided to be ourselves, trusting that Merle would respect that. We were given instructions from Merle's booking agent, Lance, to wait next to the backstage doors outside the theater so that Merle could stop and meet us on his way to the stage. We got there much earlier than was necessary and took our post outside the doors, anxious to not say or do anything stupid when we saw him. Standing there for close to an hour, we had figured out just the right angle for a picture with him, making sure the lighting would be perfect for this Mythical moment we had anticipated our entire lives.

**LINK** Eventually, the door of the bus opened, and out came our hero, dressed head to toe in black. He slowly walked toward us. My palms were pouring sweat. I braced myself for eye contact with him. Then, with his head down, he walked right past the door and right past us. There was another door. We were standing next to the wrong door. We panicked.

Thankfully, Lance saw all this go down, and chased in after Merle. We followed him. He said, "Merle, hold on! I've got some boys I want you to meet!" When we entered the theater, it was pitch-black, the only light coming from a crack in the curtain leading to the stage. Merle's band was already playing the intro to the first song, waiting for him to join them onstage. As our eyes adjusted, we realized that Merle was standing right next to us. I could smell him. I can't describe the smell—but it was good. I froze.

To his credit, Lance was on top of things. "Let's get a picture!" he said. We each put an arm around Merle—not 100 percent sure which side was his front and which his back—and faced Lance. We were touching Merle. I, like a little boy, said, "Is it really you?" It was an appropriate question because it was still extremely dark, and Merle was wearing all black, resembling more of a shadow than a music icon. Merle let out a little chuckle in response to my question, and Lance snapped the first picture. But there was no flash.

Time was running out. Lance said, "OK, now I got the flash on," and proceeded to snap the picture. We didn't make eye contact with Merle, focusing on finding the camera instead. Before we knew it, he was trotting out to the stage and picking up his guitar. We stood there, silent. It had all happened so fast.

Our first-ever photo with our hero, Merle Haggard.

Our second-ever (and properly lit) photo with our hero, Merle Haggard.

Getting some quality time with Merle. Our conversation was so intense he needed to break out the sweat towel.

**RHETT** After the show, we had the opportunity to spend some time with Ben, Merle's youngest son and guitarist. Ben was gracious enough to give us special passes to allow us to come backstage (and even on the tour bus!) for any future Merle show. We were blown away. He ensured us that next time, we could have a proper meeting with his dad. And he made good on that promise, because the following year when Merle came back to play a show near L.A., we finally had the opportunity to actually board the tour bus.

We weren't nearly as anxious this time around, having expended so much emotional energy during our first meeting. We were able to contain ourselves and have a conversation with Merle. We told him about our wall dedicated to him, and the time we had chased his bus through South Carolina. He had watched our episode of *GMM* where we described our first meeting with him. It was all so surreal, to be sitting on the tour bus with the man whose work had influenced us so dramatically. I think we kind of expected him to think we were crazy, but we got the sense that there are lots of people out there who have expressed the same kind of admiration for him. He took it all very humbly, and this time, we were able to get decent pictures.

In late 2015, Merle was scheduled to play the Saban again, and we were preparing for another chance to see him. He had to cancel the show at the last minute because of an illness, and was never able to reschedule it, as his illness got progressively worse. On his birthday, April 6, 2016, Merle passed away at the age of seventy-nine. We each sat at home that night, listening to Merle and contemplating the influence he'd had on our lives and friendship.

MERLE'S ORIGINALITY AND musical genius was what initially drew us to him. But once we became superfans, we learned that a shared admiration for someone can be an incredible way to build and strengthen a friendship. There are few things more connecting than experiencing someone else "getting" a work of art that you also "get." It's an indirect way of saying that, in some way, you get each other. It's Mythical.

Being lifelong fans of Merle has also informed the way we think about our own work. We're inspired by the fact that Merle delivered a nearly unending string of songs that served as the soundtrack of our lives. To think that it's possible for us to affect others in even a fraction of the way Merle impacted us is mind-blowing and humbling. When we think about how much we connected with his music, it reminds us that we're not creating our work in a vacuum. There's an audience who has chosen to watch the videos we've made (and read the book we've written). Of course, it's doubtful that videos with titles such as "Amazing Butt Facts" or "Will It Deep Fry?" can move people as much as Merle's music has moved us, but we're nevertheless floored that many out there refer to themselves as our "fans." We prefer the term Mythical Beasts.

**When we were kids, celebrity selfies weren't really a thing. We wanted autographs. If you were lucky, you could get a signed publicity photo, book, or baseball glove. Today, with the Internet and drones and conventions and virtual reality, the opportunities are endless for worshiping your pop-culture heroes. However, with opportunity comes great responsibility.**

**There is a very fine line between superfan and stalker. Here's the line and what lies on either side of it.**

**SUPERFAN:** You see your idol wearing a particular brand of underwear in a picture, so you buy a pair of that same brand.
**STALKER:** You see your idol wearing a particular brand of underwear in a picture, so you buy a pair of that same brand and send it to them with a request to wear it and return it to you.

---

**SUPERFAN:** You sneak onstage and find one of their hairs . . . and you frame it.
**STALKER:** You sneak onstage and find one of their hairs . . . and you make tea out of it.

---

**SUPERFAN:** You visit the hometown of your idol and buy a sweatshirt with the name of their high school.
**STALKER:** You visit the hometown of your idol and walk the halls of their high school while wearing a mask made of human skin.

---

**SUPERFAN:** You see your idol at the movies, and as they exit the theater, you ask for a picture.
**STALKER:** You see your idol at the movies, so you have a friend pose as a theater employee, directing them to a special seat. The special seat is you dressed as a seat.

---

**SUPERFAN:** You have jury duty and learn that your idol's cousin is the prosecuting attorney, so you excuse yourself from the jury for potential bias—but only after taking a selfie with the cousin.
**STALKER:** You have jury duty and learn that your idol's cousin is the prosecuting attorney, so you trade your swing vote, condemning an innocent man to a life sentence in exchange for your idol's garage code.

---

**SUPERFAN:** You send a handwritten letter to your idol, detailing the ways in which they have changed your life for the better.
**STALKER:** You attach a handwritten letter to the windshield of your idol's car, but then you discover that the door is unlocked and you decide to bed down in the backseat for the night. The next day, you stay completely silent as your idol runs errands around town. Four hours in, as the sweat from your body begins to overwhelm the car's "orange dream" air freshener, you begin to imitate the middle-aged British voice on the GPS and miraculously navigate your idol out to the desert, where you have constructed a twenty-five-foot-tall sand sculpture of the two of you embracing . . . And if you do it again, Terry, we'll have to press charges.

# *Mythical Fan Art*

**One of the coolest things about having fans is the amazing fan art. You really can't complain about too much when there are people across the globe who are willing to draw pictures of you.**

Column 1: Janelle Rosal (@jannelle-o); Casper Stewart (@TheRoyallyPurple); Meredith Danner (@MKDrawings) Column 2: Corey Kramer (@CoreyremarK); Jade Galler (@jade_iemr_galler); Amy Whitaker (@amcoffeeart) Column 3: Juanita Rodriguez (aka Fluffycawwot); Maddy Wingrave-Manns; Fatin Fikriyah (@cookiecoasters); Jasmine Pilkinton (@pinkcherryprincess); Aiyani

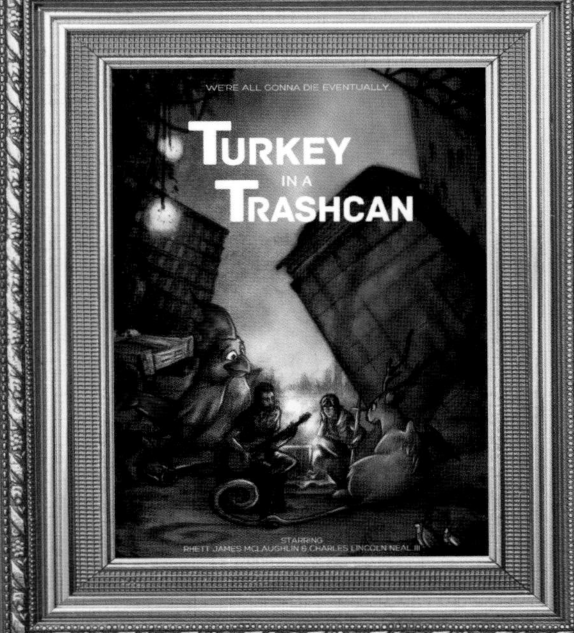

Column 1: A.H. Valderhaug (@tusletangen); Cioccolatodorima; Eleanor McHugh Jewell (@dealwrought); Gisela Beer (@herospy) Column 2: MONKPANDA (@iammonkpanda); Itzel Garza
Column 3: Anna Focke; Falco Verholen (@lifemachine84); Edward Hildreth

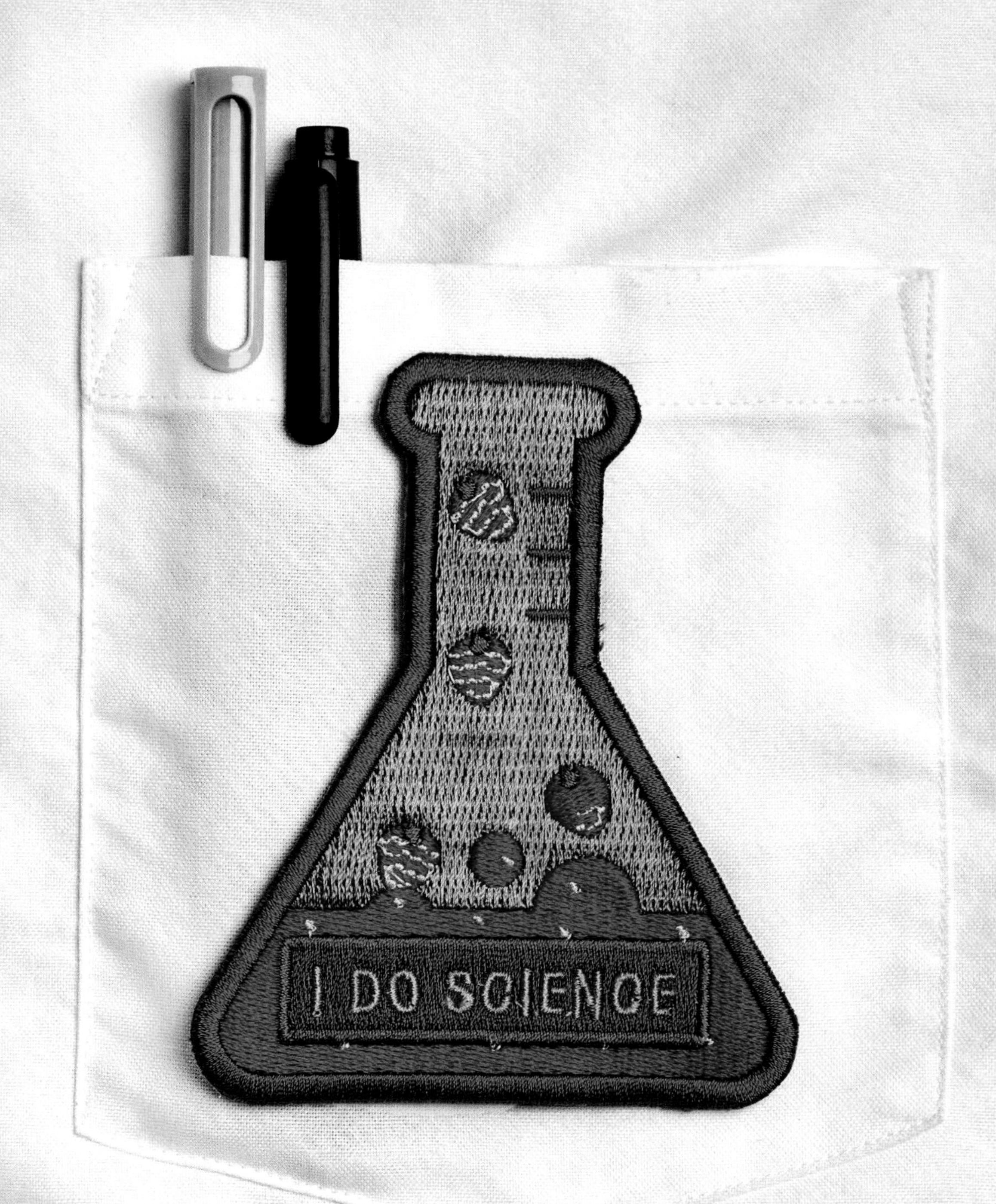
I DO SCIENCE

# CONDUCT A WEIRD EXPERIMENT

"WHEN WE UNSCREWED THE TOP, THE UNMISTAKABLE, SWEET SMELL OF FERMENTED STRAWBERRIES AND BANANAS FILLED THE CAMPSITE. LINK VOLUNTEERED, 'YOU GO FIRST.'"

DISCLAIMER: THIS CHAPTER CONTAINS STORIES OF PLAYING WITH MATCHES AND MAKING HOMEMADE WINE, WHICH WE DON'T RECOMMEND. BUT AT LEAST WE DIDN'T DO THEM AT THE SAME TIME.

**EXPERIMENTATION AND DISCOVERY** have always been two major pillars of our friendship. Decades before we conducted the Psychopath Smell Test, tried to give ourselves the hiccups, or wondered "Will It Shoe?" on *Good Mythical Morning*, we were conducting amateur experiments within the confines of Buies Creek. Without smartphones or the Internet to enchant us, we were left with our own curiosity.

**LINK** Our pseudoscientific career began with a cloud of smoke. One afternoon when we were about ten, we were standing in my garage watching my rock tumbler. This was a favorite pastime of mine. I couldn't actually see the rocks themselves—just the red cylinder that slowly turned them over and over—but I could hear the rocks tumbling inside. It was mesmerizing to me. Rhett, not so much.

Rhett insisted that "Smokey the Man in a Bear Costume" wouldn't mind very careful boys striking a few matches.

After about twenty minutes or so, he couldn't take it anymore and asked if I had any matches. I reminded him of the many times Smokey the Bear had implored us not to play with matches, but he wasn't having it. Rhett explained that Smokey the Bear wasn't an actual bear, just a man in a bear suit with a puppet mouth. Look, he said, we weren't going to be lighting matches in a forest, Smokey's primary area of expertise and concern. We would stay on my deck, where the trees were already dead. Plus, Smokey the Bear commercials were for "kids who aren't careful." Made sense to me. I went to the forbidden kitchen drawer and grabbed a box of matches.

Walking the matches outside, I couldn't completely shake the image of Smokey the Man in a Bear Costume standing disapprovingly with his arms crossed, so I insisted that we immediately throw the matches into an old Coke bottle after striking them. Rhett thought that I was being too careful, but reluctantly agreed.

**RHETT** This is probably an appropriate time for me to step in and mention that my attitude toward Smokey the Bear has softened considerably with age. While I still suspect that he's not a real bear, I feel his mission is a worthy one, and his advice to not play with matches is sound. I'm also reasonably sure he is not a fan of deck fires, which we could have easily started that day.

**LINK** We then took turns striking matches. The match striker would hold up his freshly lit stick like the Statue of Liberty while the other guy watched in awe (again, kids were easily impressed pre-Internet). Then, just before the flame reached our fingers, we would toss the matches into the bottle.

We quickly burned through most of our matches, and I explained to Rhett that I didn't think it would be wise to confiscate another box. My stepdad Jimmy probably wouldn't notice one missing, but two would be pushing our luck. So, we struck our last few matches with extra-special care, cherishing the majesty of each flame. And because we were trying to milk every ounce of entertainment value out of each match, we paid close attention as we tossed them into the bottle—which is when we noticed that the entire bottle would fill with smoke when a match was extinguished.

"We should trap the smoke!" Rhett said excitedly. I agreed. We took our last two matches, lit them together, tossed them into the bottom of the bottle, then grabbed the top and screwed it down tightly. We leaned in to investigate, and inside the bottle hung a thick gray haze perfectly suspended in midair. We had trapped the smoke! We set the bottle on the back deck.

Rhett slept over that night, and we returned to the bottle to check in on our smoke-trapping experiment a good twenty times. For all we knew, this experiment had never been done before, certainly not by children. Surely we would gain some sort of renown for our research. We could see the headlines in the local paper.

VOLUME 16 NO. 127 TUESDAY MAY 12, 1987

The Daily Record 50¢

Buies Creek, NC

In Scientific First, Local Boys Trap Smoke!

We went to sleep that night wondering what state our experiment would be in the next morning. I awoke at the first sign of daylight and poked Rhett's sleeping bag. After a couple of groggy seconds, his face lit up. "Smoke bottle!" We sprang up and ran down the hallway like it was Christmas morning.

The bottle sat in the morning light, filled with that same gray haze as the night before. The smoke had been trapped forever. Then it hit us: We could unscrew the top and watch the smoke escape the bottle. We had nothing to lose. We could always just trap more smoke. I grabbed the bottle and slowly unscrewed the cap. We both sat in anticipation and waited for the smoke to billow out of our bottle like a chimney. But nothing happened. I looked down into the bottle and all I saw was a pile of expired matches. I was confused, because smoke was clearly visible from the outside of the bottle. Turns out the smoke had created a gray film on the inside of the bottle, merely giving it the appearance of being trapped.

While disappointed that our bottle didn't spew smoke like exhaust from a big rig, we were equally fascinated with what we had learned: Smoke wasn't a gas; it was just a collection of fine particles left over after something burns. It was more like a dust.

We were officially scientists!

**RHETT** Our affinity for experimentation and discovery carried through to high school. One of our classmates and friends, Jeff Autry, was a self-described "good ol' boy" from a farming family. His tractor-accident stories were far more captivating than AP European history, but he particularly sparked our interest when he revealed that he knew how to make homemade wine.

Neither Link nor I drank alcohol while in high school, but I still begged Jeff to share his secret recipe. I was gripped by the thought that I could simply follow a series of steps and create a consumable alcoholic beverage. Jeff smiled at my request, scribbled a set of instructions on a sheet of notebook paper, and handed it to me. As I hid it in my pocket, he said, "If you don't follow this exactly, you might go blind." A look of concern sprouted on Link's face. I, on the other hand, was sold. The possibility of me and Link losing our eyesight only enhanced my interest in the process.

In an effort to curb the potential proliferation of winemaking among Mythical Beasts, I will refrain from sharing Jeff's recipe here. All you need to know is that the recipe was remarkably simple and had a line that read "add your fruit of choice." While one might assume that the best "fruit of choice" for a first-time winemaker would be grapes, it's important that you know that country singer Deana Carter had recently released her hit single "Strawberry Wine" and the song was very popular at Harnett Central High School.

Jeff Autry, contemplating homemade wine recipes.

Rhett's mother, Diane, was too busy writing with vinegar to pay attention to her son making wine in the bathroom.

Even though Deana's song was about losing her innocence in the woods, we were subliminally compelled by the fact that we—just like the girl in the song—were seventeen. In a sense, we were also losing our innocence, in that we would be manufacturing an alcoholic beverage without a proper license. The choice had been made for us. Our wine would be strawberry. However, we also wanted to maintain some sense of originality. I asked Jeff, "Do you think we could add bananas?" He looked at me and said, "Well, it ain't yogurt, but I guess it won't hurt." That's all I needed to hear.

Since Link was still a little apprehensive about this entire endeavor, we decided to manufacture the wine in my upstairs bathroom. When my mom saw us ascending the stairs with a two-liter of Coke, a basket of strawberries, a bunch of bananas, and an entire one-pound bag of sugar, she started to ask what we were up to. Before she could even finish the question, I calmly said, "We're gonna eat some fruit and have some Coke upstairs. Link likes sugar on his strawberries." She knew something else was going on, but probably also figured it couldn't be too nefarious based on the ingredients. She simply returned a skeptical, "Okaaaaay."

Once the secret recipe had been executed, we had to find a good spot to store our homebrew so it could ferment. I didn't exactly want to carry our bottle of pre-wine around the house, so I determined that the best place for fermentation would be on top of the AC unit inside the storage closet in the bathroom. My parents never went in there, and I could easily check on the concoction from the privacy of my own bathroom.

As the weeks passed, the intensity of the very obvious alcohol smell grew. It's difficult to communicate just how exciting this was. We had simply followed Jeff's advice, and now there was a metabolic process happening in my bathroom whereby bacteria was consuming sugar and converting it into alcohol. I felt like a mad scientist. At the same time, I was a bit worried about whether the AC was blowing the smell of strawberry-banana wine all over the house. But my parents never said a word.

When it appeared that the fermentation process was complete, I filtered the sweet tonic and called Link to let him know the wine was ready. We decided that it didn't seem right to just stand in a bathroom and drink wine together. After all, this would be the first time either of us would be consuming alcohol, and it wasn't just any alcohol. It was our special alcohol. We had made it. And it might make us go blind.

We decided to plan a camping trip so that we could drink our homemade wine on the banks of the Cape Fear River. (As with "Strawberry Wine," we were likely influenced by country songs that caused us to think that all significant life events happen on riverbanks.) The next Friday night, we laid out our sleeping bags under the stars at a small sandy patch right next to the water. The location was remote, dramatic, and beautiful—the perfect spot for what we anticipated would be our passing from boyhood into manhood.

I had removed the plastic bottle's label so our special hooch could be easily seen in all of its cloudy pinkish-brown glory. We waited until the sky turned dark and the large southern moon floated above us, shedding a blue light on our illicit ceremony. When we unscrewed the top, the unmistakable, sweet smell of fermented strawberries and bananas filled the campsite. Link volunteered, "You go first." He was still consumed by the thought of us going blind and being stuck in the woods with no hope of finding our way back home. At least he could lead me out if he kept his vision. I slowly brought the bottle to my lips, tipped it back, and let the fruits of our labor fill my mouth. Once my tongue had a chance to process this strange new beverage, it sent my brain a very clear message: *You're drinking rotten Kool-Aid.* I tightly closed my lips, determined to swallow it. I was not about to spew our precious creation into the river. After a few seconds of breathing through my nose to regain my composure, I force-swallowed our special strawberry-banana wine. The aftertaste was even worse. I conjured up a smile and held the bottle out to Link. He just sat there and stared, waiting for me go blind.

A few minutes passed. I hadn't vomited or lost my sight, so Link bravely took a sip, going through the same process of overcoming his body's insistence that he not swallow the potentially poisonous liquid he had just put in his mouth. He shot me a smile that was more of a grimace, and handed back the bottle. Without speaking, we passed the sauce back and forth a few times, hoping that our palates would acclimate to the sugary battery acid. They didn't. We eventually gave up and resealed the container, and sat silently on the banks of the Cape Fear with a sense of accomplishment—and nausea. We felt like men.

An early attempt at making grape wine that turned into a spontaneous photo shoot.

WE NEVER FINISHED that bottle, but we did go on to make additional batches of wine, eventually using grapes. Link even got to a point where he was willing to ferment it in the crawlspace of his house. We never made anything worth drinking, but again, it was less about the product and more about the process. We learned something every time we adjusted an element of the technique.

When we started *Good Mythical Morning,* we knew that experiments would be an integral part of the show, because experimentation starts with a sense of curiosity. Mythicality is characterized by wanting to find answers to questions. Granted, our questions are not always very sophisticated. The "Will It?" series is based on trying to find out if certain unexpected food combinations will end up being a pleasant surprise. Learning that toothpaste doesn't pair well with pancakes isn't necessarily as groundbreaking as finding the cure for the common cold, but it's more fun and much less expensive.

We've satisfied our curiosity by asking a number of questions on *GMM.* Some of our favorites are presented on the following pages.

# PSYCHOPATH SMELL TEST

**September 26, 2012** **Episode #167**

## Question:

**Who is more of a psychopath?**

## Background:

**A study suggested that psychopaths have below-average senses of smell.**

## Experiment:

**While blindfolded, Rhett and Link each smelled a series of items, including (among other things): markers, pickles, and beef jerky.**

## Conclusions:

- **Link is more of a psychopath, but it's close.**
- **Rhett thinks cookie dough smells like dog food.**
- **Link thinks ground red pepper smells like shoes.**
- **Link still has Yoo-hoo at the forefront of his memory.**

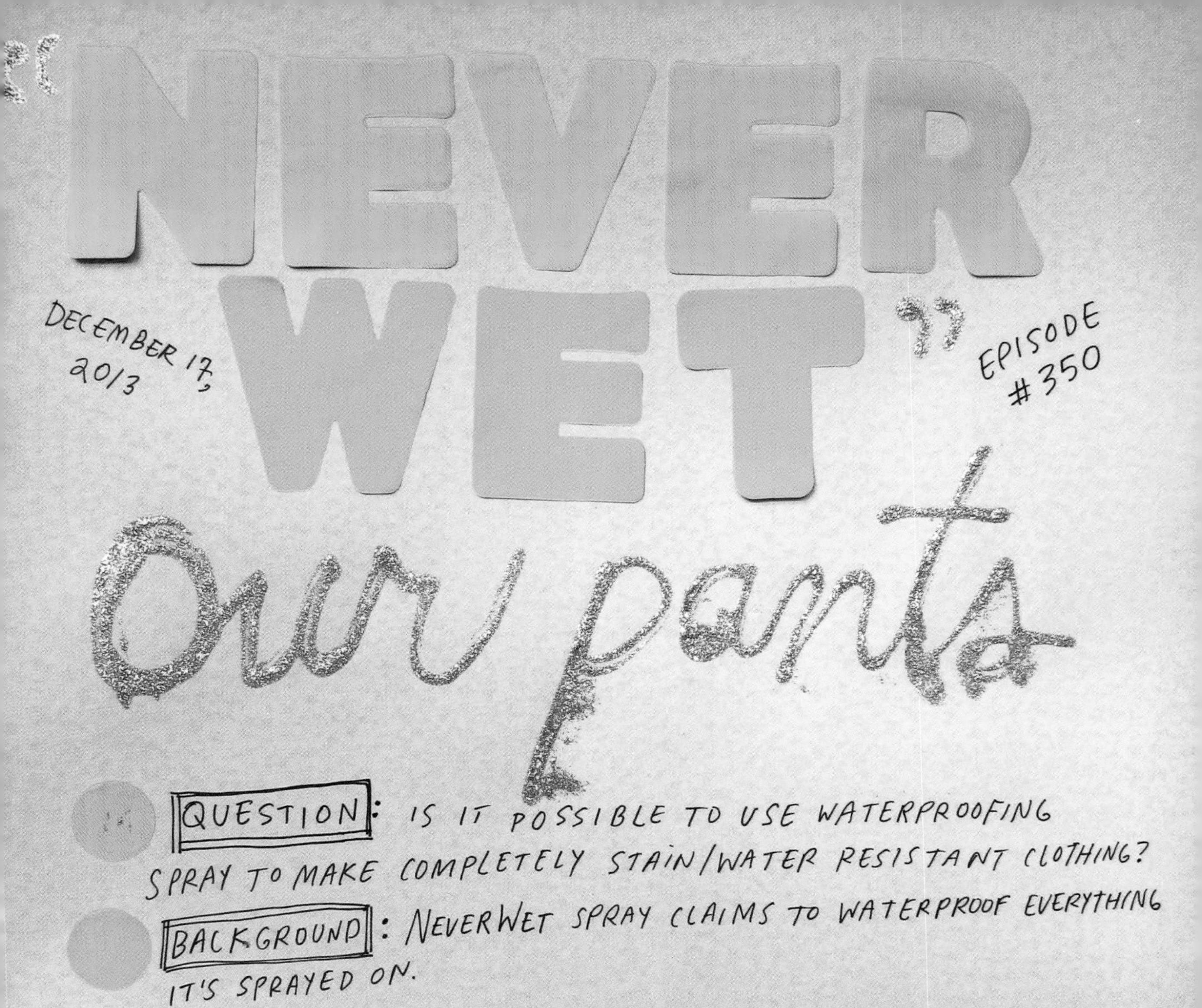


**QUESTION**: IS IT POSSIBLE TO USE WATERPROOFING SPRAY TO MAKE COMPLETELY STAIN/WATER RESISTANT CLOTHING?

**BACKGROUND**: NEVERWET SPRAY CLAIMS TO WATERPROOF EVERYTHING IT'S SPRAYED ON.

**EXPERIMENT**: RHETT SERVED AS THE CONTROL GROUP, WEARING UNSPRAYED WHITE CLOTHES. LINK'S CLOTHES WERE SPRAYED WITH NEVERWET. THEY BOTH APPLIED WINE, BBQ SAUCE, AND MUSTARD TO THE CLOTHES.

**CONCLUSION(S)**:

- NeverWet, when applied to clothing, actually does work! It repels most liquids, causing them to visibly roll up into balls on the clothing and fall off
- The process of watching liquids and sauces bounce off Link's clothes caused Rhett to achieve unnecessary levels of excitement that are not becoming of respectable scientific experimentation.

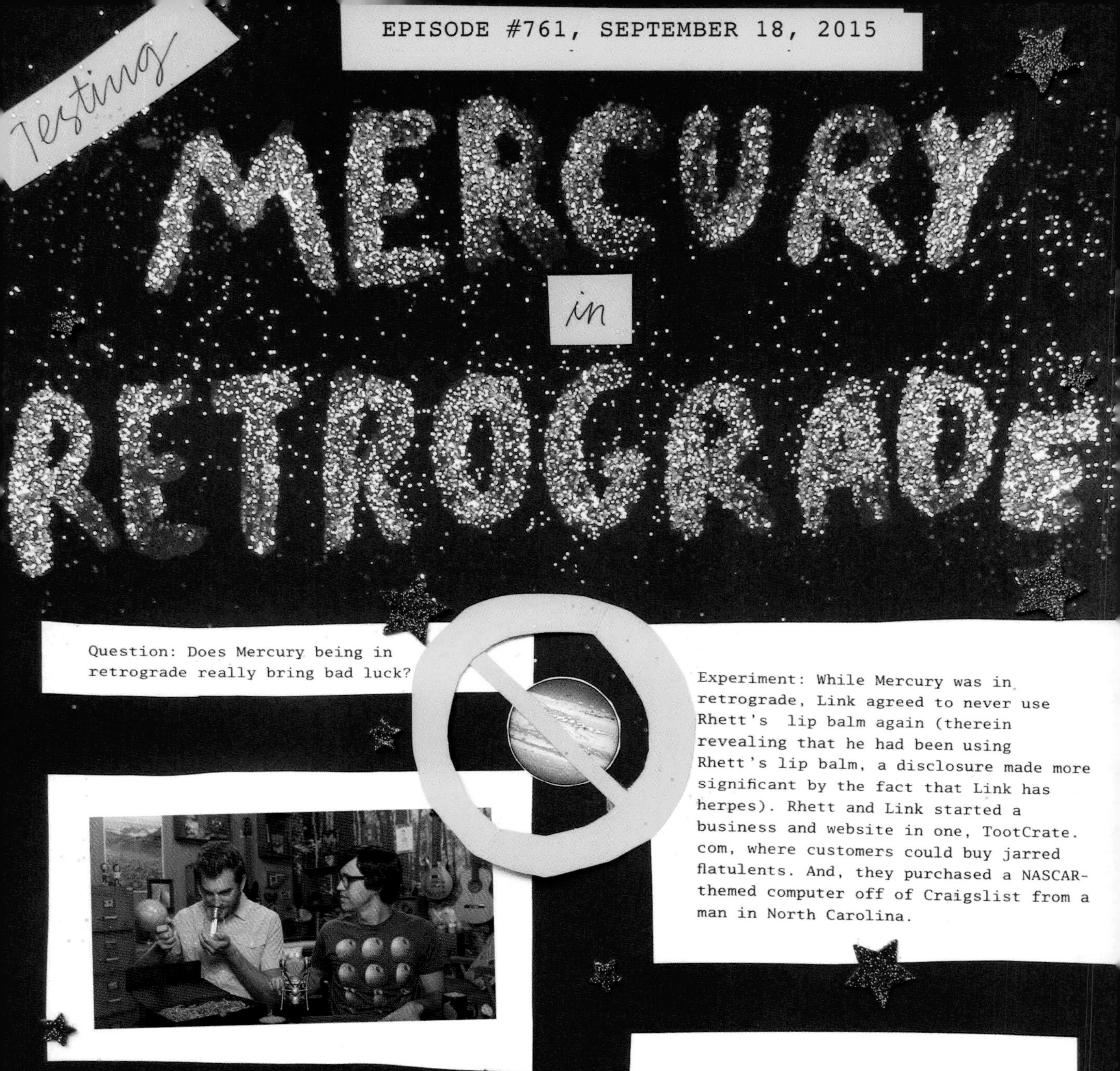

EPISODE #761, SEPTEMBER 18, 2015

# Testing MERCURY in RETROGRADE

Question: Does Mercury being in retrograde really bring bad luck?

Experiment: While Mercury was in retrograde, Link agreed to never use Rhett's lip balm again (therein revealing that he had been using Rhett's lip balm, a disclosure made more significant by the fact that Link has herpes). Rhett and Link started a business and website in one, TootCrate.com, where customers could buy jarred flatulents. And, they purchased a NASCAR-themed computer off of Craigslist from a man in North Carolina.

Background: The nature of Mercury's solar orbit with respect to Earth's results in an optical illusion that it is moving backward. This is the period in which Mercury is said to be in retrograde. It is purported that there are a number of actions that will have negative outcomes if performed during this time, including: making an agreement, starting a business, launching a website, and making large purchases.

Conclusion(s):
TootCrate probably isn't a desirable subscription service.

TootCrate.com, WeFartInJars.com, RipItAndShipIt.com, and PootCrate.com were all available domain names.

People in North Carolina who own NASCAR-themed PCs don't know what "Mercury in retrograde" means.

CAN YOU SMELL FEAR?
EPISODE
#641
2/4/2015


## QUESTION:

- Is it possible for Rhett and Link to determine if the other is experiencing fear or happiness by only smelling them?

## BACKGROUND:

- One scientific study determined that smelling the sweat of another person can indicate that person's level of fear.

## EXPERIMENT:

Rhett and Link were each subjected to things that they are typically frightened of – or alternatively, things that make them happy. For Rhett, fears included heights and roaches, and for Link, a fear was crew member Chase dressed like a psycho killer. Link was also subjected to something that traditionally makes him happy: a bowl of Frosted Mini-Wheats. Rhett and Link smelled each other's armpits after each item was introduced.

## CONCLUSIONS:

- Rhett and Link cannot smell fear. They were wrong 100 percent of the time.
- Link's armpits smell really bad without deodorant. Especially the left one.
- Rhett's armpits are at perfect smelling height for Link.

# COLE McLAUGHLIN'S SCIENCE PROJECT DISASTER

MY BROTHER, COLE, WAS THREE GRADES AHEAD OF ME AND LINK. ALL OF BUIES CREEK ELEMENTARY (KINDERGARTEN THROUGH EIGHTH GRADE) PARTICIPATED IN THE ANNUAL SCIENCE FAIR, BUT THE EIGHTH-GRADE WINNERS WERE LARGELY CONSIDERED TO BE THE SCHOOLWIDE SCIENCE CHAMPIONS. SO, WHEN COLE ENTERED HIS LAST YEAR AT OUR SCHOOL, I PUT A LOT OF HOPE IN HIM REPRESENTING THE SCIENTIFIC APTITUDE OF THE McLAUGHLIN FAMILY. AS YOU ARE ABOUT TO LEARN FROM THE FOLLOWING COMIC STRIP THAT RETELLS HIS LEGENDARY SCIENCE PROJECT, THINGS TURNED OUT DIFFERENTLY FROM HOW I PLANNED. THIS IS ALL TRUE.

COLE'S SCIENCE PROJECT

AS YOU MIGHT IMAGINE, COLE DIDN'T WIN THE SCIENCE FAIR. IT'S A WONDER HE WASN'T ASKED TO LEAVE, CONSIDERING THAT THE BIRD HE DISMEMBERED AND TAPED TO A POSTER BOARD WAS NONE OTHER THAN THE RED-COCKADED WOODPECKER, A PROTECTED SPECIES THAT MR. EVERHART WAS VERY FAMILIAR WITH. WE CAN'T ALL BE SCIENTISTS, I GUESS.

# LINK'S SCIENCE PROJECT: NATURE IN THE BALANCE

My eighth-grade science project was a jarring experience for me. Literally. I filled eight jars with water, added in various combinations of a waterweed (Elodea) and snails (Gastropoda), and sealed on all the lids. And then I watched. I was determined to answer the pressing question plaguing all of mankind: "What magical combination of weeds and snails doesn't turn into a putrid brown mess after three weeks?" My hypothesis: This was blue-ribbon material. It turned out to be red-ribbon material thanks to Sam Cluck's analysis of Drosophila fly reproduction that I swear his parents did for him, but whatever.

Here's some excerpts from my log, chronicling the sad downward spiral of nature happening in my garage:

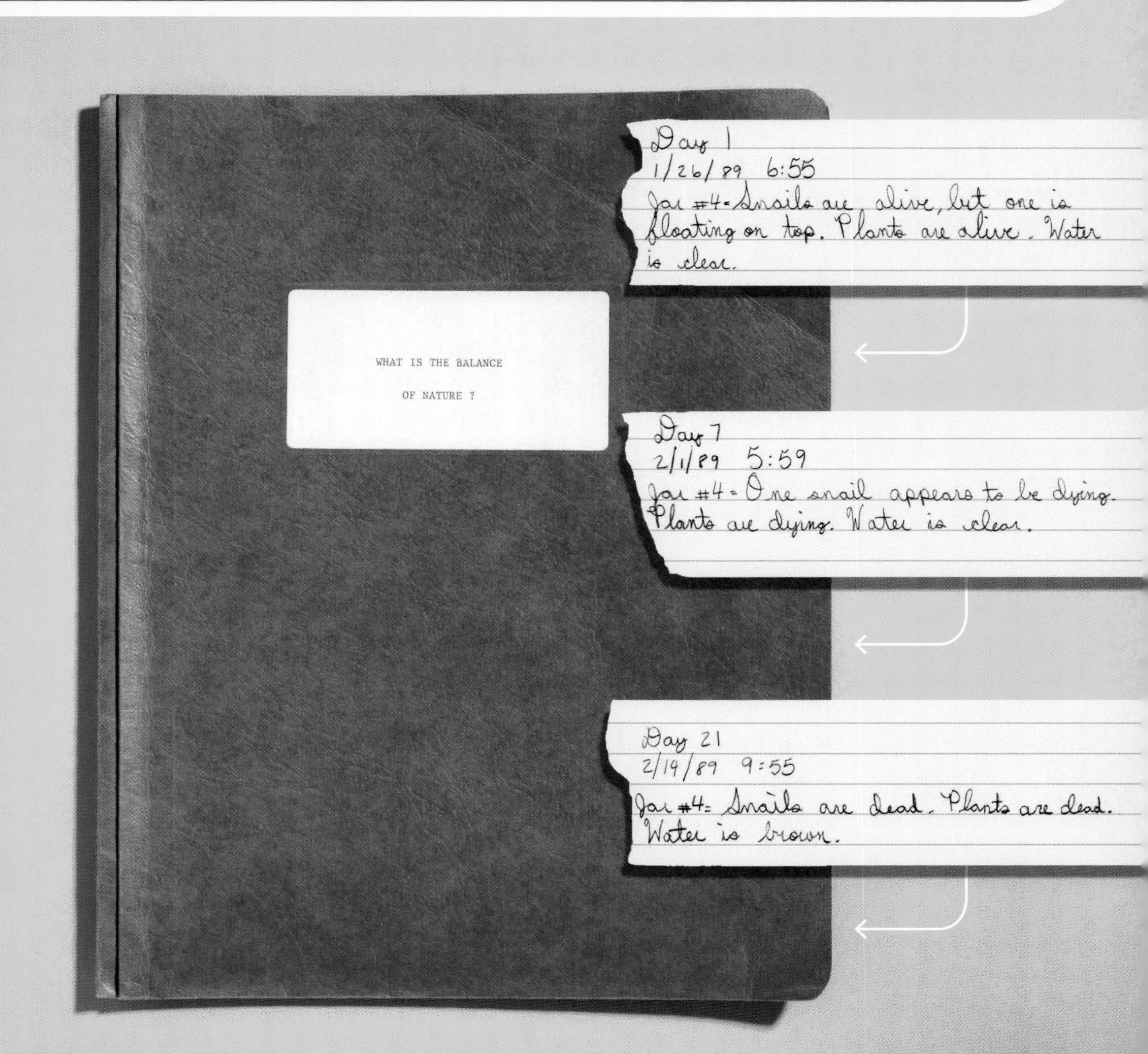

WHAT IS THE BALANCE
OF NATURE ?
Day 1
1/26/89 6:55
Jar #4 = Snails are alive, but one is floating on top. Plants are alive. Water is clear.
Day 7
2/1/89 5:59
Jar #4 = One snail appears to be dying. Plants are dying. Water is clear.
Day 21
2/19/89 9:55
Jar #4 = Snails are dead. Plants are dead. Water is brown.

PARTY
ANIMAL

# THROW A PARTY THAT DOESN'T SUCK

"I FULLY EXPECTED THAT THEY WOULD BE SERVING SUSHI RIGHT OFF OF PEOPLE'S BODIES, AND THAT WE WOULD EVENTUALLY GET INTO A HOT TUB FULL OF JELL-O. I WOULDN'T HAVE BEEN SURPRISED IF THERE HAD BEEN A CAGED BEAR ON DISPLAY, A FLAMING COUCH BEING TOSSED OUT A WINDOW, AND AT LEAST ONE PERSON GETTING STABBED. I WAS READY FOR A PARTY."

**PARTIES ARE SUPPOSED** to be awesome—a time to get together with the right people in the right place and have fun. When people want to celebrate appreciation, inauguration, coronation, graduation, procreation, and a whole lot of other words that end in "-ation," they throw a party. But if parties are supposed to be among the highlights of our lives, then why is it that they are—more often than not—a total letdown?

**LINK** One fine June day, my mom asked me to get into the car and then wrapped a T-shirt around my face to blindfold me. I was an anxious nine-year-old, so this didn't exactly set my mind at ease. *Why is Mom blindfolding me? Is she really my mom? Could she be an alien, secretly monitoring my way of life all this time? Am I gonna be ground up into pet food for alien pets? Is this really how it all ends?* Sensing my concern, she assured me that we were going someplace fun. "Remember," she said, "today's your *birthday*!"

As we zoomed down winding country roads, my anxiety was replaced with car sickness. I wanted out. No surprise was worth this much suffering. My mom continued to comfort me, assuring me, "Rhett will be there!" Didn't help. She broadened her promise to "All your friends and family will be there!" Still sick. Finally, she revealed, "We're having a party at one of your favorite places!" None of this caused the nausea to subside.

In retrospect, the blindfold had been rendered mostly unnecessary, seeing as she had disclosed a significant number of pertinent details leading to one inevitable conclusion: she was taking me to a surprise birthday party. But, determined to at least keep the location a surprise, my mom insisted that I keep my 100 percent cotton veil on while she kept winding down the road.

"Mom, I think I'm gonna barf," I said.

"We're almost there!" she assured me, "It's gonna be great!" All I could think about was how *not great* it was gonna be to throw up into a T-shirt tied around my face. Then, at the moment I was convinced that I couldn't hold it in any longer, the car came to a stop.

"Can I take off the T-shirt now?" I asked.

"No!" she snapped. She came around and opened the door, took my hand, and escorted me across a parking lot and into somewhere with a familiar smell. When she removed my blindfold, there they were: all my family and friends sitting in . . . McDonald's. They began to yell "Surprise!" but then quickly lost confidence and volume once they saw my pale face. It came out as more of a "Surpriiiiii . . ." that trailed off as I bolted for the bathroom. My mom never blindfolded me again. Come to think of it, she hasn't even really surprised me since.

I'm sure I'm not the only one who's been to a party that turned sour. In fact, I'm convinced that pretty much every party suffers from the same problem. People have a tendency to bring unrealistic expectations to them. When they hear the word "party," they think, *It's gonna be great!* Which means that, most likely, it's going to be a disappointment.

**RHETT** One of the most highly anticipated parties of my life was at Redfoo's house. He was a guest on an episode of *GMM*, and after the show, he invited me and Link to a party the following week. We were excited.

This dude has a song called "Party Rock Anthem" and his house is called the "Party Rock Mansion." I could only imagine the extreme party shenanigans we would experience, the kinds

The photo booth at RedFoo's party was not meant to accommodate freakishly tall people.

of things you only see at parties in the movies, where the cops show up and they're so entranced by the vibe that they come inside and begin performing perfect renditions of the "YMCA" dance. I fully expected that they would be serving sushi right off of people's bodies, and that we would eventually get into a hot tub full of Jell-O. I wouldn't have been surprised if there had been a caged bear on display, a flaming couch being tossed out a window, and at least one person getting stabbed. I was ready for a PARTY.

But when we showed up, there were no cops banging on the front door and no smoldering sofas sitting on the front lawn. There was just a nice man out front asking to see our IDs. Upon entering, we were asked to remove our shoes. This was less like dropping into an epic party and more like entering the home of an elderly couple who wants to preserve their new carpet. We noticed that there was a pair of very flashy canvas Vans shoes on each step of the stairs. We figured, *Oh, this is why we had to take our shoes off.* So, we each squeezed tightly into a pair of size-10 Vans (they were all size 10), and moved deeper into the party. It didn't take long to notice that no one else was wearing shoes. It turns out that the Vans were just Redfoo's personal shoe collection, not something he intended for partygoers to wear. But at that point, we were committed.

Inside, no one was eating sushi off of anyone's body, there were no caged bears, and not one person was being assaulted. There were just a bunch of cool-looking people talking to one another. We went out back, and the hot tub was full of water—not Jell-O. We returned inside, where people were now dancing in their socks, and saw Redfoo. It was hard to hear him over the music, but he seemed to say "Thanks for coming!" and then looked down at our feet and chuckled a little, as if to say *Why are you wearing my shoes?* Given that we didn't really know anyone else, and that my size-12 feet were really beginning to feel the effects of walking around in Redfoo's size-10 shoes, we made a few more rounds, snapped some pictures in the photo booth, and decided to head home. It wasn't that the party was lame. It was that it was just . . . a party.

WE HAVE DEVELOPED a theory that the natural momentum of every party moves toward suckage. This is due not only to the fact that we typically bring unrealistic expectations to them but also because it only takes one miscalculated party factor to create a forgettable experience. What's the answer? Just give up and cease partying? Far from it. Parties are planned moments of celebration. They present opportunities for highly concentrated Mythicality. We owe it to our species to get this right, because humans are destined to continue throwing parties until we die out and are replaced with cockroaches. Cockroaches may then evolve the ability to party, and assuming that they will also evolve the ability to read twenty-first-century English and one of them will find this book in the distant future, they are invited to take note as well.

While you can't do much to shape the parties you attend, you do have control over the parties that you personally throw. The most important rule of parties is: parties are only as good as the planning. If your party sucks, it's probably your fault. The following are a number of the party pitfalls we've witnessed, along with some proposed solutions designed to ensure maximum Mythicality at your next soiree.

**Party Pitfall #1: Incorrect Friend-to-Stranger Ratio.** Nothing kills party potential like the wrong ratio of friends to strangers. If you don't know anyone, you end up like us at Redfoo's house—walking around with the person you came with, talking only about the lack of Jell-O in the hot tub. It's pathetic. On the other hand, if you know everyone, you're forced to hear your friends Doug and Allison tell their "Finding True Love at a Phish Concert" story for the twelfth time. We get it, Allison. You love a man who can handle his hacky sack.

**Tip:** A good ratio of friends to strangers is 60/40. This gives you the comfort of knowing you can connect with friends, but you still have the opportunity to get to know someone new (hopefully someone who isn't a Phish fan). How do you get people you don't know at your own party? Tell your friends to bring friends. Duh. (We've been looking for an excuse to use "duh" this entire book. Please forgive us.)

**Party Pitfall #2: Wrong Kinds of People.**

In our opinion, a Mythical party is one where the guests stand a good chance of getting into an interesting conversation, and that usually involves learning something new from someone with a unique perspective. If you're a proctologist, and you go to a proctology conference, no doubt there's going to be some kind of party at the hotel restaurant, most likely featuring a pianist playing Journey songs. And at that party, you're going to end up talking to a bunch of buttholes about buttholes. Yawn.

**Tip:** The key is to invite the kinds of people who would make great Reddit "Ask Me Anything" hosts, like an exterminator or an ER doctor. These people have seen unspeakable things in unspeakable places, and they're dying to speak about them in a casual setting.

**Party Pitfall #3: Food Faux Pas.**

Never, under any circumstances, throw a party without food. Even if all your friends are on weird diets that preclude them from eating anything other than specially prepared meals they carry around in their own Tupperware (this is much more common in Los Angeles than you might expect), serve food. People on fun-free diets are known to relax their standards at parties, and famished people are incapable of sustaining positive party vibes.

**Tip:** The overarching solution for party food is heavy hors d'oeuvres. The one question everyone asks themselves prior to attending a party is "Should we eat before?" Heavy hors d'oeuvres answers that question regardless of the decision your attendees made. And, although "hors d'oeuvres" is a fancy term, they themselves don't have to be fancy. Meatballs are perfect. When the meatballs come out, everyone will be happy, even people stuck in conversations about Phish with Doug and Allison. Just make sure you provide enough, because you don't want your guests to suffer from Anticipated Meatball Disappointment, the acute condition of watching some jerk eat the last meatball. In an ideal party world, you're sending people home with baggies of meatballs.

**Party Pitfall #4: Boredom.**

A Mythical party has no lulls. You have to be ready for the real possibility of conversation tapering off by providing activities to keep people engaged. These should be optional, though, because you don't want to be the party dictator who forces everyone into a forty-person game of Twister. (Although we have seen this done to great success with minimal injury, and it spawned at least one marriage.)

**Tip:** You want simple activities that are fun to do and entertaining for spectators. Avoid horseshoe tournaments. They are not only boring, but dangerous. While conversational games like "Two Truths and a Lie"—or its more time-consuming cousin, "Three Truths and Two Lies"—can be perfect in the right crowd, providing a competitive team game is often the best strategy. We recommend "Hide the Meatball".

## HIDE THE MEATBALL!

OBJECT: Be the last team standing by finding your opposing team's meatballs.

RULES:

1. Divide into two teams of equal size. Name your teams, because it's fun. If your party size is uneven, have one person play the "talker."
2. Each team picks up one meatball. (Take note of who chose the larger meatball.)
3. Each team turns away from the opposing team, at which point one player on each team is selected to place a meatball in his/her mouth but does not chew or otherwise consume it.
4. Each team turns back toward the other when the talker says so. If there is no talker, it may be hard to determine when to turn around. But you'll figure it out.
5. The team (in this example, Team 1) that chose the larger meatball goes first. Using only grunts and gestures, Team 1 must agree on choosing one player from the opposing team that they think has the meatball in his/her mouth.
6. The accused player opens his/her mouth.
7. If Team 1 guessed correctly, the person with the meatball eats it and is eliminated (sits out). Team 1 then turns away in order for one of the remaining members to secretly take a meatball. Play continues to Team 2. If the opposing team guesses incorrectly, they must eliminate someone on their own team who does not currently possess their meatball. Play continues for Team 2.
8. Play continues until the losing team is entirely eliminated or everyone gets tired of eating meatballs.

**Party Pitfall #5: The Dwindle.**

Known in some circles as the "fizzle," this is the inevitable waning to lameness to which parties seem to be ultimately doomed. It can be signaled in a number of ways, such as the DJ restarting his playlist, the cool people beginning to leave, or you finding yourself in a corner alone, nibbling on a cold meatball. This is not how you want your guests to remember your party. Instead, you want to abruptly end it just after a peak, before any hint of the dwindle.

**Tip:** We advise that you let people know up-front, either using several large signs (feel free to use the sample sign below) placed throughout the venue, or on the invitation (if applicable) that the party is over when a particular sound is heard. We've found that an air horn works in almost every environment. It can't be mistaken for a doorbell, a phone ringing, or a fire alarm, and it easily pierces through even the loudest pumping bass. As the party planner, you are responsible for sensing when to abort, but know this: very few parties have more than three peaks. The conservative approach is to sound your horn immediately after the second peak, but you may want to gamble for a third peak because a three-peak party that ends at just the right time is the kind of party that people tell their grandkids about.

WELCOME TO
THE PARTY!!!
ENJOY THE MEATBALLS.
WHEN YOU HEAR THE HORN,
PLEASE LEAVE.
(WE'RE NOT TRYING TO BE RUDE. WE JUST DON'T WANT
YOU TO HAVE TO SUFFER THROUGH A DWINDLING PARTY.
IT'S FOR YOUR OWN GOOD.)


IF YOU CAN avoid these pitfalls at your upcoming party, you will notice that the people who attended will start calling/texting you to ask when your next bash is. This is a sign that you have indeed thrown a Mythical party, and it's a huge accomplishment. We would even go as far as to say that it's a service to humanity.

You see, a party can provide one of those rare moments when you can experience every aspect of Mythicality simultaneously. A party can pique your curiosity and make you laugh if the right people are there. A party can bring more good into the world if you're partying to bring awareness or support to a cause. A party can even have a sense of adventure and originality if you choose to do the right activities. (Hide the Meatball alone can accomplish this.) If you can provide a setting where this kind of Mythicality is experienced by a group of people, you're making a difference.

May all your parties be Mythical.

# Rhett & Link's Party Startin' T-Shirts

IF YOU'D LIKE TO TAKE THE EASY WAY OUT IN GUARANTEEING THAT YOU THROW A MYTHICAL PARTY, YOU CAN ALWAYS USE THESE T-SHIRTS. THE FIRST TEN GUESTS TO SHOW UP DRAW A T-SHIRT OUT OF THE BOX AND HAVE TO WEAR IT FOR THE DURATION OF THE PARTY.

GUESS MY PERFECT PIZZA ORDER

Slow Dance INSTRUCTOR

DESIGNATED PHOTOBOMBER

FEEL THE BABY KICK
PLACE HAND HERE
ASK ME ABOUT MY LAST MEDICAL PROCEDURE
thoughtful conversation
hot pockets
POKE YOUR PERFECT PARTY
caviar
running from the police
truth < DARE
PICK ONE:
SUGARY
SALTY
SPICY
SWEATY
CAN I GET YOU A MEATBALL?
MY SPIRIT ANIMAL CAN BEAT UP YOUR SPIRIT ANIMAL

# Party MVPs

This could be the ER doctor who removed a weird something from a weird place on a weird person, the woman who does spot-on *Sesame Street* impressions, or the Frisbee instructor. You may not want to be her lifelong companion, but she sure makes a ten-minute exchange at a party memorable.

He'll get everyone on the dance floor, sing the first karaoke song, eat the first hot wing of unknown spiciness, and introduce people who have been staring silently at each other from across the room.

She can't handle clutter and feels compelled to clean up after everyone, but she isn't obvious or dramatic about it because she's self-conscious about the compulsion.

"Who wants to play Charades, liar's dice, or set up a Ping-Pong tournament?" As long as this person doesn't pressure people to participate, he's great to have around.

Whatcha talkin' 'bout? Herbal remedies? Video games? First kisses? Cool. He's got some hilarious-but-not-overbearing thoughts on that.

She might not live in the house, and it might not be her birthday party, but her mission in life is to make sure everyone feels included and special. Sure, she can be controlling, but if you just let her play sheepdog, everyone will benefit.

# Party LVPs

He feels compelled to one-up your amazing story before you've even uttered the last words of said story.

One is way too intimate, the other couldn't be less engaged.

The Pinot is her permission slip to start "keepin' it real" with her opinions.
Glass 1: "THAT's an interesting dress."
Glass 2: "Did you make this dip? Because it tastes weird."
Glass 3: "You guys need to get divorced already."

To him, actual arguments are normal conversations and actual normal conversations are stupid.

She's got the perfect products for you to sell to your friends for her.

# NO BUDGET BLOWOUTS

THE GLOBAL PARTY SCENE IS COMPLETELY OUT OF CONTROL. Million-dollar weddings, kids' birthday parties with swag bags, red-carpet retirement parties... Everywhere you look, people are mortgaging their life in order to throw a record-setting shindig that will hopefully induce mass FOMO across their social media networks.

THIS IS ALL UNNECESSARY. When it comes to throwing a party, creativity trumps cash every time. To prove it, here are three different themed parties that will wow your friends and generate crazy buzz (and, if you want, online FOMO) and they won't cost a thing.

## POSTAPOCALYPTIC POTLUCK

The key to this party is that none of the guests eat for three days before the event, and then everyone brings unmarked canned foods that the host hides all over the house.

GAMES INCLUDE: How Far Will You Go for a Can Opener?, Celebrity Zombie Charades, and Touch Those Baked Beans and I'll Kill You.

PARTY #2

# MOST SATISFYING PARTY EVER

Have every guest bring their most comfortable clothes and blankets, along with any leftovers they currently have in the fridge.

Create a YouTube playlist of those "Most Satisfying" videos – featuring things like cutting Play Doh with a knife, fresh pasta crawling out of a machine, or skilled baristas doing incredible latte foam designs – all set to hypnotic music. Have everyone sit back and experience pure, unadulterated satisfaction.

PARTY #3

# MENNO-NITE-OUT

The Mennonites have a tradition of inviting the community over to buid a barn in just a day, which is known as a barn raising. Borrowing from that idea, the Menno-Nite-Out is when you invite your friends over to celebrate a meaningful life event and get them to renovate your garage. Win-Win.

FUR
THE LOVE

# RISK YOUR HEART FOR AN ANIMAL

"THIS WAS OUR FIRST BURIAL. WE TRIED OUR BEST. AND WHILE WE DIDN'T FIND A PERFECT COFFIN, DIG A FITTING HOLE, OR DELIVER ARTICULATE EULOGIES, I DID RUN INSIDE AND GRAB MY TRUMPET SO I COULD PLAY 'TAPS.'"

FOR THOUSANDS OF years, human-animal relationships were limited mostly to either humans chasing animals so they could eat them or animals chasing humans so they could eat them. Then, one glorious day, an especially Mythical individual decided that, instead of running from the wolves, we should try to pet them. That person was probably eaten by a wolf. But eventually, when the right person petted the right wolf, it opened the door for a bond that has brought Mythicality into millions of people's lives.

Since those early days of wolf-petting, humans have gone on to find companionship with thousands of different animals. Even though some people may feel a special connection with an iguana that never makes eye contact or a cobra that can kill you during feeding time, we have found our animal friends in the canine species—specifically those who have been selectively bred as cute companions we can carry around in a backpack. These are the kinds of dogs that couldn't eat us unless we chopped ourselves up into bite-size pieces and added "real cheese flavor," and they have become members of our families. However, our journey to this current state of camaraderie with man's best friend was filled with some lowlights. It turns out that choosing to love an animal is not without its risks.

**LINK** My childhood dog was named Tucker. He was a big, yellowish-brown border collie mix with a head so pointy it was like he had a horn that never quite broke through. Tucker lived outside, because in rural North Carolina in the 1980s, that was a dog's proper place. Sure, there were a few families that had "house dogs" as we called them, but those were also the families that talked funny and ate Lean Cuisine. We local folk knew that dogs descended from wild animals, which meant that the backyard would do just fine.

As with most things in my life, I had a specific daily routine with Tucker. I would venture out into the backyard, approach his house, and fill his bowl with Gravy Train. Then I would pet him on his pointy head exactly five times. This was definitely an indicator of my future OCD, though I justified it by telling myself that five pets allowed me to both bond with Tucker and easily wash the smell of dog off my hands later. We didn't really bathe our dogs back then. As long as they jumped into a creek or pond a couple of times during the summer, we considered them clean. As a result, all backyard dogs achieved a distinct dog smell, and you knew that you'd get it all over you if you petted them too much (more than five times).

Tucker (left) and Link (right).

I loved Tucker. As an only child, he was kind of like a brother to me. A really hairy, naked brother who wasn't allowed in the house. Tucker would accompany me on treks through the woods. I felt safe knowing that he could pierce the vital organs of any predator with a swift head-butt from his sharp skull. And Tucker loved me back. He never judged me. He even accepted me in my Jams shorts phase, never shunning me no matter how ridiculous the pattern.

One day when I was in middle school, I went out to feed Tucker and caress his subdermal horn. But that day he wasn't standing by the door in anticipation of his five head pats. Instead, he was lying down with his eyes open, stiff as a board. I sat down next to him and cried. My old pointy-headed friend had taken his last ride on the Gravy Train.

I chose not to bother my mom with the news of Tucker's death or with questions about what to do with him. I felt it was my duty to dispose of his body, so I called up Rhett, who soon arrived on his bike, ready to go to work.

The idea of simply throwing poor Tucker into a hole in the ground didn't seem right to me, so we found a large box that could serve as a makeshift coffin. Tucker was a pretty big dog, and the only box we could find that would work was a giant refrigerator box. In all likelihood, the cavernous box could have accommodated at least five dead Tuckers, but hey, a dead pharaoh got an entire pyramid. We gently placed his stiff body into the box and then carried it to a good "burying spot" in my backyard. With every step, Tucker slid around in his oversized cardboard sarcophagus.

It's worth noting that we didn't say a word to each other throughout this entire process. It just seemed right to remain silent out of respect for Tucker.

We dug for hours until we reached some very rocky soil that was impossible to break up with a shovel. We had excavated a large cube of earth, and using only a series of hand motions to communicate, decided to place the giant box into the hole to see if it would fit. It didn't. The top of the box was sticking about six inches out of the ground. Knowing that we had dug as deep as we were capable of, Rhett looked at me and, maintaining his stoic expression, placed his foot on the top of the box, then raised his eyebrows as if to ask, "Is it OK if I step on the box?" Seeing no other option, I somberly nodded. I silently joined him, pushing the box down until the crumpled coffin sat about a foot below the surface. We then proceeded to cover it with dirt.

*"If we stop now, at least we'll always know where we buried him."*

Just as the dirt level was getting even with the surface, there was a sudden crashing noise as the top of the box gave way even more, dropping down another few inches. We looked at the hole, looked at each other, looked at the pile of dirt beside us, and then kept shoveling. A few minutes later, the box failed again, and this time, we heard the sound of dirt pouring into the box with Tucker. It wasn't exactly a comforting sound, but we continued to add more dirt. Had we been burying a human in this way at some sort of graveside service, the entire family would have been crying and gasping with each audible collapse of the cardboard box. But this was our first burial. We tried our best. And while we didn't find a perfect coffin, dig a fitting hole, or deliver articulate eulogies, I did run inside and grab my trumpet so I could play "Taps." Ultimately, I'm proud of the way my friend and I worked through broken hearts to honor that pointy-headed pooch.

My mom and I never got another dog.

**RHETT** I had two backyard dogs during my childhood who, like Tucker, taught me about both love and loss. Or, more specifically, love and lost.

My first dog was Sandy, an extraordinarily sweet but stupid mutt. She was my parents' answer to their sons' endless pleas for dog ownership. I had always dreamed of having a dog that I could teach a bunch of cool tricks, like having it fetch a cold Dr Pepper out of the fridge when I licked my lips. Unfortunately, Sandy only ever learned one trick, and that was running away like a prison escapee every time she got a chance.

One day when my dad was taking Sandy to the vet in Dunn, she caught him daydreaming about *Matlock* and bolted past him as soon as he opened the minivan door. She ran behind the Belk department store and we never saw her again. I was devastated. Where had she gone? Did she finally find that new family she'd been searching for? For years, every time we went to Belk, I would walk around back hoping I might find Sandy curled up in a pair of 30-percent-off pleated khakis, but she was never there.

Rhett and his brother, Cole (left), trying to keep Sandy from running away.

Rhett and Cole with their replacement dog, Beauty (apparently at Easter time).

I guess my parents sensed their sons' grief, because it didn't take them long to bring home a small black Lab mix. We named her Black Beauty. I'm not sure why my family chose the name, since we had never read the book *Black Beauty*, or seen the movie. All I know is that after a few awkward instances of having to call her Black Beauty in front of strangers, we shortened her name to Beauty and never spoke of it again. The early days with Beauty were promising. She wasn't constantly trying to run from us like Sandy. But when we decided to bring her out with us to pick peaches at a local orchard, she vanished. We searched for her for hours, and I cried as we drove home empty-handed. My parents told me that they suspected that she had been stolen, which instilled in me a deep distrust of peach farmers that I still carry to this day.

These two deeply unsettling dog disappearances in my childhood left me hesitant to get a dog as an adult. Even if a third dog didn't vanish, I knew I was going to outlive another little creature I loved. What kind of sense does that make? Why begin a relationship that you know is going to come to a tragic end? This defensive strategy kept me and Jessie from getting a dog after we got married.

Rhett and pregnant Jessie with Gypsy.

But fate wouldn't allow me to go on without a dog. While driving through the town of Erwin in 2003, I decided to stop and grab a bite to eat. I took my lunch down to the Cape Fear River, where Link and I had made lots of childhood memories. While I ate, a tiny puppy emerged from the woods, walked over, and crawled up in my lap. Seriously. Any commitment that I had to remaining petless melted. I looked around to make sure that she hadn't just wandered off from a peach-picking family, but it was soon obvious that she had been abandoned.

We named her Gypsy, and once she made it through puppyhood, I started to feel like my dog curse had been reversed. Wrong. When she was only a little over a year old, Gypsy jumped a fence when we were staying at the beach and was hit by a car and instantly killed. Jessie was pregnant with our first child, Locke, at the time, and Gypsy's death didn't help her already emotionally fragile state. We both sat in bed and cried. My heart had been crushed again. I told myself—for real this time—I would never own another dog.

My wife's parents' dog, Rosie, had other plans. Specifically, she had plans to break out of the house and explore the neighborhood in order to make a canine love connection. That tendency to roam, coupled with Rosie's still very functional reproductive organs, created the perfect storm. Long story short, Rosie hooked up with Sparky, a vicious little Chihuahua who spent most of his time tied up to a stake in his owner's backyard. Rosie and Sparky's passionate liaisons produced a litter of the cutest puppies I'd ever seen. I actually filmed Rosie's delivery and instantly fell in love with the runt of her litter.

Thus, even though Jessie and I were one month away from having our second child, we found ourselves in possession of another dog. We knew our baby would be a boy and had decided on the name Shepherd. Since our son was already going to have a dog's name, we determined the dog needed a human name, so we named it Merle. I had always wanted to name a dog after Merle Haggard, and even though the puppy was a girl, we went for it. We called her Merle the Girl and we even let her stay in the house. It wasn't exactly easy having a five-year-old, a newborn, and a puppy under one roof, but we were happy . . . until another dog convinced Merle to drink our neighbors' antifreeze. I found them both lying lifeless in a yard a few houses down the block. I was a wreck.

Merle and Shepherd. These are moments that justify having babies and puppies at the same time.

Clearly, I was cursed. Dogs weren't safe with me. Every relationship I had with them had ended in tragic tears.

But then I moved to Los Angeles. For our first five years in L.A., we rented a house and the landlord didn't allow pets. Even though my kids begged me every year to get a dog, I would say, "We're not allowed to get a dog. Maybe when we get our own house." When we finally did get our own place—and my excuse evaporated—I tried to convince myself that I wasn't the root cause of the canine curse. Maybe it was a regional thing. Maybe the curse stayed in North Carolina. This is the West Coast! Dogs are different here. You don't keep them in roughshod houses in the backyard. They get baths and haircuts and dress up as Yoda for Halloween. Plus, there's no such thing as curses! After a long break from dog ownership, I told my family that we could get a dog.

**LINK** What Rhett might not have fully realized at the time is that he was making a dog decision for me as well. You see, our wives and kids are close friends, and we have to take those relationships into account whenever either family makes a major change, like getting an Xbox, another newborn, or a puppy. When Rhett gave his family the green light for a dog, he simultaneously put me in a trap. I had always thought that we just weren't going to be a dog family. Over the course of fifteen years of marriage and three kids, and I had already seen enough poop and vomit from human children to last a lifetime. Plus, every time I thought about having my own dog, I pictured Tucker and heard echoes of his cardboard casket collapsing. But I also saw an opportunity to be a hero. I knew my kids would be thrilled if I were to come home and say, "Hey kids! Guess what? We're getting a dog!" So, before Rhett even had a chance to get a dog for his family, I got one for mine.

Link texted Christy this pic to let her know "Jade chose us."

Link's gift to Christy on their sixteenth wedding anniversary. The frame plays an audio recording: "With love from your two favorite people."

My pet-adoption scenario is outlined explicitly as "what not to do" in all of those books you're supposed to read before you get a dog. Just a couple of days after telling my kids they could finally have a dog, my family and I walked past a pen full of pooches in need of rescue at the local farmer's market. My daughter Lily, seizing the opportunity, ran up to the pen and knelt down. A ridiculously cute little black dog walked right up to her and started licking her hand. "Dad, she chose me!" she said. We brought Jade, a miniature dachshund/Papillon mix, home with us that day.

It's hard to believe that I was considering never getting a dog for my family. Christy and the kids love that little dog, and she has more than won me over too. When she crawls up into my lap, there's a connection that's even stronger than the one I felt every time I petted Tucker's horn, and I pet her way more than five strokes a day. It might border on unhealthy. And while she occasionally poops on the rug and licks her privates in front of guests, she's a family member.

**RHETT** Link's hair-trigger acquisition of Jade put the pressure back on me. After all, I was the one who had promised my family a new furry sibling, and all of sudden, the Neals had one and we didn't. Jessie and I found a pet-rescue center and learned that they recently had someone bring in a litter of what they thought were Maltipoo puppies in need of homes.

I dropped Jessie and the kids off at the place and then embarked on a quest to find a parking space, something that can take a while in L.A. By the time I went inside the adoption center, Jessie had a cute little white fur ball sitting in her lap. Even though we went through the motions of acting like we were thoroughly considering whether this dog was "right for our family," the decision had been made as soon as the puppy sat in her lap. We named her Barbara Mandrell McLaughlin to continue our tradition of naming dogs after country singers, and we took her home with us, but not before the people at the center took a picture of us with her "for their Facebook page." Apparently their Facebook page is *TMZ*, because Jessie was alerted by her friends two days later that we were featured on the site.

Barbara has changed my life more than I anticipated. I was never one to do much "baby talk" with my actual babies, but the way I talk to Barbara is embarrassing. I hope the public never has to witness it. When she jumps up next to me and begins clawing at my hand until I show her some love, I can't resist it. She's a friend who offers more consistent love and loyalty than most humans are capable of. Sure, maybe she just likes me because I feed her grain-free organic dog food, but I don't care.

Barbara pensively hoping that the McLaughlin dog curse has been broken.

**YOUTUBE STAR RHETT MCLAUGHLIN**
**I GOT A NEW 'POO ...**
**and It's Adorable!**

f 867 | 45 | 2/14/2016 12:20 AM PST BY TMZ STAFF

TMZ reported that Rhett "dropped nearly a grand on toys and outfits" for Barbara. And by "reported" we mean "totally fabricated."

**JADE AND BARBARA** have captured our hearts and brought joy to our families. However, the sad truth is, even if the McLaughlin curse has been broken and the Neal OCD "five strokes only" method has relaxed, we will still almost certainly outlive both dogs. However, even with the knowledge that our current canine love affairs are destined to end in one way or another, we've gladly made the Mythical choice to put our hearts—and our children's hearts—on the line. We think you should too (unless you're allergic).

# SHOULD I GET A DOG?

## A BRIEF ASSESSMENT

So you've decided that you want a dog, but you're not sure if you can handle the commitment or responsibility. This quiz will help you determine whether you are up to the task of bringing in a full-time canine companion.

1. **Why do you want a dog?**
   a) Because dogs love me.
   b) I'm lonely and I want to commit to one best friend for the next 10 to 15 years.
   c) I saw a wild one at the zoo and felt like we bonded through the glass.
   d) I don't have enough chores in my life.
   e) Dog videos get tons of hits on YouTube.
   f) I just bought a super cute bag for my puppy to ride in.
   g) All of the above.
   h) None of the above.

2. **Which dog name is the best dog name of all time?**
   a) Jaws
   b) Woofy
   c) Bobo
   d) Mr. Peekaboo
   e) Skoogie Woogie
   f) Mom
   g) Dakota
   h) None of the above

3. **How do you feel about training and discipline?**
   a) Expecting a dog to listen to me is counter to its essential wildness.
   b) A few good kicks'll teach him.
   c) I will establish myself as the alpha in our group and discipline will be less important than suppressing challenges.
   d) "Discipline" is such a militaristic word.
   e) None of the above.

4. **How do you feel about cleaning up poop?**
   a) I thought you could train them to, like, not do that.
   b) Why would I feel dog poop? Gross! Wait . . . what? OH! How do I feel ABOUT it? How do I feel about what again?
   c) I prefer to throw feces as a way to emote.
   d) Nobody actually picks it up except for, like, the type of people who volunteer.
   e) None of the above.

5. **Where should your dog sleep?**
   a) On my bare chest.
   b) In a kennel near the ring where I'm teaching her to become a canine matador.
   c) In a large nest of sticks and leaves that she builds outside by the trees.
   d) In her own bed, in her own room, in the addition we build onto our house for her.
   e) With my parents, because they're going to take care of her anyway.
   f) None of the above.

**ANSWER KEY**

If you answered anything besides "none of the above" to any of these questions, you shouldn't get a dog. Trust us.

If you answered "c" to more than one question, you actually want a gorilla, not a dog. Note: you should not get a gorilla.

If you answered "f" to question #2, you should be in therapy.

If you answered "b" to questions #3 or #5, we are going to report you to the authorities.

# MYTHICAL BEASTS' MYTHICAL BEASTS

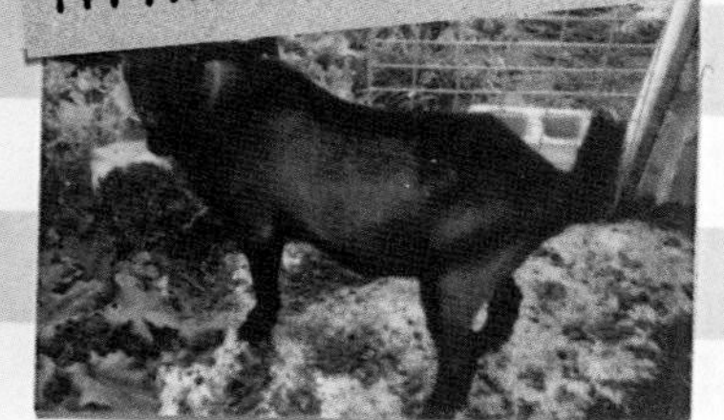

This is my goat, Itty Bitty. I bottle fed him so he thinks of me as his momma. He's always happy to see me and loves hugs, but now that he's grown up he gets very stinky during breeding season.

- Christena Warner

This is my rat, Cheese. He loves to cuddle but also smells weird.

- Angel Miller

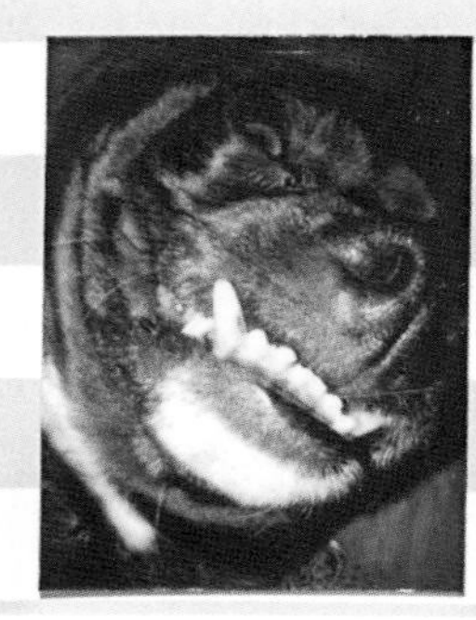

Satchel, my huggable pug-a-bull (pit bull pug mix), is always there for me and even meditates with me. He has really bad gas, but I still love him more than anything

- Amy Marx

Sir Crab is a purple pincher hermit crab. He's a great listener, especially while I study, but he's really stubborn and picky with his food and living space. (In loving memory of Sir Crab.)

- Jamaila Craig

Julien, my panther chameleon, can quickly change through a range of beautiful colors, but any time he comes out to play, he just climbs up onto someone's head and stays there.

- Emily Alexander

My Mexican Red Head Amazon, Weeki, is a loyal little snuggle bug, but when he doesn't get his way, he shrieks like a fire alarm.

- Noor Hakim

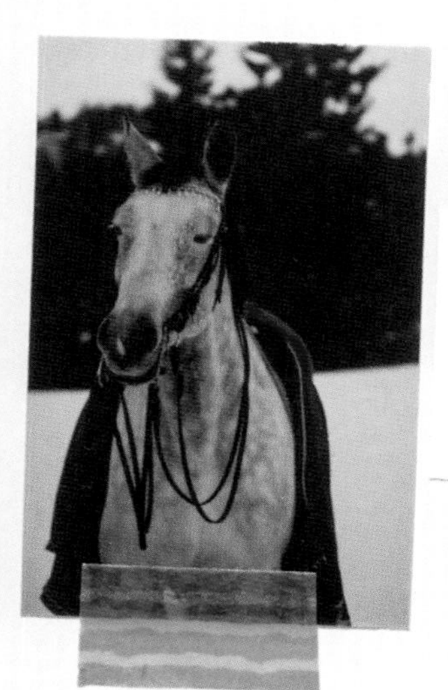

Quite High, the horse, is really laidback. However, when she's mad, she's REALLY mad!

- Tonje Aarsand

Hiccup is a central bearded dragon. He likes to sit with me, he's totally easygoing and makes big poops.

- Jazmin McHugh

HERE ARE SOME OF OUR FAVORITE PETS FROM THE WORLDWIDE COMMUNITY OF MYTHICAL BEASTS.

My guinea pigs, Zelda and Lorhetta, are soft and adorable, but very demanding. When they hear the refrigerator door open, they always squeak loudly for more food.

-Amanda Louise Alger

My pet rock, Excroto, is quiet and chill, but he's the laziest pet ever - he never moves.

-Miguel Muralha

My ball pythons, Mooshoo and Cricket, like to kiss your cheek and don't need to be fed often, but they do need to stay in a warm climate, so I can't take them out as much as I'd like.

-Kaden Peppers

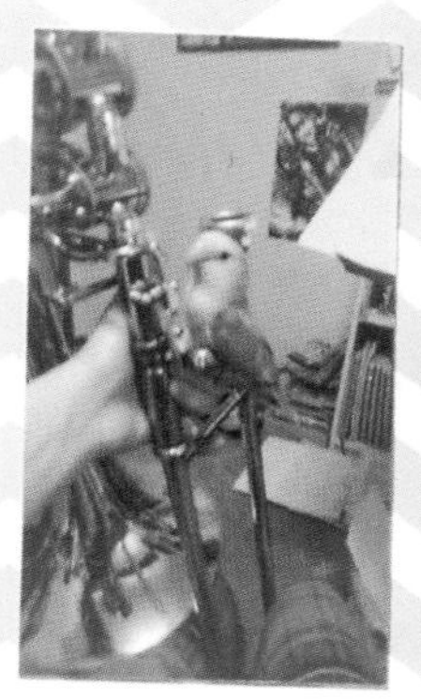

This is Lamarr the lovebird. The best thing he does is give me kisses and nibble my ears, but the worst is when he gets all cozy right next to my ear and lets out a terrible, piercing scream.

-Erin Windish

I love that my cat, Elise, is basically a dog, but unfortunately she's not very bright.

- Stephanie Lynn Chastek

This is Rocky - he's a miniature pinscher. I love that he has my whole family's schedule memorized - he gets worried if someone is late! The worst thing about him is that he needs to be carried up and down stairs every night, multiple times.

- Kati Yau

Layla is a Siberian Husky mix. She's a huge goofball and always makes me laugh, but she does acrobatics on my bed until I wake up in the morning, so I can never sleep in.

- Logan O'Rourke

We have two mischievous bunnies named Oberlix and Asterlix. They're super soft, very affectionate, love to snuggle and lick, but they leave tiny poops everywhere.

-Persephone and Ethan Burgess

# THE STORY of CRAIG OUR OFFICE PYTHON

IN 2016 WE DID AN EPISODE OF GMM FEATURING SPECIAL GUEST TONY HALE CALLED "WHAT AM I PETTING?"

THE GAMEPLAY WAS SIMPLE. WE, ALONG WITH TONY, PUT ON BLINDFOLDS AND HAD TO PET THINGS IN ORDER TO GUESS WHAT THEY WERE. THAT'S COMEDY, PEOPLE.

THE MYTHICAL CREW INITIALLY PLANNED TO HAVE TEAM MEMBER CHASE BRING IN HIS PET CHINCHILLA, A.J. HOWEVER ON THE DAY OF THE SHOOT, THEY DECIDED IT WOULD BE FUNNIER IF LINK HAD TO PET A SNAKE, GIVEN HIS WELL-KNOWN FEAR OF THEM THAT HE HAD DEMONSTRATED DURING A PREVIOUS EPISODE CALLED "TRAPPED IN A SNAKE TANK!"

WHILE TWO COMPLETELY HARMLESS SNAKES SIT QUIETLY ON THE OTHER SIDE OF THE TANK, LINK HOLDS RHETT'S HAND FOR COMFORT.

SO, CREW MEMBERS ALEX AND LIZZIE WENT OFF TO FIND A SNAKE WITH ONLY HOURS BEFORE THE SHOOT. ALTHOUGH THEY WERE ABLE TO RETURN THE BABY CORN SNAKES USED IN THE EARLIER EPISODE WITHOUT INCIDENT, THE STORE HAD A STRICT NO-RETURN POLICY ON THE ONLY SNAKE AVAILABLE THAT DAY: A PYTHON.

THEY WERE CAUGHT BETWEEN A ROCK AND A HARD PLACE. ALEX + LIZZIE QUICKLY MADE UP A STORY ON THE SPOT THAT THEY WERE A COUPLE BUYING A SNAKE FOR ALEX'S YOUNG COUSIN, AND THEY WANTED TO RETURN IT IF HE DIDN'T LIKE IT. AS CONVINCING AS THIS STORY SURELY WAS, IT DIDN'T WORK. SO, INSTEAD OF SETTLING FOR A CHINCHILLA, THEY BOUGHT THE SNAKE, ALONG WITH ALL THE NECESSARY EQUIPMENT FOR KEEPING IT AS A PET, AND BROUGHT HIM TO THE SET.



LINK DISLIKES BIG SNAKES EVEN MORE THAN SMALL SNAKES. MAKES SENSE.

WE NAMED HIM CRAIG—

(CONT ON NEXT PAGE)

ALTHOUGH WE'RE NOT SURE IF HE'S A MALE AND WE'RE NOT SURE HOW TO CHECK FOR THAT. SO FAR, HE HAS ONLY MADE THE CLEANING LADY SCREAM ONCE, AND HE MADE AN EPIC APPEARANCE ON RHETT'S NECK FOR AN EPISODE OF GMM

CRAIG HAS MADE A FEW APPEARANCES ON *GMM*. SO HAS RHETT'S BELLY BUTTON.

AT THIS POINT, THE CREW HAS A COMPLICATED RELATIONSHIP WITH CRAIG.

·ALEX·

"I KINDA REGRET LYING WHEN WE WERE GETTING CRAIG BECAUSE EVERYTIME I GO BACK TO THAT PET STORE I KEEP EXPECTING THE GUY TO ASK ME HOW MY COUSIN LIKED THE SNAKE."

·LIZZIE·

"I ALSO REGRET LYING WHEN GETTING CRAIG BECAUSE EVERY TIME I GO BACK TO THAT PET STORE I KEEP EXPECTING THE GUY TO ASK ME HOW MY MARRIAGE TO ALEX IS GOING."

·EDDIE·

"CRAIG AND I SPEND A LOT OF TIME TOGETHER... LOUNGING ON THE HAMMOCK, OR JUST SCARING MIKE. WE'RE INSEPARABLE... UNTIL IT'S TIME TO GO HOME AFTER WORK."

·MIKE·

"CRAIG SEEMS LIKE A CHILL DUDE, BUT EDDIE ALWAYS INSISTS ON BRINGING HIM OVER TO MY DESK UNINVITED, SO I DO HATE HIM."

·ALLIE·

"THANKS TO CRAIG, I ONCE PICKED UP A BOWL WITH A DEAD RAT IN IT IN THE KITCHEN. IT WAS **HIS** FOOD DEFROSTING. I STILL LOVE HIM THOUGH, BECAUSE IT WASN'T HIS FAULT.

ME MYSELF
AND ISOLATION

# ISOLATE YOURSELF WITH YOURSELF

"AS THE SKY GREW DARKER, I GOT EVEN MORE AFRAID. LOOKING INTO MY FIRE, I BEGAN TO WORRY ABOUT ALL THE THINGS THAT MIGHT SNEAK UP BEHIND ME. ARE COYOTES AFRAID OF FIRE OR ARE THEY ATTRACTED TO IT?"

NEITHER ONE OF US has ever had much alone time as adults. We both went directly from living with our families to rooming together in college to getting married and living with our wives. Furthermore, the fleeting moments of solitude we were afforded during our first few years of marriage were quickly eviscerated by the rapid and repeated arrival of baby bundles of joy. As if constant interaction with humans in our houses was not enough, we proceeded to add animals to the mix. Long story short, we are now at the point where our only refuge at home is an unnecessarily long bathroom break, and even that is usually interrupted by a lost tooth or request to murder a spider.

Work offers us no more privacy than home. Most weekdays, we carpool to the office together. When we arrive at our studio, instead of retreating to separate offices for a few minutes of seclusion, we both enter our shared office, just like we've done ever since we started working together. For most of our career, we've had desks that face each other. We even sit at the same desk during every episode of *GMM*. We spend a lot of time together.

Nothing to see here. Just two guys working at desks facing each other.

To be clear, we are incredibly thankful for the time we spend with our families. We couldn't imagine our homes not being filled with the sounds of door slams, valuables being broken, and heated arguments about who the dog loves most. Furthermore, we think our professional success is largely related to the amount of time we've spent in direct collaboration with each other. But due to our family and work environments, we rarely spend any time truly alone.

It's important for us to get time to ourselves in order to be the Mythical husbands, fathers, best friends, and internetainers we need to be. When we get the opportunity to experience moments of pure, unadulterated self-reflection, it can be thoroughly reinvigorating.

Ironically, one of our most memorable experiences with isolation occurred on *GMM*, when we entered a sensory deprivation tank (or "float tank"). By allowing you to float effortlessly in a super-buoyant salt solution within a completely dark and silent enclosure, a sensory deprivation tank leaves you utterly alone with nothing but your own thoughts.

There is a dude named Ed not too far from us in L.A. who has a float tank at his house. He also has a T-shirt that says PREPARE TO EVOLVE and a wall full of inspirational quotes that include fortune cookie papers he has taken pictures of and printed out much larger than the originals. Bottom line: he seemed legit enough to trust. Under Ed's direction, we each disrobed (and then re-robed in actual robes) and prepared for entry.

**RHETT** I went first. Once I leaned back and began to float, I noticed that there was only about an inch of clearance above my head and below my feet, and I was gently but repeatedly floating into the sides of the tank. I was worried that I was—yet again—too tall for something. But as the water settled down, I began to experience something foreign to me: nothing at all. The lack of stimulation and extreme feeling of disconnection from my environment was a little disconcerting. Then something strange happened. I began to see . . . people. More specifically, I began to see people's faces. They floated in front of me, one by one. They would stop in front of my face for a few seconds, then float away, only to be replaced by another face. They weren't scary faces, mostly bearded men who looked like royalty, like what I would guess the Knights of the Round Table resembled. I like to think that I was making some kind of connection with distant ancestors of mine who were perhaps warrior kings. Or I may have just been experiencing indigestion from the gyro I had for lunch. Either way, it was unlike anything I've ever experienced. When my hour was up, I didn't want it to end.

Rhett entering the void.

Link readying himself to repeatedly choke on salt water.

**LINK** My experience in the tank was a bit different. I didn't see any King Links from the past, but I did begin to fall asleep several times, which involved my head turning and my open mouth dipping below the surface and filling with water. (Which is awesome because it was the same water Rhett had just floated in naked.) I must admit, though, that when I wasn't choking on saltwater, I was having an amazing time. I was totally relaxed. I had no one to answer to. It was just me, alone with myself, nearly drowning every twelve minutes or so. Eventually I quit falling asleep and had a good thirty-minute run of pure peace. This total commitment to nothingness induced a weird sense of euphoria, captured perfectly in the uncontrollable laughter that I experienced upon opening the tank. I remember thinking, *I gotta do this again. I need it.* However, as awesome as the experience was, I haven't been back to Ed's—and it's not because it was a little awkward sitting in a bathrobe in Ed's garden, eating grapes with him for an hour while waiting for Rhett's turn to end. I haven't returned because it's difficult to make time for myself, even if I have every intention to do so.

If you were wondering what Rhett looks like after seeing ghost-royalty, this is it.

Link either had the time of his life, or was just extremely relieved to have not encountered any floating bearded men.

Link took his special binoculars with him everywhere. He still does.

It was easier to find time for myself when I was a child. I was the weird kid who roamed the neighborhood alone in army gear. My stepdad, Jimmy, frequently bought me items from the army supply store. Based on the wide array of military accoutrements he gave me, he must have thought that a war could break out in Harnett County at any moment. He outfitted me with an army belt, high-powered camouflaged binoculars, and my prized possession: a giant bowie knife with a compass built into the handle. I would gear up and head out into a horse pasture behind my house, going "on patrol." A compass isn't particularly helpful for navigating a small, fenced horse pasture, and I was never sure what exactly I should be stabbing with my knife blade. But I felt ready for anything.

I would sit in a corner of the pasture and survey the grass with my discreet binoculars. Occasionally, there was a teenage girl who would ride a horse there. I think her name was Amy, and I'm pretty sure she did pageants. She would see me crouching in the corner, ride up to me, and ask, "What are you doing out here?" Never removing my eyes from the binoculars, I would just sit there and say nothing. I thought that if I remained perfectly quiet and still, she wouldn't be able to see me. After a while, she would trot away on her horse. I remember thinking that she had nice hair and wishing that she would ask me to ride the horse with her. She never did. I never accomplished anything particularly notable while on patrol, but it was my time. I was connecting with myself.

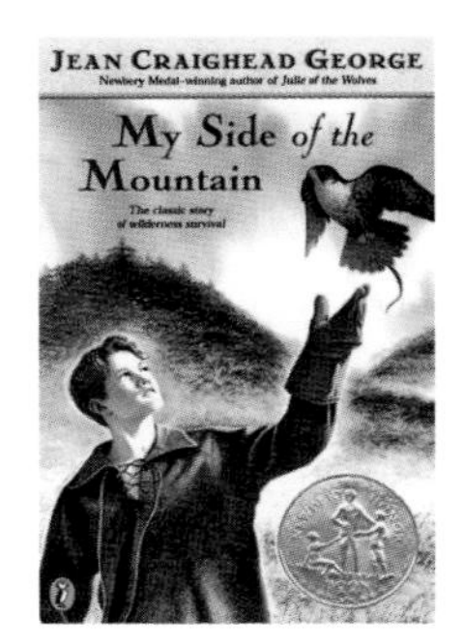


Sam inspired many kids to exert their independence . . . and master falconry.

**RHETT** As far back as I can remember, I've always been drawn to the idea of solitude, and I've always loved stories about people who were alone for long periods of time. One of my favorite books as a kid was *My Side of the Mountain,* a novel about a twelve-year-old boy who runs away from his family and lives inside a hollowed-out tree. I consider it to be one of the best books ever written for kids, even if it inspired a whole generation of us to run away from home.

Despite my romantic idea of solitude, up until recently, I had never spent a night alone in the wilderness. That changed in early 2016 when my wife and kids were back in North Carolina visiting family. I knew it was time for me to finally do it: I would spend a night alone in the desert. I would not simply go to a campground where I would be surrounded by other people in tents. No, I would head deep into the desert and set up my camp in a place where I wouldn't come across another person. I found the perfect spot outside of Joshua Tree National Park. As I set up my camp in the daytime, I was loving every minute. Sure, I still had cell service, and my car was less than twenty feet away, but I was alone. I was going to just sit with myself and think, and it was going to be glorious. But then, it began to get dark. And I got scared. I'm ashamed to say, in order to fight that isolated, vulnerable feeling, I went on Instagram.

Rhett's campsite in the daytime (before it got scary).

As the sky grew darker, I got even more afraid. Looking into my fire, I began to worry about all the things that might sneak up behind me. Are coyotes afraid of fire or are they attracted to it? Are there bears in the desert? What about crazy people with machetes? Then, my mind truly went wild. I began to ponder that, if the many-worlds interpretation of quantum physics is true and there are an infinite number of alternate realities branching off from my reality, then there actually is a world in which I am currently being attacked by a pack of coyotes, and another world in which I'm being ripped apart by a desert bear, and yet another world where I'm being killed by a machete-wielding desert maniac. There's even a world where all three of these things are happening at the same time to one Rhett. As I began to get scared for the version of me that was being triple-teamed by this awful coyote-bear-man gang, I reached my breaking point, retreated into my tent, and watched *Superbad* on my laptop to make the fear subside. I woke up the next morning feeling better. I then posted a shirtless selfie that I somewhat regret.

Rhett escaped an attacking desert bear. But not before it took his shirt.

**IF THESE STORIES** prove anything, it's that things can get weird when we're alone. It leads to strange, binoculared interactions with women on horseback and face-to-face meetings with bearded ancestors. Despite the nature of our experiences, we want to be alone more so we can get better at solitude. Alone time can help a friendship, because being apart from someone often makes you better at being with them. (If this brings back memories of the time your high-school sweetheart went to college across the country, telling you, "We need some time apart so we can be better together," only to return the next summer with her hand in the back pants pocket of someone who looked exactly like you, we're sorry. That is not our intention.) Plus, being alone creates the mental space for us to recharge individually, sparking our creativity and helping us recapture a fresh perspective on our work.

Despite all the benefits, making a commitment to find time for yourself isn't easy. If you're like us, it only happens if you plan it. As we write this chapter, we are scheduling a return to the float tank. Link will be fully caffeinated to avoid sleep-drowning, and Rhett will be prepared with questions for his ancient royal uncles to find out exactly who they are. And, we promise that the next time either of us willingly spends a night alone in the wilderness, there will be no pseudo-sexy self-portraits. (Well, there will probably be a lot, but we will share them only with our wifes.)

## PLANNING YOUR PERFECT DAY OF SELF-SECLUSION

Picture this: after months of work/school commitments, family responsibilities, social functions, and so on, your schedule is finally clear. You wake up in the morning with no appointments on the calendar and no people around. How do you feel? Free? Excited? Anxious? Confused? For some people, just the thought of having a day to themselves can be overwhelming, which is why we have taken the liberty of planning your day of self-seclusion for you. What's more, we've given you three environments for living out your perfect day alone.

| TIME | GLAMPING | A RAINY DAY INSIDE | MILES FROM CIVILIZATION ON THE AFRICAN SAVANNAH |
|---|---|---|---|
| 6 A.M. | Zip up your polar performance fleece, grab an espresso to go from your battery-powered Keurig, grab your self-propelled microlattice walking sticks, and set out for an early morning walk as the forest begins to wake up. If you're lucky, you might catch a glimpse of a rare bird or perhaps a mother doe taking her fawns to the side of the river for a drink. | Roll over, scratch your butt, and resume snoring. | Having not had any protein since your jeep broke down two days ago, you wake up famished. You should head to the river, where, if you are lucky, you will be able to kill a rare bird or a weak deer who has walked to the river for a drink. If not, you must choose between another day without food or some of the mysterious yellow berries that have given you explosive diarrhea for the past thirty hours. |
| 8 A.M. | Look for a couple sturdy trees between which the staff can hang the hammock you bought from Brookstone. You're probably pretty tired from your walk and you deserve a nap. Better yet, you deserve the prepackaged Paleo snacks from the "roughing it" section at Whole Foods. | Begin the ninety-minute process of considering whether or not to get out of bed. | If you don't build a protective shelter, you will likely not survive another night. Not with that family of African lions prowling about. Start building now. You have roughly three hours to construct your crude attempt at shelter before the sun reaches its peak, at which point the oppressive heat could kill you, or at least cause you to black out and become susceptible to a rock python attack. |
| NOON | Wait a minute, did you just fall asleep, silly? You promised yourself that you wouldn't take a nap until after your moderate hike to the waterfall. No matter. When it's just you versus the elements in nature, rules go out the window. Now, hurry up or the golf cart will leave without you and you'll have to walk the quarter mile to the trailhead. | Stare at the expiration date on the cottage cheese until the numbers change. | Consider fashioning a crude spear. There's no way you will be able to kill anything with it, and potential predators will view your spear as less of a threat than a Nerf gun, but at least it will occupy your mind for a few minutes and distract you from the pain of your stomach eating itself. |

| TIME | GLAMPING | A RAINY DAY INSIDE | MILES FROM CIVILIZATION ON THE AFRICAN SAVANNAH |
| --- | --- | --- | --- |
| 3 P.M. | Stop FaceTiming. Seriously. And turn off Netflix. Just because your $10,000 Forcefield-backed pop tent has multimedia features, that doesn't mean you need to use them all concurrently. Go back outside for at least another thirty minutes before you walk up to the lodge for happy hour. | Roll over, scratch your butt, and resume snoring. | Stare ominously at the impending storm clouds on the horizon. Your shelter might be able to shield you from the lions and leopards, but your roof is not waterproof and will offer no protection from the rain. Take off your clothes. They will become a danger to you when they are soaking and cold. On the bright side, the weather will deter the insects from attempting to burrow into your orifices like they did last night. |
| 6 P.M. | Well, now you've done it. Your inability to say no to the seafood tower guarantees that you will underappreciate your soup course, let alone the prime rib. Slow down. It's raining outside, which means you might as well stay at the restaurant for a few more hours. | You realize that you haven't showered in a week. But you also haven't watched all seven Fast and the Furious movies back-to-back. | The rain pounds your starving body as the temperature drops twenty degrees. If nature doesn't give you a break, hypothermia is a real possibility. You consider peeing on yourself for warmth but decide against it, not because it will only provide temporary relief, but because there is no liquid in your bladder since you didn't catch any of the rain runoff. |
| 9 P.M. | Once your complimentary camping assistant, Gerald, lays out your self-inflating mattress in the tent, lie down and let the sounds of nature (along with the wine and martinis from dinner) help you drift off to sleep. Remember to tip Gerald before he returns to the lodge. | Vin Diesel is an even better actor than you remember. Bring on Tokyo Drift! | You fell asleep for a minute but the sounds of two lions slaughtering a wild boar startle you awake. The boar's screams are like nothing you've ever heard and you can't help but think that the only thing preventing you from screaming like that is a weak perimeter of thorny bushes and a poorly made spear. |
| MIDNIGHT | Let's not kid ourselves, a pack of lions couldn't even wake you up before 8 a.m. #foiegrasmakesmesleepy. | More disruptive: getting up to use the bathroom or not getting up to use the bathroom? | You are startled awake by a pack of lions. The sky is an unnatural shade of purple. The hunger pains have subsided. Are you dead? You must be dead, otherwise you would feel more afraid. . . . Maybe you are losing your mind. Not a bad thought actually, considering the alternatives for you once the big cats discover the weak joints in your shelter. Then again, what if this was all a dream . . . ? |

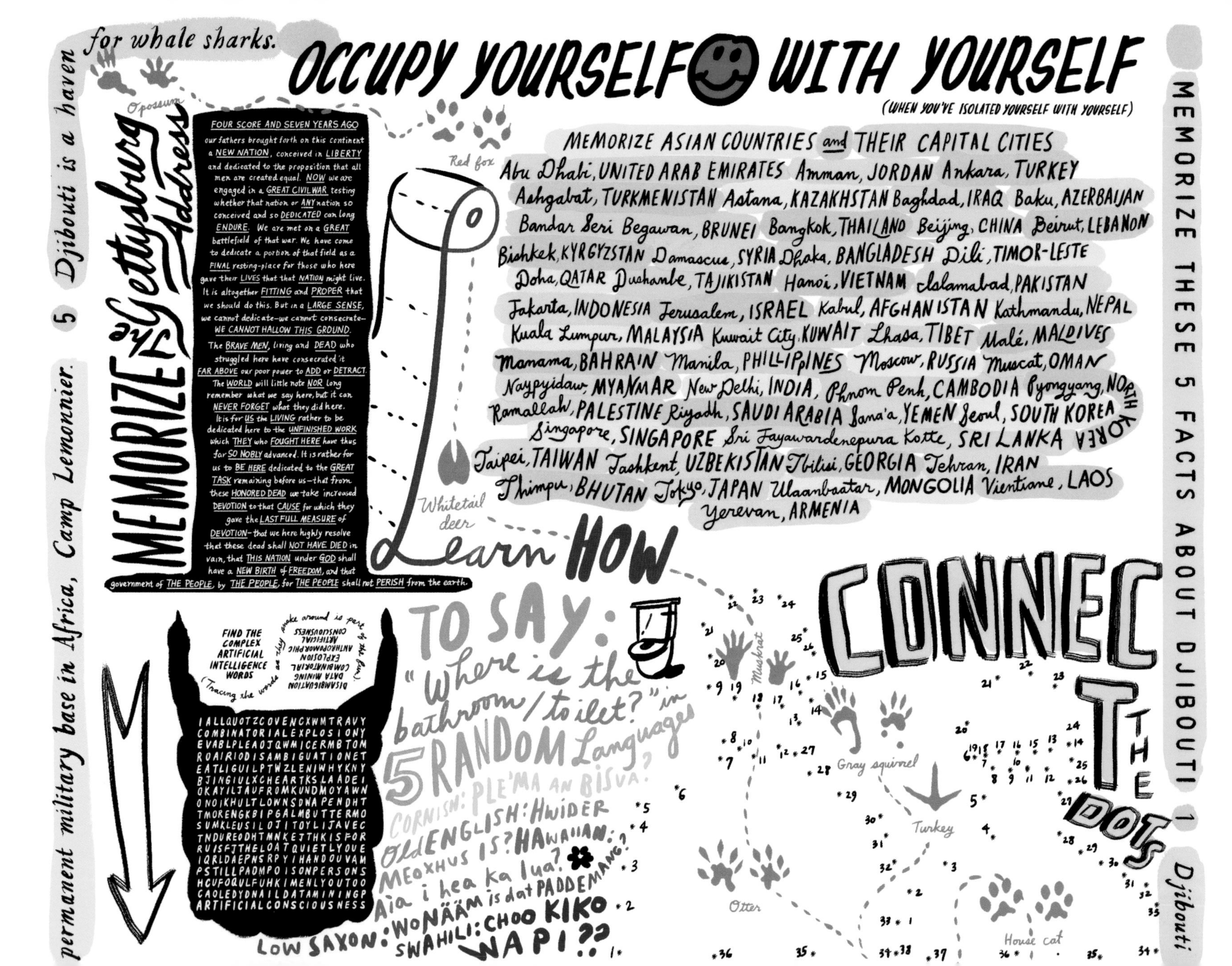

MEMORIZE THESE 5 FACTS ABOUT DJIBOUTI
1
Djibouti
permanent military base in Africa, Camp Lemonnier.
5
Djibouti is a haven for whale sharks.
OCCUPY YOURSELF WITH YOURSELF
(WHEN YOU'VE ISOLATED YOURSELF WITH YOURSELF)
MEMORIZE ASIAN COUNTRIES and THEIR CAPITAL CITIES
Abu Dhabi, UNITED ARAB EMIRATES Amman, JORDAN Ankara, TURKEY
Ashgabat, TURKMENISTAN Astana, KAZAKHSTAN Baghdad, IRAQ Baku, AZERBAIJAN
Bandar Seri Begawan, BRUNEI Bangkok, THAILAND Beijing, CHINA Beirut, LEBANON
Bishkek, KYRGYZSTAN Damascus, SYRIA Dhaka, BANGLADESH Dili, TIMOR-LESTE
Doha, QATAR Dushanbe, TAJIKISTAN Hanoi, VIETNAM Islamabad, PAKISTAN
Jakarta, INDONESIA Jerusalem, ISRAEL Kabul, AFGHANISTAN Kathmandu, NEPAL
Kuala Lumpur, MALAYSIA Kuwait City, KUWAIT Lhasa, TIBET Malé, MALDIVES
Manama, BAHRAIN Manila, PHILLIPPINES Moscow, RUSSIA Muscat, OMAN
Naypyidaw, MYANMAR New Delhi, INDIA, Phnom Penh, CAMBODIA Pyongyang, NORTH KOREA
Ramallah, PALESTINE Riyadh, SAUDI ARABIA Sana'a, YEMEN Seoul, SOUTH KOREA
Singapore, SINGAPORE Sri Jayawardenepura Kotte, SRI LANKA
Taipei, TAIWAN Tashkent, UZBEKISTAN Tbilisi, GEORGIA Tehran, IRAN
Thimpu, BHUTAN Tokyo, JAPAN Ulaanbaatar, MONGOLIA Vientiane, LAOS
Yerevan, ARMENIA
MEMORIZE The Gettysburg Address
FOUR SCORE AND SEVEN YEARS AGO our fathers brought forth on this continent a NEW NATION, conceived in LIBERTY and dedicated to the proposition that all men are created equal. NOW we are engaged in a GREAT CIVIL WAR testing whether that nation or ANY nation so conceived and so DEDICATED can long ENDURE. We are met on a GREAT battlefield of that war. We have come to dedicate a portion of that field as a FINAL resting-place for those who here gave their LIVES that that NATION might live. It is altogether FITTING and PROPER that we should do this. But in a LARGE SENSE, we cannot dedicate—we cannot consecrate—WE CANNOT HALLOW THIS GROUND. The BRAVE MEN, living and DEAD who struggled here have consecrated it FAR ABOVE our poor power to ADD or DETRACT. The WORLD will little note NOR long remember what we say here, but it can NEVER FORGET what they did here. It is for US the LIVING rather to be dedicated here to the UNFINISHED WORK which THEY who FOUGHT HERE have thus far SO NOBLY advanced. It is rather for us to BE HERE dedicated to the GREAT TASK remaining before us—that from these HONORED DEAD we take increased DEVOTION to that CAUSE for which they gave the LAST FULL MEASURE of DEVOTION—that we here highly resolve that these dead shall NOT HAVE DIED in vain, that THIS NATION under GOD shall have a NEW BIRTH of FREEDOM, and that government of THE PEOPLE, by THE PEOPLE, for THE PEOPLE shall not PERISH from the earth.
Opossum
Red fox
Whitetail deer
Learn HOW TO SAY:
"Where is the bathroom/toilet?" in 5 RANDOM Languages?
CORNISH: PLE'MA AN BISVA?
OLDENGLISH: HWIDER MEOXHUS IS?
HAWAIIAN: Aia i hea ka lua?
LOW SAXON: WONÄÄM is dat PADDEMANG?
SWAHILI: CHOO KIKO WAPI??
FIND THE COMPLEX ARTIFICIAL INTELLIGENCE WORDS
(Tracing the words as they snake around is part of the fun).
DISAMBIGUATION
DATA MINING
COMBINATORIAL EXPLOSION
ANTHROPOMORPHIC
ARTIFICIAL CONSCIOUSNESS
IALLQUOTZCOVENCXWMTRAVY
COMBINATORIALEXPLOSIONY
EVABLPLEAOJQWMICERMBTOM
ROAIRIODISAMBIGUATIONET
EATLIGUILPTWZLENIWHYKNY
BJINGIULXCHEARTKSLAADEI
OKAYILTAUFROMKUNDMOYAWN
ONOIKHULTLOWNSDWAPENDHT
TMORENGKBIPGALMBUTTERMO
SUMKLEUSILOJITOYLIJAVEC
TNDUREODHTMNKETTHKISFOR
RUISFTTHELOATQUIETLYOUE
IQRLDAEPNSRPYIHANDOUVAM
PSTILLPADMPOISONPERSONS
HCUFOQULFUHKIMENLYOUTOO
CAOLEDYDNAILDATAMININGP
ARTIFICIALCONSCIOUSNESS
CONNECT THE DOTS
Muskrat
Gray squirrel
Turkey
Otter
House cat

is a small nation located in the Horn of Africa. 2 The capital city of Djibouti is Djibouti City. 3 Hussein Ahmed Salah won the country's only Olympic medal in 1988, winning bronze in the men's marathon. 4 Djibouti is home to America's largest
MAKE A LOON CALL
1
2
3
4
START HERE
JUST BECAUSE YOU'RE FINALLY ABLE TO FIND SOME TIME TO YOURSELF DOESN'T MEAN THAT YOU'RE GOING TO KNOW HOW TO MAKE THE MOST OF IT. IN FACT, A LOT OF PEOPLE actually get BORED when they're ALONE. IN ORDER TO PREVENT YOU FROM HAVING A NEGATIVE EXPERIENCE WITH YOURSELF, WE'VE CREATED A COLLECTION OF THINGS TO KEEP YOU OCCUPIED WHEN YOU'RE ALL BY YOUR LONESOME.
Identifying Animal Paws & Claws
Dog
Coyote
Beaver
Raccoon
Crow
Mink
Cottontail rabbit
Striped skunk
Woodchuck
BUILD YOUR OWN EMOJI CRYPTOGRAM WHEEL
A B C D E F G H I J K L M N O P Q R S T U V W X Y Z
TONGUE TWISTER
"pad kid poured curd pulled cod"
In 2013, MIT researchers dubbed the following tongue twister—"pad kid poured curd pulled cod"—the world's toughest. Say that ten times fast and you will be deserving of a prize. Say the word "toast" 243 times or until you taste toast, whichever comes first.
THE KEY TO SOUNDING SMART
HERETOFORE: BEFORE NOW
THEREINBEFORE: BEFORE THAT
NOTWITHSTANDING: AGAINST WHICH
LEARN ABOUT PRONOMINAL ADVERBS
PRONOMINAL ADVERBS
happen when you combine a pronoun with a preposition. When injected into casual conversation, these "VOLTRON WORDS" earn major style points. The following are a few of our favorites, along with their definitions:

STAY WOKE
AT YOUR WAKE

# SPEAK AT YOUR OWN FUNERAL

"OF COURSE, THERE WERE SOME THINGS THAT I NEVER GOT TO DO, LIKE WATER-SKI OFF A RAMP THROUGH A RING OF FLAMIN' HOT CHEETOS THAT WERE ACTUALLY ON FIRE. UNLESS, OF COURSE, I DID FINALLY GET TO DO IT AND THAT'S WHAT KILLED ME."

**LESLI PEEBLES WAS** our first girlfriend. (We say "our" not because we dated her at the same time, but because she was the first girlfriend each of us had, independently. Buies Creek was a small town). One of the alluring things about Lesli was the fact that her parents ran a funeral home. The whole place was cloaked in mystery. We both wondered if, by entering into a relationship with Lesli, we'd gain some secret knowledge about what happened there—or at least see a dead body.

Lesli never had much patience for our inquiries about the finer aspects of body preparation. If we asked her a question about sewing mouths or other orifices shut, she changed the subject. Ultimately, she dumped both of us after about a month (Rhett in sixth grade, Link in seventh grade). Apparently, four weeks of constant badgering about the embalming process was all she could handle.

Thankfully, Lesli's mom liked both of us. And years later, in 2007, she even allowed us to make a video at the funeral home—and more specifically, get inside a coffin. We know. It's weird.

The video didn't amount to much, but we learned something important that day: all the nice white quilting that lines a coffin may make it look like dead people are resting on a comfortable cloud, but it's not comfortable at all. It's cold, it's hard, and it features two unforgiving crossbeams. Not that deceased people give a rip. The frilly decoration isn't for them—it's for the people left behind who hope that their casket fashion choices would have pleased the dearly departed.

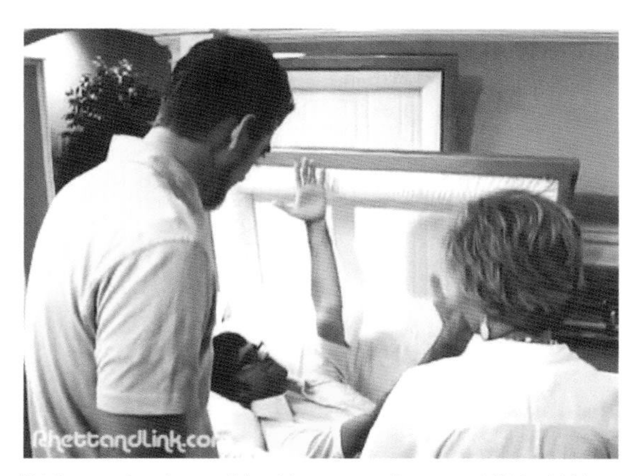

We've made plenty of bad Internet videos, and "Would You Get in a Casket" is one of them.

In fact, everything about funerals is up to the folks left behind to worry about. Not just the coffins, but also the music, the guest list, the fried chicken, the Jell-O mold, and unfortunately, the stories. This is a problem.

When a person passes away, they immediately relinquish control of how they'll be remembered. This is like a filmmaker working on a movie for years, getting every detail of an epic adventure right, and then suddenly handing the final scene over to someone else, who decides to reveal that the whole thing was just a dream. (This cheap trick will forever be acceptable only in *The Wizard of Oz.*) Your funeral is your last chance to control the narrative of your life, and we personally think that most people get it dead wrong.

Let's start with the obituary. You can't leave this up to grieving relatives. They're in no position to pen your masterpiece, especially if your death was unexpected. You need to write your own obit, or at least seek out someone who once blogged for a few months. Keep it short, sweet, and of course, funny. The people you leave behind are going to appreciate a laugh during this time, and they'll probably be even more grateful that you took care of this beforehand. As far as what to write, maybe our draft obituaries can serve as an inspiration. Naturally, there is a fair amount of guesswork involved, but the pertinent details can be updated later depending on the circumstances surrounding our deaths. Anyway, here goes:

OBITUARY

**RHETT JAMES MCLAUGHLIN,** 99, died Sunday when his self-driving, flying automobile became sentient and self-destructed by flying into some seaside cliffs, creating a massive fireball that could be seen for miles.

He leaves behind his beautiful and loving wife, Jessie, who will no doubt soon be on the prowl for a significantly younger (and shorter) man, and two sons, Locke and Shepherd, who continue to valiantly serve in our ongoing struggle against the robot overlords.

Mr. McLaughlin was one of the hosts of *Good Mythical Morning*, which featured him and his lifelong best friend, Link Neal, talking to each other about various topics of interest, and occasionally eating things like bull testicles and pig anus. Apparently, this kind of thing was considered humorous in the earlier parts of the twenty-first century.

In more recent years, Rhett and Link had completely lost their relevance, never fully adjusting to the "new comedy." Rhett had turned to whittling in order to ease the pain of a floundering career, and he even went on to win several awards, including Best Duck at the 2051 Greater Los Angeles Whittling Expo. Of course, he was stripped of all his accolades when it was discovered that he was just 3-D printing all of his entries, but he never lost the sense of accomplishment.

OBITUARY

**CHARLES LINCOLN "LINK" NEAL III** died peacefully in his sleep on Sunday at the age of 98. He was taking a power nap beneath some seaside cliffs and was struck by flying automobile debris.

He is survived by his beauteous and splendid wife, Christy; their three children, Lily, Lincoln, and Lando; their nine grandchildren, Charles Lincoln Neal V, Lofton, Lork, Landa, Lerry, Liquids, Lavarock, Lojan, and Lychee; and their great-grandchildren, Loofa, Loufus, Lufrus, Lasper, Linda, Lason, Lichael, Larbara, Lorax, Lsteven, Lsheila, Ladarius, Lolcano, LL Cool L, L'entrancé, Lookylooky, Lequinox, Lriangle, Levitate, Lebronjenames, Leather, Loaves, Lobe, Limb, Lob, Lop, Lab, Li, Lu, Lo, and Tom.

Mr. Neal gained semi-notable fame as cohost of the Internet program *Good Mythical Morning*, along with local duck whittler Rhett McLaughlin, in the 2010s. Then, in 2021 he embarked on his masterwork: manufacturing intelligent refrigerators that suggested exactly the right food to eat when you opened them. This inadvertently led to his pioneering advancements in the worlds of both car and robot consciousness. He is known globally as the Father of the Robot Overlords.

An obituary is only the beginning. It's the funeral service that holds much more weight. Your family and friends will gather together and summarize your entire life in less than an hour. Contrary to popular belief, the details will not take care of themselves. No sir. So many things can go wrong. The person best equipped to handle the particulars of your funeral is the person being funeralized. That's you. Our condolences.

Let's start with the number-one funeral mistake: the open casket. This is never a good idea, even if you die in your sleep fully toned and tanned (with no crazy battle wounds). You don't want the last image that people remember of you to be you sleeping in caked-on makeup with your butt sewed shut. Sure, they can't see the sewn-up butthole, but everyone will know it's there, and you don't want them thinking about it. Go with a closed casket—or better yet, cremation. A fail-safe strategy is getting a nice urn for your ashes and placing it next to a framed picture of you from your physical peak—or right after you returned from Hawaii.

Making sure nobody sees your dead self is only half the battle. Since the turn of the century, it has become customary for a slideshow accompanied by music to play on repeat prior to the funeral service. If you let your surviving family and friends choose these photos, they will select pictures that make them and their children look good, not you. You risk having a slideshow full of lazy-eyed, half-mouth-opened pictures of yourself. We suggest hiring a photographer every couple of years to take pictures of you doing interesting things, like sharing a milkshake with a chimpanzee, delivering a baby in a cave, or being knighted by the queen of England. If you can't afford a photographer, tasteful photo editing is passable. Pepper these intriguing pictures into the slideshow to leave people with a sense that there was even more to you than there actually was. If this seems disingenuous, remember that it will be super inspiring, and that makes it worth it.

Rhett may have never actually had a milkshake with a chimpanzee, but all that matters is that the people at his funeral think he did.

In reality, Link wasn't even in the room when his own children were born. But in the fabricated reality of his funeral slideshow, he will be a cave doctor extraordinaire.

The importance of music cannot be overemphasized. If you leave this to chance, it's not unlikely that your slideshow will feature Pachelbel's "Canon in D" on repeat. This is unacceptable. There are two recommended strategies for building your funeral playlist. The simple method is choosing music that you would have on a personal playlist, the kind of music that represents you and your musical taste. A more involved plan, assuming you've included the right pictures in your slideshow as described above, is to sync your music to the pictures to elicit maximum emotional engagement from the audience. For example, Randy Newman's "You've Got a Friend in Me" would be the perfect companion to your Milkshake with Chimpanzee photo series, while the original *MacGyver* theme would play well with the cave baby delivery.

You could get the obituary, slideshow, and music perfect, but if the words spoken about you at the service don't deliver, your funeral will be a fail. Naturally, friends and family will want to say something, and they should go for it. Hopefully you'll have lived the kind of life that generates good stories, as opposed to a series of thinly veiled grievances. However, a Mythical funeral should definitely include a word from the person who died and brought everyone together. Again, that's you. Sorry.

Hopefully, by the time you die, hologram technology will have progressed to a place where it will seem like you are actually standing up front at your funeral. But assuming that's still years away, the best you can do at the moment is make a video. Do it however you want. If you'd prefer to do a jump-cut-filled vlog while sitting on the edge of your bed, that could work. Or you may want to memorize a soliloquy and deliver it in a rich Shakespearean tone. How you deliver your words is not nearly as important as what you say. On the following pages we offer up our own self-eulogies in hopes that they might provide a bit of inspiration.

## *Link*

*Goooood Mythicaaal Funeraaal! Thanks so much for being here. That makes one of us. HA-HA-HA. [I recommend starting with a joke.] Anyways, I want to go ahead and apologize for the non-skippable ad on the front of this video. Papa gotta pay for that custom-made me-shaped urn.*

*Listen, I don't want this to be a solemn affair. I've rented out this entire Cheesecake Factory and Lionel Richie's "All Night Long" is playing in the background for one reason. To have FUN! So, let's all stand and follow along with the words on the screen:*

*Deceased: Tom bo li de say de moi ya!*

*Congregation: Yeah! Jumbo jumbo!*

*Deceased: Way to parti' o we goin'!*

*Congregation: Oh, jambali!*

*Thank you; you may be seated. Truly, I have lived a jumbo jumbo life. My job was making Internet videos with my best friend. Of course, there were some things that I never got to do, like water-ski off a ramp through a ring of Flamin' Hot Cheetos that were actually on fire. Unless, of course, I did finally get to do it and that's what killed me. Man, that would be quite ironic/tragic/awesome.*

*I got old, but I never grew up; like a Lost Boy . . . or an old bush. I loved my wife and my kids with everything I had. And I loved many of you with what was left over. I probably should've said that differently but, of course, I didn't script this out ahead of time.*

*Tonight, let's celebrate the love and life we shared. Thank you for the difference you made in my life. Enjoy the cheesecake.*

## *Rhett*

*Hello everyone. I wish I could be here under different circumstances, specifically circumstances in which I am not dead. But apparently I am gone, and I'm guessing that it was sudden and unexpected. Actually, I know it was, because this is the "sudden and unexpected death" version of my funeral speech. I also have a "saw it coming for months" version available if you're interested. It's pretty much the same as this one, but it starts a little differently.*

*While it's never easy to say goodbye, I'd like you to take comfort that I died with few regrets. Well, I regret clicking on that YouTube video "20 Year Old Blackhead Removed," but other than that, things were pretty good.*

*I'm incredibly thankful to my wife, Jessie, but I won't be going into too much detail about that, because I made a special private video just for her. If I showed you all some of the things that I did for that video, it would probably make you feel very uncomfortable, and everyone under seventeen would have to leave the room. I'm also extremely proud of my sons, Locke and Shepherd. They only embarrassed our family a handful of times.*

*I'd also like to take a moment to thank my best friend, Link. Of course, there's a chance we died together doing something stupid to entertain people. If so, please don't forget to play the joint funeral video that we made in preparation for just that situation. It's very entertaining and involves a coordinated dance number that we worked on for weeks. You'll love it. Well, anyway. Don't die on the way home. That would be a real bummer . . . dying on the way home from a funeral. Now I'm rambling. Farewell!*

As you can see, we've put quite a bit of thought into our sign-offs. However, a Mythical funeral doesn't necessarily have to include shout-outs to Cheetos and blackheads. Ultimately, what makes a funeral Mythical is you taking some time to think about the way you want to be remembered instead of leaving it up to your loved ones alone. We know—nobody likes to talk about dying, and it seems unnecessarily morbid to consider your death if you don't know it's right around the corner. Just remember that if you don't discuss it now, you may end up lying there in that velour suit you absolutely hate while everybody sits and looks at you, thinking of nothing other than your sewn-up tuchus. Don't let that happen.

# Rhett and Link Funeral Hymn

Given the amount of time we spend together, it is not unlikely that we will die at the same time. Of course, we are requesting a joint funeral if this happens. (We are requesting separate urns, however. We do not want our ashes mixed.) We have written a song to lighten the mood for the occasion. It isn't like our typical songs: no pop chord progressions and no funky beat. This is a funeral dirge.

## We're Still Here

BY RHETT & LINK

# DEAD LIBS
## EULOGY GENERATOR

Of course, sometimes other people die before you do. In those cases, you need to be prepared to say something about them at their funeral that adequately honors the deceased and doesn't make you look like an idiot. This is not easy, so we've created a generic eulogy below that you can personalize by filling in the blanks. You're welcome.

| | |
|---|---|
| name (of dead person) ________ | location ________ |
| plural noun ________ | city near you ________ |
| verb ________ | plural noun ________ |
| adjective ________ | deceased's significant other ________ |
| bodily function ________ | body part ________ |
| verb ________ | hobby ________ |
| noun ________ | adverb ________ |
| event ________ | verb ________ |
| liquid ________ | plural noun ________ |
| verb ________ | verb ________ |
| celebrity ________ | adjective ________ |
| place of business ________ | plural noun ________ |

**THE WONDERFUL LIFE OF ________ (NAME)**

There will never be another person like ________ (NAME). ________ (NAME) loved life almost as much as he/she loved ________ (PLURAL NOUN). The way he/she would always ________ (VERB) when he/she was ________ (ADJECTIVE), the way he/she would whistle and roll his/her eyes when someone ________ (BODILY FUNCTION)ed, the way he/she would ________ (VERB) a ________ (NOUN) when it was time for ________ (EVENT), all the while never spilling a drop of his/her ________ (LIQUID). ________ (NAME) taught me so much about life. And about love.

I remember one time we went ________ (VERB)-ing and he/she told me the story about how he/she met ________ (CELEBRITY) at a ________ (PLACE OF BUSINESS) in ________ (LOCATION). The war had just ended and he/she had taken a Greyhound from ________ (CITY NEAR YOU) with only a suitcase, twelve dollars, and a pocket full of ________ (PLURAL NOUN).

I was continually inspired by the way that ________ (NAME) loved ________ (DECEASED'S SIGNIFICANT OTHER). Even though ________ (DECEASED'S SIGNIFICANT OTHER) had an unnaturally large ________ (BODY PART) and a weakness for ________ (HOBBY), ________ (NAME) was always faithful. Every time I saw them together, they would be ________ (ADVERB) holding hands and ________ (VERB)-ing.

With ________ (NAME) you always knew where you stood. He/she was never afraid to speak his/her mind, even when his/her mind started failing him/her and he/she became convinced that we were all ________ (PLURAL NOUN). More important, he/she was always willing to ________ (VERB) people who were less ________ (ADJECTIVE) than he/she was. ________ (NAME) made the world a more colorful place and I will think of her/him whenever I see ________ (PLURAL NOUN).

I DID
INSERT
ACCOMPLISHMENT
HERE

# STOP AND CELEBRATE

"WE HAD FINALLY COMPLETED SOMETHING THAT WE'D BEEN WORKING TOWARD OUR ENTIRE CAREER, AND ALL WE DID WAS SHAKE HANDS LIKE TWO OLD FARMERS AGREEING ON WHERE TO BUILD A FENCE."

**B**ACK WHEN WE were kids, there was a cow pasture that we often visited. We weren't aspiring farmers. We just enjoyed chasing the cows, and getting the whole herd to run across the field made us feel like we were accomplishing something big. After running around, we would sit down on some large rocks in the middle of the pasture and have overly earnest conversations about our future. We always had a sense that our friendship would last, and that we were destined to do something together. One day, in the midst of an especially serious talk, we found the sharpest rock we could, cut our hands with it, and swore a blood oath to each other, promising to "work together creating something." If you had told us then that more than twenty-five years later we would be living in Los Angeles making a show where we did things like deep fry sunglasses in front of millions of people, we would probably respond, "Really? That's the something we're gonna do together?" But here we are.

The stroller we pimped out for our very first YouTube video, complete with spinning rims and built-in chocolate milk dispenser.

Although we had a tendency to do things as ceremonious as blood oaths as kids, now that we're actually in the middle of living out our childhood dream, it seems we rarely stop to really appreciate the moment. Instead, we all too often just let the years fly by, moving hastily from one thing to the next.

The day that we wrapped season 1 of our comedy series *Buddy System* provides a perfect example of our tendency to move on without pausing to take it all in. *Buddy System* represented a huge step for us. We had always dreamed of telling a story full of weird ideas (like creating a second version of ourselves in a hallucination, then, after singing a barbershop quartet with our alter egos, murdering and burying them). We had the privilege of conceptualizing this crazy story, and then spending a month and a half bringing those ideas to life on screen. After acting, dancing, and singing for twelve hours a day, it came down to our last scene, the flashback of our high school prom.

It was over 100 degrees outside that Friday, and the crew had to turn off the AC in the gymnasium every time we rolled camera in order to capture clean audio. We were performing the BFF song, our '90s boy-band throwback dance number, and sweating profusely in our white tuxedos. When we finally ran out of time, our director, John, yelled, "Cut!" and our assistant director, Matt, shouted the traditional "That's a wrap!" Everyone cheered to celebrate a successful shoot and began to hug one another. It would have been the perfect time for us to stop and make a heartfelt speech about how great of an experience it was for us, and to take a second to express our appreciation for our amazing crew. But our line producer, Marcy, made the mistake of telling us we had finished twenty minutes early. That meant we still technically had more time to shoot. We told everyone to stop hugging and proceeded to sing and dance until the last possible minute, hoping we could get just a little more footage.

Performing the BFF song on stage during the prom reenactment scene in *Buddy System*.

That night, we rode together back home, barely talking because we were so exhausted. When we parted ways, Link said, "We did it," and then we shook hands. That was all. No ceremony, no Champagne. Just a handshake. We had finally completed something that we'd been working toward our entire career, and all we did was shake hands like two old farmers agreeing on where to build a fence. The very next Monday we were already discussing *GMM* season 10 and beginning to work on this very book.

We made sure to schedule a time to go shamelessly stare at the *Buddy System* billboards around Los Angeles.

It's easy to get caught up in your responsibilities, buying into the belief that something might slip through the cracks and receive inadequate attention if you don't move right to it as soon as you have the chance. And it doesn't matter what your job is. We're not international ambassadors negotiating peace between warring nations. We're two dudes who drink each other's urine through a filter; this isn't life-or-death stuff. But we take it seriously, and we get so engrossed in our work that we often forget to appreciate the experience.

We also tend to be highly critical of ourselves. When we finish a project or an episode of *GMM*, we're usually thinking, *We'll get it right next time.* This leads to us living in a constant state of anticipation, always looking to the next opportunity to do something well.

It goes without saying that this is not a particularly Mythical way to approach life. One of the key tenets of Mythicality is bringing more good into the world, and that involves a willingness to direct some goodwill toward yourself. We're not talking about gloating about your accomplishments, but rather recognizing that it's perfectly OK—and even recommended—to take time to reflect on a personal achievement. Ironically, pausing to reflect on something you're proud of is a great way to develop a sense of humility. For instance, when we stop to think about another season of *Good Mythical Morning* wrapping, we're struck by all the amazing people who enable us to pull off this work. That fills us with a deep gratitude.

Of course, just like a lot of Mythical things, this is all much more easily said than done. But it's not impossible.

We're committed to adding some Mythicality to our lives by making sure to actually schedule a time to sit down and appreciate the present as it's happening. When we finish this book, we're not just going to move right along to the next thing. At the moment we hold the final product in our hands, we're going to do something ceremonial, something substantial to celebrate and reflect. It won't involve any animal sacrifice, chants, or tattoos. But we'll at least take the book out to a restaurant, set it in between us on the table, and try to enjoy a hearty steak dinner without spilling any hollandaise sauce on it. And we'll let it all sink in. (The feeling of finishing a book. Not the hollandaise.)

We've missed quite a few opportunities to celebrate the present in the past, so we've created the following timeline of milestones, along with how we would mark those moments if we could go back in time. We've avoided significant milestones, like getting married or having our kids, because we think we actually did a pretty good job of stopping to appreciate those moments.

# CELEBRATION RECTIFICATION TIMELINE

1987

**WHAT HAPPENED:** Rhett beat *Super Mario Bros* using only one life while Link watched in amazement.

**WE SHOULD HAVE:** dressed up in overalls and shared some mushroom linguini.

1992

**WHAT HAPPENED:** We successfully dammed the small creek running behind Ben Greenwood's house with rocks and tree limbs. The dam held for a full three hours.

**WE SHOULD HAVE:** had a dam ceremony.

Our best childhood friend, Ben Greenwood (second from left). Ben was not willing to join the sweatpants brigade.

1995

**WHAT HAPPENED:** We, along with nine of our friends (who were all piled in the back of Link's truck), survived a fairly serious wreck while egging houses on Halloween night in the upscale community of Neill's Creek Farms in Angier, North Carolina.

**WE SHOULD HAVE:** invited all of our friends who were with us that night to a big omelet breakfast where we reflected on the fragility of life and then went door to door to apologize to the recipients of our eggs.

Our high school band, the Wax Paper Dogz, convincingly pretending to perform.

1996

**WHAT HAPPENED:** Our high school band, the Wax Paper Dogz, came in second place in the Buies Creek Battle of the Bands, finishing just behind the aptly named, short-lived local phenomenon, 15 Minutes of Fame.

**WE SHOULD HAVE:** participated in a fifteen-minute-long back-massage circle.

1998

**WHAT HAPPENED:** We invited approximately fifty girls we didn't know to come to our apartment to watch the original *Planet of the Apes* by splitting the signal from a VCR to three TVs.

**WE SHOULD HAVE:** invited them back over for four consecutive weekends to watch *Beneath the Planet of the Apes, Escape from the Planet of the Apes, Conquest of the Planet of the Apes,* and *Battle for the Planet of the Apes.*

College. These ties almost match, but they don't. Our loss.

**2001**

**WHAT HAPPENED:** We wrote one of our first comedy songs, "The Unibrow Song," and performed for a crowd of college students who actually laughed at it.

**WE SHOULD HAVE:** temporarily grown our unibrows back in.

Trying very hard at one of our first musical comedy performances.

**2003**

**WHAT HAPPENED:** We each separately spearheaded projects at our respective engineering companies, all while wearing khakis.

**WE SHOULD HAVE:** had a cake made with the words WE ARE OFFICIALLY ADULTS NOW. PEOPLE MAY DIE IF WE MADE MISTAKES IN OUR CALCULATIONS written on it.

**2006**

**WHAT HAPPENED:** Our first YouTube video got 1,000 views.

**WE SHOULD HAVE:** grabbed a drink with the person who ripped the video from our website and posted it on YouTube, thanking them for helping us to understand why it didn't make sense to have our videos only on our own server, and then kindly asking them to take it down.

**2009**

Apparently making a furniture commercial about racial reconciliation is enough to get you on CNN.

**WHAT HAPPENED:** We were interviewed on CNN after the success of our commercial for Red House Furniture, which featured the tagline "Where black people and white people buy furniture."

**WE SHOULD HAVE:** had a party at the Red House with lots of black and white people.

**2011**

**WHAT HAPPENED:** LMFAO asked us if they could use our Dope Zebra in their "Sorry for Party Rocking" music video. We said yes, if we could be in the video too—and it worked!

**WE SHOULD HAVE:** taken a celebratory trip to the zoo while wearing the zebra costume.

**2016**

**WHAT HAPPENED:** We made it to our 1,000th episode of *Good Mythical Morning.*

**WE SHOULD HAVE:** . . . Actually, we did pretty good with this one. A fan-montage video even made us cry on the show.

A heartfelt (and drafty) performance during our 1,000th episode of GMM.

**WE HOPE THAT** our reminiscing will inspire you (and us) to begin taking the time to stop and celebrate life's little victories. Remember, you don't have to wait for major stuff—like birthdays, marriages, and promotions—to celebrate. Most of us already do a pretty good job of recognizing those achievements. Instead, make it a habit to congratulate yourself for the stuff that often goes unnoticed, like finally making a properly proportioned milkshake, living through a second heart attack, or enjoying a successful one-wiper.

And just like we have promised to celebrate the day we finally finish writing this book, we want to give you an opportunity to celebrate when you finish reading this book—which is basically right now. On the next page, you'll find a picture of us, along with the bottom half of a face. We encourage you to line the top half of your face up with the face provided, and then snap a selfie. You may find it odd that the authors of a book would ask you to take a picture of yourself with the book using a nondescript half-face, but we're guessing that—if you made it this far—you probably understand that it's pretty Mythical too. If you post your selfie, use #BookOfMythicality so we'll see it. Or just use the page to make faces in the mirror. We don't care. We're just happy you got this far, and you should be too.

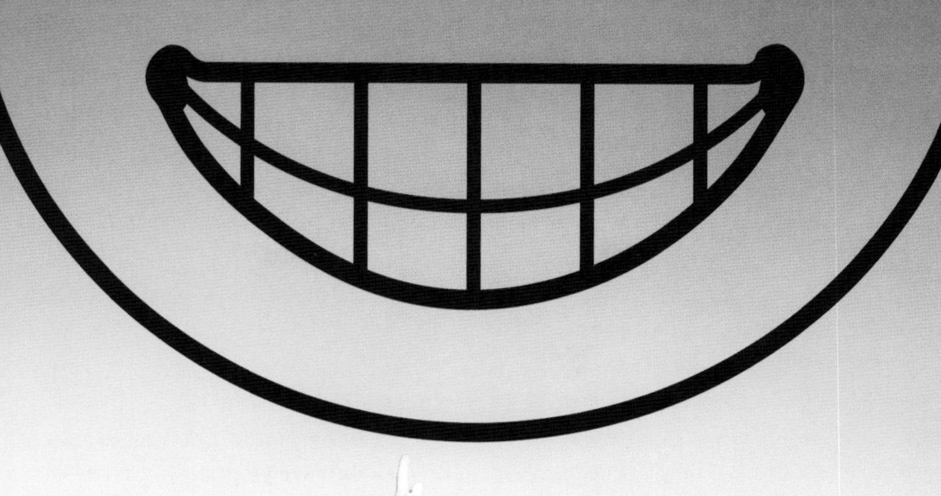

# CONGRATULATIONS TO ME!

I FINISHED RHETT & LINK'S BOOK OF MYTHICALITY! WELL, I BASICALLY FINISHED IT. THERE'S, LIKE, ONE MORE PAGE. OF COURSE, I MAY HAVE NOT ACTUALLY READ THE BOOK, BUT INSTEAD JUST FOUND THIS PAGE, BUT LET'S NOT FOCUS ON THAT.

IF ANY OF our stories about poorly placed time capsules, lost dogs, cereal baths, tobacco sickness, bad haircuts, homemade wine, or isolation-tank hallucinations have made you laugh or think, we have succeeded in our mission of bringing some Mythicality into the world through this book. If you have not laughed or thought, but instead passively digested this book like a zombie who, despite its lack of blood flow and inability to walk without a limp, has somehow retained reading comprehension skills, then congratulations. That is really impressive. We're surprised you held on this long.

What we were really striving for, though, is that something in this book has compelled you to take the risk of bringing more curiosity, creativity, or tomfoolery into your life and friendships. If we've helped you identify an area in your life that's in need of Mythicality—and inspired you to take the Mythical action you know is necessary—then that means you're well on your way to feeding your inner Mythical Beast. That's what we're all about.

But being Mythical isn't always easy. Even though laughing, learning, and creating are at the heart of our jobs, we've seen how the busyness and challenges of life can make those things difficult to do. It's easy to get in a rut where laughter is tough to come by and creating seems like a chore. It's also tough to not let pettiness or jealousy chip away at a potentially Mythical friendship. Fortunately, as you take more Mythical actions, Mythicality becomes a more natural part of your life and your relationships.

We have no specific plans to raise an official army of Mythical Beasts. (Although it would be very cool to have matching uniforms and be strategically dropped into certain areas around the world to unleash Weapons of Mass Mythicality. We would just need to make absolutely sure that our uniforms did not make us look like a herd of furries.) However, there is little doubt that the world is in need of more people who don't take themselves too seriously and who are willing to learn, try, and create new things. And so, maybe instead of donning a Mythical uniform, you can begin to share the ways you've added Mythicality to your life, encouraging others in their own Mythical quests, and also so we can hear from you. We're all on this Mythical highway together.

We wish you well in your Mythical adventures. Now, go, and be your Mythical best.

MYTHICALITY
CURIOSITY, CREATIVITY, AND TOMFOOLERY

# SOURCES


## CHAPTER 2: GET LOST

THE "WHELEPHIGEONOLE"

Ameena Schelling, "Elephants Never Get Lost, Thanks to Their Very Own GPS," The Dodo, April 1, 2015, https://www.thedodo.com/elephants-spatial-reasoning-maps-study-1070426187.html.

Leo Polansky, Werner Kilian, and George Wittemyer, "Elucidating the Significance of Spatial Memory on Movement Decisions by African Savannah Elephants Using State–Space Models," *Proceedings of the Royal Society B*, March 25, 2015, http://rspb.royalsocietypublishing.org/content/282/1805/20143042.

James Owen, "Magnetic Beaks Help Birds Navigate, Study Says," *National Geographic News*, November 24, 2004, http://news.nationalgeographic.com/news/2004/11/1124_041124_magnetic_birds_2.html./

"Magnetoreception," Wikipedia, accessed December 13, 2016, https://en.wikipedia.org/wiki/Magnetoreception.

"Whales, Dolphins, and Sound," Australian Government Department of the Environment and Energy, accessed December 13, 2016, https://www.environment.gov.au/marine/marine-species/cetaceans/whale-dolphins-sound.

Shaunacy Ferro, "Study Shows That Moles Can Smell in Stereo," *Popular Science*, February 5, 2013, http://www.popsci.com/science/article/2013-02/study-shows-moles-smell-stereo.

Tanya Lewis, "Moles Smell the World from Both Sides," Live Science, February 5, 2013, http://www.livescience.com/26871-moles-stereo-smell.html.

## CHAPTER 4: BUILD A TIME CAPSULE

OUR GOLDEN FRIEND-AVERSARY TIME CAPSULE

Sarah Pruitt, "Time Capsule Buried by Paul Revere and Sam Adams Discovered in Boston," History Channel, December 12, 2014, http://www.history.com/news/time-capsule-buried-by-paul-revere-and-sam-adams-discovered-in-boston.

Catherine E. Shoichet, "1795 Time Capsule Opened, Centuries After Revere and Adams Buried It," CNN, January 7, 2015, http://www.cnn.com/2015/01/06/us/feat-paul-revere-sam-adams-boston-time-capsule.

"William Scollay," Wikipedia, accessed December 13, 2016, https://en.wikipedia.org/wiki/William_Scollay.

Anna Caldwell, "Carriage for Queen Elizabeth's 80th Birthday That Cost Taxpayers $245,000 Still in Australia Six Years Later," *Courier Mail*, May 21, 2012, http://www.couriermail.com.au/news/national/carriage-for-queen-elizabeths-80th-birthday-that-cost-taxpayers-245000-still-in-australia-six-years-later/story-e6freooo-1226363350289.

Amanda Killelea, "Queen's New Carriage Made from Isaac Newton's Apple Tree, Nelson's Ship, and Dambusters Plane," *Mirror*, June 3, 2014, http://www.mirror.co.uk/news/uk-news/queens-new-carriage-made-isaac-3641958.

Staff, "Queen Elizabeth Receives Best Birthday Present in British History," AOL News, June 4, 2014, http://www.aol.com/article/2014/06/04/queen-elizabeth-receives-best-birthday-present-in-british-histor/20906691.

## CHAPTER 5: EMBRACE IMMATURITY

MATLOCK RELOADED

"Matlock," IMDb, accessed December 13, 2016, http://www.imdb.com/title/tt0090481/?ref_=nv_sr_1.

"Matlock (TV series)," Wikipedia, accessed December 13, 2016, https://en.wikipedia.org/wiki/Matlock_(TV_series).

"Matlock," TV.com, accessed December 13, 2016, http://www.tv.com/shows/matlock.

"Matlock Fun Facts: Questions and Answers," Fun Trivia, accessed December 13, 2016, http://www.funtrivia.com/en/Television/Matlock-4348.html.

## CHAPTER 7: EAT SOMETHING THAT SCARES YOU

WILL IT? PIONEERS

Alaina Browne, "The History of the PBJ Sandwich," Serious Eats, accessed December 14, 2016, http://www.seriouseats.com/2007/04/the-history-of-the-peanut-butt.html.

Dan Gigler, "Munch Goes to Peanut Butter Jelly Time," *Pittsburgh Post-Gazette*, February 11, 2016, http://www.post-gazette.com/life/munch/2016/02/11/Munch-goes-to-Peanut-Butter-Jelly-Time/stories/201602100139.

"Breakfast Burrito," Wikipedia, accessed December 14, 2016, https://en.wikipedia.org/wiki/Breakfast_burrito.

Jill Magnus, "August 6, 2014: National Root Beer Float Day," National Day Calendar, http://www.nationaldaycalendar.com/2014/08/05/august-6-2014-national-root-beer-float-day-national-fresh-breath-day.

"National Root Beer Float Day: The First Black Cow," Popsugar, August 6, 2007, http://www.popsugar.com/food/National-Root-Beer-Float-Day-First-Black-Cow-485689.

"The Willett Story," Kentucky Bourbon Whiskey, accessed December 14, 2016, http://www.kentuckybourbonwhiskey.com/willett-story.html.

T. Rees Shapiro, "Jeno Paulucci, Food Visionary Behind the Pizza Roll Dies at 93," *Washington Post*, November 30, 2011, https://www.washingtonpost.com/local/obituaries/jeno-paulucci-food-visionary-behind-the-pizza-roll-dies-at-93/2011/11/30/gIQAkU4XEO_story.html.

Daniel E. Slotnik, "Jeno Paulucci, a Pioneer of Ready-Made Ethnic Foods, Dies at 93," *New York Times*, November 25, 2011, http://www.nytimes.com/2011/11/26/business/jeno-paulucci-a-pioneer-of-ready-made-ethnic-foods-dies-at-93.html.

Anna McDonald, "Big League Chew: An Oral History," Fox Sports, May 5, 2015, http://www.foxsports.com/mlb/just-a-bit-outside/story/big-league-chew-bubble-gum-oral-history-portland-mavericks-jim-bouton-rob-nelson-050515.

Dave Sheinin, "Rob Nelson Invented Big League Chew and His Bubble Has Yet to Burst," *Washington Post*, July 14, 2015, https://www.washingtonpost.com/sports/nationals/rob-nelson-invented-big-league-chew-and-his-bubble-has-yet-to-burst/2015/07/14/718ff9d2-2a26-11e5-a250-42bd812efc09_story.html.

## CHAPTER 10: SAY "I LOVE YOU" LIKE IT'S NEVER BEEN SAID

LOVE-LINE MATCH-UP

"Read Shakespeare's Top 50 Love Quotes," No Sweat Shakespeare, accessed December 14, 2016, http://www.nosweatshakespeare.com/quotes/shakespeare-love-quotes.

"Shakespeare Quotes on Love," Shakespeare Facts, accessed December 14, 2016, http://www.williamshakespearefacts.com/quotes-on-love.html.

Brendan Frederick, "The 25 Best Hip-Hop Love Songs," Complex, February 14, 2012, http://www.complex.com/music/2012/02/the-25-best-hip-hop-love-songs.

Lauren Zupkus, "12 Really Questionable Love Song Lyrics," Huffington Post, March 19, 2014, http://www.huffingtonpost.com/2014/03/18/weird-love-lyrics_n_4988320.html.

Hillary Busus and Will Robinson, "Funny Valentines: 16 Weirdly Insidious Love Songs," *Entertainment Weekly*, February 14, 2015, http://www.ew.com/article/2015/02/13/16-weirdly-insidious-love-songs.

http://www.brownielocks.com/lovequotes.html

Lucy Jones, "29 Beautiful Lyrics About Love," NME, February 13, 2013, http://www.nme.com/blogs/the-big-picture/29-beautiful-lyrics-about-love.

## CHAPTER 11: INVENT SOMETHING RIDICULOUS

BEST WORST INVENTIONS

"The 50 Worst Inventions," *Time*, May 27, 2010.

## CHAPTER 13: VISIT THE FUTURE

THE TIME WE SHOWED MATT DAMON THE FUTURE

Theodoros II (screen name), "25 Movies That Predicted the Future with Creepy Accuracy," List 25, January 27, 2016, http://list25.com/25-movies-that-predicted-the-future-with-creepy-accuracy.

Susie Poppick, "10 Back to the Future Predictions That Came True," *Time*, October 20, 2015, http://time.com/money/4076862/back-to-the-future-day-predictions-accuracy.

Susanna Kim, "How Back to the Future: Part II Scored on 2015 Predictions," ABC News, October 21, 2015, http://abcnews.go.com/US/back-future-part-ii-scored-2015-predictions/story?id=27946920.

SELFIES IN 100,000 YEARS

Michael Graham, "What Will Humans Look Like in 100,000 Years?" Mother Nature Network, July 1, 2013, http://www.mnn.com/green-tech/research-innovations/stories/what-will-humans-look-like-in-100000-years.

Zoltan Istvan, "Bionic Eyes Can Already Restore Vision, Soon They'll Make It Superhuman," Gizmodo, December 12, 2014, http://gizmodo.com/bionic-eyes-can-already-restore-vision-soon-theyll-mak-1669758713.

## CHAPTER 18: ISOLATE YOURSELF WITH YOURSELF

OCCUPY YOURSELF WITH YOURSELF

Jessica Durando, "World's Toughest Tongue Twister?" *USA Today*, December 11, 2013, http://www.usatoday.com/story/news/nation-now/2013/12/11/mit-tongue-twister/3985789/.

"Capital Cities of Asia," Nations Online, accessed December 14, 2016, http://www.nationsonline.org/oneworld/capitals_asia.htm.

"List of Asian Capitals," Countries of the World, accessed December 14, 2016, https://www.countries-ofthe-world.com/capitals-of-asia.html.

Barefoot Bushcraft, "Making a Loon Call," YouTube, August 2, 2014, https://www.youtube.com/watch?v=GsbxazgiGfc.

Jason Plautz, "The 21 Countries with One Olympic Medal," Mental Floss, accessed December 14, 2016, http://mentalfloss.com/article/31311/21-countries-one-olympic-medal.

"Ten Fun Facts About Djibouti," 10 Facts About, accessed December 14, 2016, http://www.10-facts-about.com/Djibouti/id/950.

"Djibouti Country Profile," BBC, April 9, 2016, http://www.bbc.com/news/world-africa-13231761.

"Djibouti," Wikipedia, accessed December 14, 2016, https://en.wikipedia.org/wiki/Djibouti.

"Pronomial Adverbs," Wiktionary, accessed December 14, 2016, https://en.wiktionary.org/wiki/Category:English_pronominal_adverbs.

"Sliding Scale or Cryptograph," Secret Codes for Cubs and Scouts, accessed December 14, 2016, https://sites.google.com/site/codesforscouts/sliding-scale-or-cryptograph.

# CREDITS

## PHOTOS

Jonathan Weiner: endpapers, 2, 51 (Rhett), 73, 90, 92, 146 (Link and Christy), 150, 151, 177 (Link), 188, 230–231, 235 (Mythical crew), 240, 251 (Link), 263
Peter Yang: 1, 73, 80, 106–107, 109, 115, 118–119, 122–123, 177 (Rhett), 250 (Rhett)
Eric Kelly: 6-7, 16–17, 68–69, 141, 142, 185, 234–235 (Craig)
George Baier IV: 10, 28, 42, 47–48, 58, 74, 84, 100, 112, 124, 136, 146, 148, 160, 172, 182, 194, 206, 220, 232–233, 236, 246, 256, 265
Roman Sigaev/Shutterstock (church background): 15
sd619/E+/Getty Images (background): 20–21
pixhook/iStock by Getty Images (wood background): 22–23, 66–67
Wikimedia Commons, Bull-Doser: 32
franckreporter/iStock by Getty Images: 34–35
ZaZa Studio/Shutterstock: 38–39
Robyn Von Swank: 50 (top), 249 (Rhett)
Robin Roemer: 51 (Link), 175 (top), 249 (Link)
Marie Louise Elizabeth Vigee-Lebrun/Getty Images: 55
GL Archive/Alamy Stock Photo (Napoleon); Peter Horree/Alamy Stock Photo (monk): 56
Leemage/Contributor/Getty Images (Julius Caesar); Martin Shields/Alamy Stock Photo (George Washington): 57
iDin_Photostock/Shutterstock (wood background): 62–63
Atstock Productions/Shutterstock: 62–63
dell640/iStock by Getty Images: 66
Stocktrek Images/Shutterstock (digestive tract): 109
Matthew Dwyer: 112, 180, 181, 228–229
7io/Getty Images: 118–119
Belterz/Getty Images: 132
Bryan Esler/ Getty Images: 132
Courtesy of the Mythical Entertainment Crew: 133
Featureflash Photo Agency/Shutterstock: 147
DNY59/Getty Images: 156–157
Jaap2/iStock by Getty Images (braid); RusN/iStock by Getty Images (nose); Barry Blackburn/Shutterstock (motorbike): 159
Courtesy of Lenora Locklear: 162, 163 (bottom)
Vector Bakery/Shutterstock (arrows): 158
Monkik/Shutterstock (bicycle): 166
Rangsan Paidaen/Shutterstock: 167 (directional sign), 169 (typewriter)
Fazakas Mihaly/Shutterstock (cassette tape): 168
jfmdesign/iStock by Getty Images (Metamucil): 170
Markar/Shutterstock (body builder): 171
Kisan/Shutterstock (background): 174–178
MRAOROAR/Shutterstock: 175 (top left)
Amazingmikael/Shutterstock: 175 (top right)
RosaIreneBetancourt 3/Alamy Stock Photo: 169 (top)
Colin Schot Klotzbach/iStock by Getty Images: 169 (bottom)
Pixelparticle/Shutterstock: 180
Ana Aguirre Perez (background): 181
Geerati/iStock by Getty Images (jaws, neck): 181
Giuseppe R/Shutterstock (cereal): 181
Karen Katrivan/Shutterstock (leaves): 181
Oleg Kozlov/Shutterstock (eyes, Rhett): 181
Roberto Sorin/Shutterstock (eyes, Link): 181
Titima Ongkantong/Shutterstock (Goozle): 181
Crisserbug/Getty Images: 191
Donatas1205/Shutterstock (watercolor): 192
barkarola/Shutterstock (background): 192
Frames: 192 (clockwise from top): Iakov Filimonov/Shutterstock; Kongsky/Shutterstock; Aleksei Gurko/Shutterstock; Karn684/Shutterstock; Prokrida/Shutterstock; LiliGraphie/Shutterstock; Most popular/Shutterstock; Arcady/Shutterstock; Daniel Heighton/Shutterstock; Pola36/Shutterstock; Volkova Natalia/Shutterstock; IhorZigor/Shutterstock; MikhailSh/Shutterstock

Frames: 193 (clockwise from top): LaKirr/Shutterstock; Iakov Filimonov/Shutterstock; Gillmar/Shutterstock; Gillmar/Shutterstock; Jamroen Jaiman/Shutterstock; Jamroen Jaiman/Shutterstock; Kongsky/Shutterstock; Photomaster/Shutterstock; Dmitry Skutin/Shutterstock
H. Mark Weidman Photography/Alamy Stock Photo: 196
Nils Z/Shutterstock: 212
David Crespo/Getty Images: 213
Jim Barber/Shutterstock (pig): 218
Sergey02/iStock by Getty Images: 242–243
Joy Brown/Shutterstock (cafe scene): 250
Trinity Mirror/Mirrorpix/Alamy Stock Photo (chimpanzee): 250
Age footstock/Alamy Stock Photo (baby): 251
Wedekiba/iStock by Getty Images (cave): 251
Katrusya/iStock by Getty Images (roses): 252–253
David Orcea/Shutterstock: 252
Dmytro Balkhovitin/Shutterstock: 253
Benjamin Eck: 259

**ILLUSTRATIONS**

Kristen Tillman: 3
Elsa Ienna: 10, 28, 42, 58, 74, 84, 100, 112, 124, 136, 148, 160, 172, 182, 194, 206, 220, 236, 246, 256, 265 (badges); 94–95 (video game illustrations); 110–111 (title lettering/illustrations); 263
Anna Thompson: 26–27 (lettering), 62–63 (lettering)
Mark Nerys: 36–37
Peter Arkle: 40–41, 204, 223
John Burgoyne: 38–39, 70–71
Mark Stutzman: 72–73, 83
Curtis Jenkins: 82
Chris Piascik: 109 (lettering)
Owen Gatley: 134–135
Matthew Dwyer: 175
Jen Matichuk: 214–215
Paul Windle: 216–217
Jason Oh: 232–233 (lettering)
Jessie Bright: 234–235 (lettering)
Na Kim: 244–245

All other images and illustrations courtesy of the authors/Mythical Entertainment.

**CROWN ARCHETYPE**

Senior Editor: Matt Inman
Editorial Assistant: Angeline Rodriguez
Jacket design by Christopher Brand
Interior design by Christopher Brand, Elizabeth Rendfleisch, and Elsa Ienna, with lots of help from Elena Giavaldi, Tal Goretsky, Andrea Lau, and Anna Thompson
Director of Production: Linnea Knollmueller
Pre-Press Manager: Neil Spitkovsky
Production Editorial Director: Mark McCauslin

**MYTHICAL ENTERTAINMENT**

Creative Concepting and Strategy: Mike Feldman
Coordinator and Archivist: Allie Berkowitz

**ACKNOWLEDGMENTS**

We could have never brought you a book that we're this proud of without the help of some extremely Mythical people. We are deeply grateful to:

All the Mythical Beasts around the world who have supported us in every endeavor, enabling us to make a living chasing our dreams, along with some very special Mythical Beasts who contributed directly to this book.

Jake Greene for all the questions and guidance that led to the specific approach to this book, and for his many Mythical ideas.

Matt Inman, Angeline Rodriguez, Christopher Brand, Elizabeth Rendfleisch, Tammy Blake, Tricia Boczkowski, Julie Cepler, Ellen Folan, Rachel Aldrich, Molly Stern, David Drake, and the entire team at Crown for believing in us and being there for every step.

Stevie Levine for her tireless commitment to helping to ensure the excellence of everything we create, this book being no exception.

Brent Weinstein, Ali Berman, Marc Gerald and our entire team at UTA for making this a reality.

Adam Kaller, Ryan Pastorek, Duncan Hedges, and our legal team for their guidance along the way.

Dan Weinstein and Studio71 for helping to get this idea off the ground.

Mike Feldman and Allie Berkowitz for their many hours spent helping to fine-tune this book into the final product.

Brian Flanagan for his interminable superintendence of myriad facets of the proceedings.

Jen Matichuk for her initial suggestion for us to write a Mythical cookbook, which then snowballed into this much more ambitious project.

The rest of the Mythical Crew for holding down the fort as this book came together, and a special thanks to those of you who contributed directly to the book.

Rhett's brother, Cole, for letting us create a comic strip out of one of his life's lowlights.

The many friends and mentors that have served as examples of true Mythicality, especially those of you mentioned in the ridiculous stories contained herein.

Our parents (Jim, Diane, Charles, and Sue) for making us, making us show up to first grade, and making room in our lives for Mythicality.

Our kids (Rhett's: Locke and Shepherd; Link's: Lily, Lincoln, and Lando) who are willing to tolerate having dads who are known to their friends as those guys who do weird stuff on the Internet.

Above all we would like to thank our wonderful wives, Jessie and Christy, who are directly responsible for encouraging us to pursue our passion for creating, and have been the lynchpins of our families throughout this journey. We love you and think you're sexy (respectively).

FSS